One Planet Communities

One Planet Communities

A real-life guide to sustainable living

Pooran Desai

A John Wiley and Sons, Ltd, Publication

Executive Commissioning Editor: Helen Castle
Project Editor: Miriam Swift
Publishing Assistant: Calver Lezama
Content Editor: Françoise Vaslin

ISBN   978-0-470-71557-4 (hb)
                     978-0-470-71546-8 (pb)

Cover design, page design and layouts by Artmedia Ltd.
Printed in the UK by TJ International Ltd, Padstow.

Dedicated to Sue Riddlestone

Acknowledgements

This book represents lessons learnt through the hard work of colleagues at BioRegional and BioRegional Quintain Ltd over the years. Particular thanks for work directly related to this book are due to Sue Riddlestone, Pete Halsall, Nicole Lazarus, Nick James, Ben Gill, Daniel Viliesid, Sarah Alsen, Greg Searle, Xiaohong Chen, Jane Hersey, Liz Darley, Sarah Mooney, Jennie Organ, Phil Shemmings, Alastair McMahon, the One Planet Products team, patron Professor Sir Ghillean Prance and for the long term support given by Emma Croxson and BioRegional trustees which has enabled the work to be done. I would like also to thank Emily Stott for helping with some of the research and Ronan Leyden, Jill Savery, Sam Smith and my brother, Biram Desai, for reading through the manuscript, and Gareth Williams, Climate Change Business Advisor, BITC for his contribution on climate adaptation. Constructing BedZED has been seminal and so all credit must be given to Bill and Sue Dunster and their colleagues at Zedfactory, Chris Twinn at Arup, Dickon Robinson, Malcolm Kirk and colleagues at The Peabody Trust, Gardiner and Theobald, Ellis and Moore and to London Borough of Sutton and MP Tom Brake for supporting the development.

I pass on thanks to the companies which helped crystallising the thinking behind the z-squared concept including KBR, Fulcrum Consulting, Foster and Partners and Cyril Sweett; and to those working with BioRegional Quintain Ltd including Feilden Clegg Bradley Studios, Denne Construction, MLM, Camco, Studio Egret West, Alsop, FAT, Brighton and Hove City Council, Tees Valley Regeneration and the South East England Development Agency. Thanks are also due to the companies and organisations who have worked, and continue to work, on creating One Planet Communities including Pelicano, Quintain Estates and Development PLC (especially Adrian Wyatt, Nick Shattock and Rebecca Worthington), Crest Nicholson PLC (in particular Stephen Stone), Codding Enterprises, Masdar, Tongaat Hulett Developments and China Merchant Property Developers. I would like to acknowledge the support of NGOs over the years including the Centre for Environmental Initiatives (in particular Vera Elliot), the WWF, Global Footprint Network and the Environment Wildlife Service of Abu Dhabi and well as the grant funders of BioRegional's research and educational work. I owe a great debt of gratitude to the environmentalist and thinkers who have influenced the ideas conveyed in this book and who include Sue Riddlestone, Sri Aurobindo, Bill Mollison, Kirkpatrick Sale, Bill McDonough, Mathis Wackernagel, Susan Burns, John Barrett and James Lovelock. Finally, I would like to thank John Wiley Publishers and Helen Castle for commissioning *One Planet Communities*.

Contents

Bangladesh – just one country already struggling to cope with the effects of climate change. A warning we must heed.

Foreword

Over 20 years ago the World Commission on Environment and Development, often known as the Brundtland Commission, produced its landmark report – *Our Common Future*. The response by the international community has in many ways been courageous and inspiring.

Around 95 per cent of the production of chemicals that damage the high-flying ozone layer have been cut and a greenhouse gas emission reduction treaty along with innovative carbon trading and carbon offset markets have been introduced.

Meanwhile, protected areas now cover roughly 12 per cent of the earth's terrestrial surface, and a wide variety of instruments covering issues from biodiversity and desertification to the trade in hazardous wastes and living modified organisms have been agreed.

Nevertheless, despite these successes the response has in reality failed to match the scale and the pace of environmental degradation which at its heart is a result of unsustainable production and consumption patterns. In short we have multiple market failures that now threaten the very fabric of human existence.

The challenge is crystallised in UNEP's 'Global Environment Outlook-4 (GEO-4)' report. Prepared by close to 400 experts, it argues that many 'persistent' problems remain unresolved and unaddressed while new ones are emerging, from the rapid rise of deoxygenated 'dead zones' in the oceans to the resurgence of new and old diseases linked in part with environmental degradation.

GEO-4 warns that we are living far beyond our means at a time of population increase set to climb to over 9 billion by the 2050s.

For example, fresh water availability is declining, and by 2025 water use is predicted to have risen by 50 per cent in developing countries and by 18 per cent in the developed world. The escalating burden of water demand will become intolerable in water-scarce countries unless more intelligent management is adopted and adopted fast.

Meanwhile, a sixth major extinction is under way, this time caused by human behaviour. Species are becoming extinct a hundred times faster than the rate shown in the fossil records.

The challenge is also one of equity. The total annual income of nearly 1 billion people, the population of the richest countries, is almost 15 times that of the 2.3 billion people in the poorest countries.

This book, *One Planet Communities*, is set against the landscape outlined in GEO-4 and many other sobering assessments. It is also set against a backdrop of multiple crises emerging on other fronts from climate change to the recent financial, economic and employment ones.

In crisis, however, there is also opportunity – a time for reassessing and reinventing economies towards a low-carbon, resource-efficient, Green Economy path.

One Planet Communities highlights the inordinate opportunities and gear-changing actions possible for delivering tomorrow's economy today – ones that foster innovation, imagination and decent jobs for the 1.3 billion unemployed or under-employed.

It is also about tomorrow's communities – with more than 50 per cent of humanity now living in urban centres. This new book, replete with practical experiences and centred around 10 key principles, offers some real answers to the fundamental question of how to build societies in which ordinary people and their families can lead happy, healthy and fulfilled lives.

In doing so, the book is in the vanguard of illuminating a path along which people, in their day to day activities, can fairly share the world's resources and achieve sustainable development not as an abstract philosophy, but as an on-the-ground reality.

Achim Steiner, UN Under-Secretary General and Executive Director,
United Nations Environment Programme (UNEP), Nairobi, March 2009

Figure 1
The *moai*, monumental stone sculptures on Easter Island created by the Rapanui people, are a testament and reminder that societies can collapse because of environmental destruction.

Chapter 1

Using ecological footprinting to define sustainability

Commonly used definitions of sustainability are not sufficient for us to define what is truly sustainable. The emerging methodology of ecological footprinting can help us to gain a clearer insight into how to build truly sustainable communities.

> *'Our biggest challenge this new century is to take an idea that seems abstract – sustainable development – and turn it into a reality for all the world's people.'*
> Kofi Annan, UN Secretary General, 2001[1]

Imagine a future where we can lead happier and healthier lives meeting our needs from renewable energy and having a positive impact on the natural world and its resources; where being green is the norm because the places where we live and products and services we consume have been designed to make it easy, attractive and affordable for us to do so. The possibility of such a future is emerging, but it will require us, with an honest heart, to challenge accepted ways of doing things and not to succumb to greenwash. Today, almost every project being promoted by a company or a government body claims to be a sustainable development project. We should not be facing any problems at all. That clearly is not the case, so how can we start thinking more clearly about what is, and what isn't, sustainable? At the same time, faced with a proliferation of sustainability standards and guidelines, it is sometimes hard to see the forest for the trees. There is a need and an opportunity to consolidate our thinking and to create a clear framework on which to build our communities in this still young century.

A brief history of sustainability

Human beings are an incredibly adaptable species and have conquered much of the planet's surface area. We have a long history of exploiting natural resources and our environment, sometimes to our detriment, as illustrated in the salutary tale of the collapse of the society on Easter Island following clearance of all its forests.[2] An isolated volcanic island 3,600 kilometres west of Chile, Easter Island was colonised by the Rapanui people, of Polynesian descent, in around 400 BC. However, forest clearance left the islanders unable to construct boats to fish, without wild birds to eat and with agriculture compromised by soil loss. By the 18th century, the society had succumbed to infighting and cannibalism, leaving the *moai*, Easter Island's massive sculptures, as a monument to past glories. Easter Island has, of course, become a metaphor for our current society's predicament: inhabiting an isolated planet without heed to the consequences of destroying the natural environment on which we depend.

All species interact with their environment and, to a greater or lesser extent, modify it. In the history of life on the planet, complex ecological systems have emerged, evolved and waned, each time replaced by a new set of mutually dependent species building on the history that preceded it. Ecological systems have sometimes collapsed catastrophically, either through internal forces such as when plants emerged producing oxygen on a grand scale for the first time, poisoning the existing ecosystems and creating a whole new planetary order; or sometimes through external ravages, such as an asteroid hitting the planet. Our ingenuity as human beings has turned us into a species which is modifying our environment on a massive scale. This is not a new phenomenon. Even as hunter-gatherers we changed our surroundings so, for example, the arrival of the Aboriginal people to Australia 40,000 years ago changed its ecology for ever. Our impact increased as we domesticated plants and animals and developed agriculture, often by clearing forests and diverting water courses. All the great civilisations – in the Indus Valley, the Egyptians, Romans and Mayans – transformed their environments, often degrading them. It is almost impossible for us today to believe that North Africa once had extensive cedar forests before they were cut down by the Egyptians and Romans. However, with industrialisation and population growth assisted by improvements in sanitation and immunisation (the population has more than doubled from 3 billion in 1960 to approaching 7 billion today), our impact is now at the planetary level.

Thinkers from the earliest times have urged us to consider our relationship with nature and every society has at some level recognised its dependence on the natural world. In more recent Western history, concerns about population growth and resource use were expressed by political economist Thomas Malthus in the 18th century,[3] stimulating often controversial debate which has heavily influenced our thinking about sustainability today. In the 1960s it was books such as Rachel Carson's *Silent Spring*,[4] which started to promote 'environmentalism' as a popular movement – it encouraged an awareness of the harmful impacts of humans on the environment, in particular those of artificial chemicals on wildlife and ecosystems. In the 1970s, modelling of human impacts at the global scale led to the publication of *The Limits to Growth*[5] which highlighted natural resource limits reached by exponential population growth. The decade also saw the social impacts of globalisation and industrial gigantism explored in economist Schumacher's *Small is Beautiful*,[6] which highlighted the contradictions of unsustainable growth with finite resources and questioned the appropriateness of using conventional economic measures such as GNP as indicators of human well-being.

In the 1980s, the polarised debate between human development and economic progress on the one hand, and conservation of nature and natural resources on the other, started to find a route to reconciliation in theory at least. The Conservation Strategy of the IUCN[7] argued for conservation as a means to assist development, and it was this approach which led to the defining document of modern sustainability, the Brundtland Report, or *Our Common Future*, of 1987.[8] The report contained one of the most enduring definitions of sustainable development, 'development that meets the needs of the present without compromising the ability of future generations to meet their own needs'. The United Nations' Earth Summit which followed in Rio de Janeiro in 1992 saw the adoption of Agenda 21 by 178 countries – this was a programme to create a sustainable 21st century with actions at local, national and global levels together with a commitment to reach international agreements on climate change and biodiversity.

In the 1990s, the process of 'sustainable development' saw a burgeoning in loosely related activities in private, public, academic and NGO sectors. The concept of the 'three pillars of sustainability' – namely social, economic and environmental – inspired the development of 'triple bottom line' accounting (people, planet, profit) and corporate social responsibility (CSR); and there was a flourishing of life cycle assessment (LCA) and independent certification systems such as the Forestry Stewardship Council (FSC) and Fairtrade marks.

Sustainability today

In the 21st century, we still rely on the two commonly used definitions of sustainability from the 20th century: the Brundtland Report definition and the 'three pillars' definition, both of which are 20 years old. The first is a good philosophical start and a worthy aspiration, but doesn't necessarily help us on a day-to-day, decision-making level. The second definition is more practical, but is too often interpreted as being a trade-off between social, economic and environmental factors. While there may be a subset of truly sustainable activities where social, economic and environmental factors converge – where all three criteria are met as in Figure 2(a) – and while these activities are to be applauded, other activities that lie outside this subset are often validated on the basis of economic or social benefits. There have been attempts to build on this approach, creating a model where the environmental aspects are non-negotiable. In this model, commerce cannot exist outside society and society cannot exist outside the environment, which results in a 'nested' arrangement of environmental, social and economic factors as in Figure 2(b).

However, neither the Brundtland nor the Three Pillars definition of sustainability is based on any particular set of metrics or boundaries, so ultimately it is impossible to use them to define sufficiently clearly what is and what isn't sustainable.

Figure 2
Sustainability is often described as integrating social, economic and environmental factors resulting in either a 'trade off' view (a) or 'nested' organisation (b).

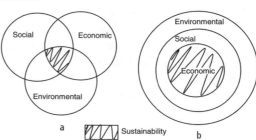

Sustainability standards

If the two commonly used definitions of sustainability cannot help us, can we determine what is sustainable by looking at sustainability standards? As the environmental agenda has come to the fore, there has been a concomitant proliferation in green guidelines and environmental standards in all areas. In food we find various certification schemes from Organic Standards, LEAF (Linking Environment and Farming), Farm Assured, Freedom Foods and Conservation Grade. With wood products we see international initiatives by the Forest Stewardship Council (FSC), Programme for the Endorsement of Forest Certification (PEFC) and Sustainable Forestry Initiative (SFI) alongside various national certification marks such as those of the Canadian Standards Association (CSA).

With respect to buildings there is a wide range of certification marks: LEED (in the US, Canada, India and Brazil), Green Globes (US and Canada), Green Star (Australia, New Zealand and South Africa), Green Mark (Singapore), VERDE (Spain), CASBEE (Japan), AQUA (Brazil), GRIHA (India), HQE (France), Estidama Pearl Rating System (Abu Dhabi) and Passivhaus (Germany). In the UK there is the Code for Sustainable Homes (which replaced EcoHomes) and standards from the Association for Environment Conscious Building.

The foremost and oldest certification schemes relating to buildings are BREEAM (Building Research Establishment Environmental Assessment Method) and LEED (Leadership in Energy and Environmental Design).

BREEAM assessment methods are available for retail, education, prisons, courts, healthcare and industrial, and a bespoke method for other types of buildings. BREEAM assesses the performance of a building in the following areas:

- Management – overall management policy and site management of contractors.
- Energy Use – operational energy including lighting, heating and cooling.
- Health and Well-Being – including indoor air quality, ventilation, daylighting, temperature control and reducing the risk of Legionnaires' disease.
- Pollution – avoiding emissions to air and water using measures such as refrigerant recovery, specification of CFC-free materials in construction and low-emission boilers.
- Transport – including use of local materials, provision of secure facilities for cyclists and links to public transport.
- Land Use – such as use of brownfield (previously built on) rather than greenfield sites and treatment of contaminated land.
- Ecology – using sites of low ecological value and/or creating new wildlife habitats.
- Materials – considering the impacts of building materials, specifying greener and healthier products such as certified timber and formaldehyde-free materials, and encouraging recycling by provision of storage for recycling.
- Water – promoting water efficiency, encouraging rainwater harvesting and waste-water recycling.

Buildings are given credits against the criteria, achieving Pass, Good, Very Good, Excellent or Outstanding ratings. Homes were assessed under BRE (British Research Establishment) EcoHomes, which has more recently been replaced by the UK government's Code for Sustainable Homes, which ranks homes on a scale of Levels 1 to 6.

The LEED rating system was originally derived from BREEAM and addresses six major areas: sustainable sites, water efficiency, energy and atmosphere, materials and resources, indoor environmental quality, and innovation and design process. Depending on the points achieved in each of the categories, the building is rated Certified, Silver, Gold or given the highest rating, Platinum. LEED versions cover New Construction, Existing Buildings, Commercial Interiors, Core and Shell, Homes, Neighbourhood Development, Schools and Retail.

Green certification systems are now often used by planning authorities as a requirement in granting planning permission. On top of certification systems for buildings we often see requirements in separate national building regulations, planning regulations and guidance notes at local, regional and national levels, and regulations covering transport and emissions to air and water. With many layers of standards, regulations and policy guidance, it is often not possible to meet the requirements of all the different and sometimes conflicting demands being made on a particular development. This is now leading to confusion, delays and excessive costs. Perhaps worse than that, sometimes the prescriptive nature of these standards prevents the adoption of the most appropriate solution.

Geof Syphers, Chief Sustainability Officer at Codding Enterprises, developer of Sonoma Mountain Village in California (described in Chapter 13), and an LEED Accredited Professional, explains with some examples of how building a sustainable community can even be illegal:

> While seeking to ensure that streets be kept clear for public safety and to provide adequate access to businesses, laws were established requiring a minimum number of parking spaces, unintentionally mandating that transportation needs be met with cars. The California Environmental Quality Act can lead to favoring development on green fields over urban infill sites because the review process can be used as the basis for lawsuits by the many neighbors of infill projects. Because of height limits, it is often easier to get permits to build low-rise sprawl than an elegant 5-storey mixed-use community, which would reduce or eliminate the need for a car. Zoning limits how different uses may be stacked vertically, such as homes over shops, and horizontally, such as factories next to daycare, and most cities do not currently have a zoning category for mixed-use buildings. The Endangered Species Act can unintentionally harm endangered species by steering developers to mitigate their impacts through buying land elsewhere to establish permanent open space and encouraging the original development to plow, spray and do anything possible to prevent endangered plants from moving back onto the construction site. The rationale is that these actions protect the developer from potential delays that would arise if endangered species were later found.[9]

In some cases, standards are also stifling innovation because they don't always recognise new approaches or products. For example, the UK's Code for Sustainable Homes has credits related to materials, but gaining them is conditional on manufacturers having their products assessed, which can be an expensive and lengthy process. This acts as a barrier to the introduction of new products, particularly by small, innovative companies that need to build market share to reduce unit costs and make their products competitive.

Standards such as LEED, BREEAM and the Code for Sustainable Homes (together with standards in other areas such Organic Standards and FSC) certainly do have a very important role to play in ensuring that the buildings, products and services we use are more environmentally friendly than they might otherwise be. However, they do not relate our consumption of products and services to the overall availability of natural resources on the planet. For example, just because a building consumes less energy, it doesn't mean that we will reduce CO_2 emissions sufficiently to avert the dangers of climate change: if all the buildings in the world were certified to the highest environmental standards, we would not necessarily have a sustainable planet. Therefore, certification systems do not provide us with an overall indicator of sustainability. To provide this insight into overall sustainability we can turn to ecological footprinting.

Ecological footprinting as a tool

Increasingly, ecological footprinting is being used to provide an insight into what is truly sustainable. It has been originated by thinkers such as Mathis Wackernagel and William Rees,[10] and development of ecological footprinting as a tool is being led internationally by the Global Footprint Network.[11]

Ecological footprinting allows us to create a simple equation comparing the availability of naturally renewing resources on the planet with the rate at which we are consuming them. From satellite imaging we know we have a total of 12.6 billion hectares of biologically productive land and sea on the planet (see Table 1) which amounts to about a quarter of the planet's surface area. The rest is deep ocean, desert and high mountain which is not of high biological productivity. Built-up areas can be biologically productive: trees growing in our gardens absorb CO_2, or we might be

Table 1
Figures from the Global Footprint Network show us the total biologically active land and sea on the planet.
Statistics 2008

Land or sea type	Billion hectares
Cropland	1.3
Grazing land	4.6
Forest	3.3
Fishing grounds	3.2
Built up areas	0.2
TOTAL	**12.6**

growing vegetables or, in some parts of the world, even keeping livestock (as we shall see later in this book, there is great scope to increase the biological productivity of our urban areas). The 12.6 billion hectares of productive land and sea on earth is our one planet's worth of biological productivity.

It is possible to get a very good idea of how much can be produced sustainably from this productive land and sea. For example, every 25 hectares of fishing grounds on the planet will yield sustainably, as a global average, about one tonne of fish per year. In other words, 25 hectares of fishing grounds are needed somewhere on the planet for each tonne of fish we consume each year. We need 1.3 hectares of forest to provide us with each cubic metre of wood, whether we use that wood for paper production or for construction. We need 0.35 hectares of forest to absorb each tonne of CO_2 we release each year from, say, burning fossil fuels – called 'energy land' by the Global Footprint Network.

Exceeding the planet's biological limits

Periodically, the Global Footprint Network produces figures which compare the biocapacity of the planet with our consumption of these natural resources. For each country in the world we can calculate how much of the planet's surface area it takes to support consumption in that country. First we look at the levels of domestic production from farming, forestry, fisheries, etc. Then we add in imports and subtract exports to get the net consumption of that country. From this net consumption we can work out the country's ecological footprint – the area of the planet's biologically productive land and sea that is needed to support it. We can add the footprints of all the countries of the world together to get the world or global ecological footprint. This sort of analysis suggests that we exceeded the carrying capacity of the planet – the highest sustainable level of consumption – in the mid-1970s, and as a global society we are now consuming naturally renewing resources at a rate of 30 per cent more than the planet can sustain in the long term. We are doing this by eating into the natural reserves of the planet. For example, globally we are still losing forests at more than 7 million hectares a year,[12] an area equivalent to the size of Sierra Leone. The area is even greater when we count land converted from natural forests to plantations. The 'Global Environment Outlook-4 (GEO-4)' report by the United Nations in 2007 suggested that the capacity of fishing fleets is 2.5 times greater than the amount of fish that can be harvested sustainably.[13] Up to 70 per cent of all the world's fisheries are fully exploited or over exploited. So, for example, in the UK we no longer have a cod fishery in the North Sea and instead are air-freighting fish from all over the world to meet our demands. And because the planet doesn't have the capacity to absorb CO_2 as fast as we are releasing it into the atmosphere, its levels are building up and causing global warming. Indeed, rising CO_2 emissions are the largest contributor to the world's ecological footprint, as shown in Figure 3.

All these figures can appear as just another set of statistics. However, had we been able to go into space and look back at the earth, we would, in a short space of time, have seen massive changes. At the very start of this century, astronaut Commander Cuthbertson had this to say as he looked out from the International Space Station:

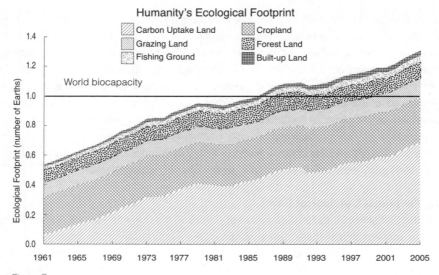

Humanity's Ecological Footprint

Legend:
- Carbon Uptake Land
- Grazing Land
- Fishing Ground
- Cropland
- Forest Land
- Built-up Land

World biocapacity

Y-axis: Ecological Footprint (number of Earths) — 0.0, 0.2, 0.4, 0.6, 0.8, 1.0, 1.2, 1.4

X-axis: 1961, 1965, 1969, 1973, 1977, 1981, 1985, 1989, 1993, 1997, 2001, 2005

Figure 3

The world's ecological footprint is steadily growing. As a global society we exceeded the carrying capacity of the planet in the mid-1970s and are currently consuming 30 per cent more a year than the planet can sustain in the long term.

'It's quite amazing to see how many people actually live down there and how much effect they are having on the environment and the land we live on. It is a cause for concern. Since my first flight in 1990 and this flight, I have seen changes in what comes out of some of the rivers, in land usage ... we are losing lots of trees ... We have to be very careful how we treat this good Earth we live on.'[14]

A fair share of the earth's resources

We can use ecological footprinting to generate the concept of a fair share of the earth's resources. If we take the total 12.6 billion hectares of the planet's productive land and seas, leave 10 per cent for wildlife and use 90 per cent primarily to meet human consumption, we have a budget of 11.3 billion hectares from which to meet our needs. If we divide this budget of 11.3 billion hectares by the global population of 6.7 billion people, we get a fair-share ecological footprint of 1.7 hectares per person. Another way of looking at this is that if we were living sustainably on the planet, the average global citizen would have an ecological footprint of 1.7 hectares.

Taking first a UK perspective: the average person in the UK has a footprint of 5.3 hectares.[15] This is three times the global fair share. In other words if everyone on earth consumed as many resources as the average person in the UK, we would need three planets to support us.

So the challenge for those of us living in the UK is to find ways of living where we can increase our quality of life, but reduce our consumption of virgin materials and fossil fuels by two-thirds to adopt 'One Planet Living'[16] or a one planet lifestyle. This way to communicate sustainability and create a practical approach to achieving it has been pioneered by environment organisation BioRegional Development Group, whose work is described in more detail in the next chapter.[17] To create sustainable communities we should create places where it is easy for people to lead happy and healthy lives within a fair share of the earth's resources.

We can take the same approach to look at the challenge from the perspective of any country. Different countries are consuming resources at very different rates. The ecological footprint of the US is 9.6 hectares per person. If we all lived like Americans we would need over five planets to support us. Other countries with what we might describe as an American lifestyle characterised by large homes in sprawling suburbs, a high level of car dependence and a high meat diet – countries like Canada and Australia – also have a four to five planet lifestyle. This is not to cast blame or demonise these countries. As these countries and their cultures were built, land and space were not scarce resources, so the need for compact cities, towns and suburbs was simply not an issue. Back then no one had any inkling of the global effect of burning fossil fuels.

The highest consuming country in the world today is the United Arab Emirates with an ecological footprint of 11.9 hectares – an enormous seven planet lifestyle: very car dependent, very high consuming and using huge amounts of energy, for example, for air conditioning and desalinating water in the desert climate.

China overall has a one planet level of consumption. It is, of course, an emerging economy and so its ecological footprint is growing rapidly. Cities like Shanghai are now high-consuming places where people have a three to four planet lifestyle.[18] The poorest countries in the world like Eritrea (0.7 hectares per person), Mozambique (0.6 hectares per person) and Afghanistan (0.1 hectares per person) have ecological footprints which are a one-third planet lifestyle or less. The One Planet Living approach – where we all move to using closer to a fair share of the earth's resources – means that we can leave space for these poorest of countries to increase their levels of consumption and their ecological footprint to attain a comfortable material standard of living.

It is not just differences between countries that should be considered. There are differences within countries, especially those with a marked disparity between rich and poor. South Africa, for example, overall has a footprint of 2.3 hectares per person. However, it is a country with a mix of high-consuming, 'American' five planet lifestyles, such as in the gated suburbs of Midrand in Johannesburg, existing side by side with very poor communities with a quarter planet lifestyle or less in the nearby townships such as Ivory Park.

Most of Western Europe has a footprint between 4.5 and 6 hectares – around a three planet lifestyle. This is interesting as we often think of countries like Sweden as more eco-friendly than countries like the UK. They may well be in some regards, but the Swedes have a Western European lifestyle – living in similar homes, driving similar amounts, having similar diets – which means overall footprints are similar. Sweden's footprint per capita is 5.1 hectares compared with the UK's 5.3 hectares. As we shall see in Chapter 2, it is *lifestyle* which drives ecological impact and therefore lifestyles are the best way of looking at ecological footprints and approaches to building sustainable communities. In Chapter 8, we will also look at the relationship between ecological footprint and happiness, and how the emerging science of happiness can give us a particular insight into creating sustainable communities. Levels of consumption, even in Europe, are far greater than we need to be happy, and in many ways increasing levels of consumption are actually reducing overall levels of happiness, even in the short term.

Limitations of ecological footprinting

Ecological footprinting is a good headline indicator for sustainability. In Chapter 3 we explore in more detail how ecological footprints relate to CO_2 emissions and other indicators such as 'carbon footprint'. However, every indicator has its limitations. From an environmental perspective, ecological footprinting does not take into account toxicity or water, for instance. Therefore pollutants and water need to be considered separately. Chemicals such as dioxins produced by burning certain plastics in poorly regulated incinerators, for example, are carcinogenic. Other examples include polychlorinated biphenyls (PCBs) used, for instance, as fire retardants in PVC wiring. PCBs don't readily break down in the environment, persist for long periods and are linked to liver damage. To create a sustainable future, we will need to reduce and ultimately aim to eliminate the release of toxins, particularly persistent ones, into the environment.

Methods have been developed to account for environmental impacts such as toxicity. The EcoPoints system developed by the Building Research Establishment enables comparisons to be made between different construction materials, taking into account a range of factors from embodied energy to pollution released into water. For example, in deciding cladding materials for the BedZED eco-village in south London (described in more detail in the next chapter), the EcoPoints system was used to compare various options (Figure 4). Untreated, but resilient, oak weatherboarding from local woodlands was selected on this basis.

Ecological footprinting also does not take into account impact on water resources. In many parts of the world, such as the Middle East and southern Europe, access to water and its availability is becoming the most pressing short-term environmental issue. The approach to sustainable water use is very much a local and regional issue and, although it is wise never to be profligate with any resources, the amount of effort we focus on water varies – even between Kent in the south of England and Middlesbrough in the northeast where local water availability is hugely different.

Sustainability is not just about environmental factors. It is also about economic and social issues and we might want to use a range of other indicators (employment, education, health, etc) in defining a strategy for sustainability. The engineering company Arup employs a system called SPeAR (Sustainable

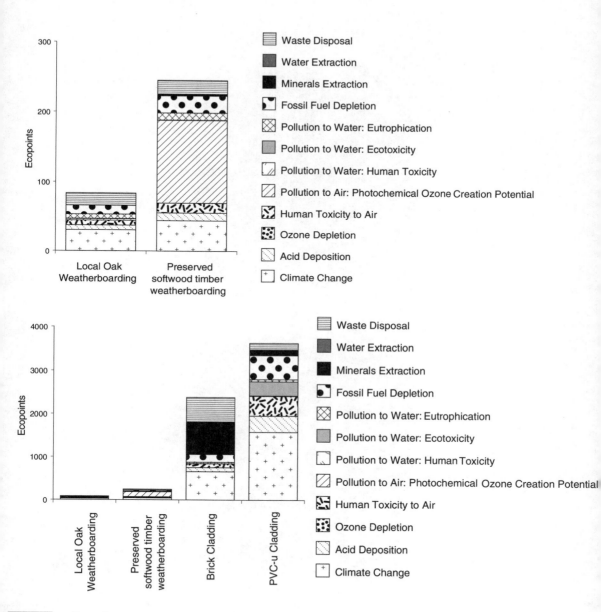

Figure 4

EcoPoints can be used to assist decision-making. When specifying materials for the BedZED eco-village in south London, an EcoPoints comparison showed local oak weatherboarding to be the best environmental choice. The lower the points, the less the environmental damage.

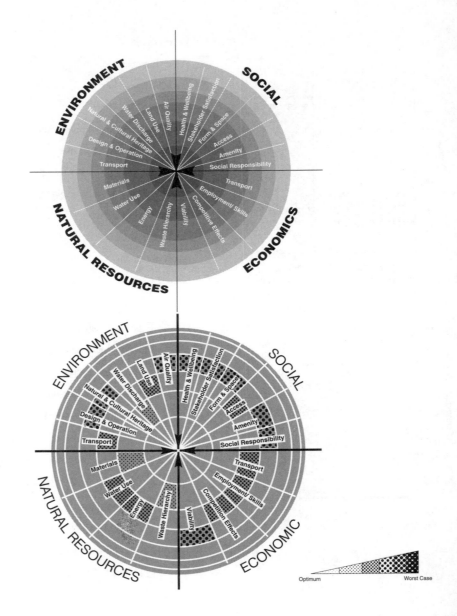

Figure 5

The SPeAR system is based on sets of environment, natural resources, societal and economic indicators (top image). Any project can be assessed on these indicators and graphically represented (bottom image). The aim is to hit the 'bull's eye' with all indicators being optimum.

Project Appraisal Routine) to compare a wide range of sustainability indicators grouped into four key areas: environment, natural resources, societal and economic. Any particular project or area such as a city can be assessed against the range of indicators to provide a mechanism for comparison (see Figure 5).

We must learn how and when to use different tools and indicators. They give us different views on the impacts and potential advantages of making different choices from environmental, social and economic perspectives. However, the real value of ecological footprinting as a headline indicator remains. It is the indicator which gives us a clear insight into our consumption of naturally renewing resources compared with their global availability. Not to be underestimated is also the relative ease with which ecological footprint can be communicated to a wide professional and lay audience. As someone remarked to me once, 'Number of planets to support a lifestyle: I can talk about it down at the pub!'

Some commentators discuss sustainability as a trade-off between environmental, social and economic factors. However, headline environmental indicators such as ecological footprinting must always be at the heart of any discussion of sustainability. Environmental sustainability must be non-negotiable because without environmental sustainability our economic and social systems cannot exist. All of us depend on the integrity of the planet – ultimately for our lives.

The UK's three planet lifestyle

To provide us with an example, let us consider in more detail how the three planet lifestyle in the UK is made up. We can break down our footprint in various ways, but an emerging standardised way of reporting ecological footprint is emerging (see Figure 6).[19]

The footprints are calculated by a combination of so-called mass balance studies and economic flow models. Mass balance studies very accurately measure the footprint of a particular product – such as a T-shirt, for example, or a solar panel – from detailed information on the materials and energy used to produce it. However, mass balance studies are very labour- and time-intensive. Estimates of the ecological footprint using economic flows – using data collected on the sales of goods and services – are now used to get a good broadbrush indication of ecological footprint. For example, we know the CO_2 emissions associated with electricity generation in the UK, so we can get a good estimate of the ecological footprint associated with each unit (kWh) of electricity sold – tracking the ecological footprint through the economy as a whole. Using economic flows allows us to relate ecological footprint to standard categories used by economists and can help in modelling government policy. These categories are defined in Table 2.

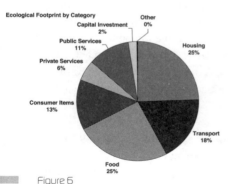

Ecological Footprint by Category

Capital Investment 2%
Public Services 11%
Private Services 6%
Consumer Items 13%
Other 0%
Housing 25%
Transport 18%
Food 25%

Figure 6
How our ecological footprint is made up in the UK. Data from REAP Version 2, October 2008, published by Stockholm Environment Institute, available from www.sei.se/reap.

Table 2
Definitions
of ecological
footprint
categories.

Category	Definition
Home and energy	Energy used in the home including gas and electricity consumption, energy and materials in the building and maintenance of our homes
Transport	Fuel consumption, car ownership, public transport and flying
Food	Food and drink consumed at home and out at restaurants
Goods	Consumer products we purchase, such as large household objects like furniture and appliances, plus smaller products such as newspapers, clothing and electronics
Services	Services that we use such as recreation, financial, telephone, insurance, private schools and private medical care
Government	Central and local government activities, the health service, schools, universities and social services
Capital assets	Investment in capital assets such as factories, machinery and other buildings and structures that isn't covered in the sectors above

Energy in the home for appliances, space heating and hot water accounts for 25 per cent of the UK ecological footprint. The amount of energy consumed in any home varies enormously depending, for example, on how well insulated the home might be, what appliances are in the home and how much these are used. The greater the number of people living in the home, generally the lower the energy consumption per person because things like cooking and watching television might be shared. In new homes, space heating is becoming a smaller proportion of overall energy consumption. Therefore the measures we might take to build a new sustainable community could differ markedly from the approach to 'retrofitting' existing communities to make them greener.

Personal transport accounts for 18 per cent of the average person's footprint in the UK. The greatest proportion of this is for private car use. Food is a large part of our ecological footprint comprising 25 per cent of the total. Our food choices greatly affect footprint – for example, intensively reared meat makes up a disproportionately large part of the footprint. We explore the footprint of food further in Chapter 7. Goods and consumer items make up 13 per cent. This includes everything we end up throwing away, with almost 70 per cent of household waste in the UK still ending up in landfill.[20] Increasing recycling rates and using more recycled products can help us to reduce our ecological footprint.

Individual choice, local infrastructure and government spending – a planet apiece

Approximately one-third (or one planet's worth) of the UK footprint arises from areas over which people have more direct control – such as personal choices with regard to goods, transport and food, as well as behaviour such as whether people choose to switch off appliances when not using them. A second planet's worth is determined by what we might call local or community infrastructure – recycling facilities and public transport, provision of energy-efficient homes and appliances, and whether schools and offices are within walking or cycling distance. The final third planet's worth is spent by central government on our behalf in delivering services such as health provision, defence spending and large infrastructure projects like major road building programmes. This division of personal choice, local infrastructure and government spending is paralleled in all countries although the relative contributions of each may vary. As a theme that runs through this book, we need all three to line up in order to ultimately achieve our aim of One Planet Living.

Ecological footprinting tells us clearly that if we are to create a sustainable community it is not enough to build an eco-friendly house. We need to address all the different areas of our lifestyles – energy, personal transport, food, waste and holidays.[21] In creating these communities we also need to align individual choice, local infrastructure and government spending so all that we need for a happy and healthy life can be met within a one planet footprint. We can greatly influence ecological footprint by making the green choice easy, attractive and affordable. As we shall see in the next chapter, we cannot control ecological footprint as it ultimately depends on the choices individuals make, but we can certainly create places where it is much easier for us, and the people around us, to lead more environmentally friendly lifestyles.

Let us turn now to BedZED eco-village, a pioneering UK example of a sustainable community, to see how it measures up as a place where residents can reduce their ecological footprint – and also what it is like to live there.

Notes
1 Kofi Annan, Dhaka Speech, 2001.
2 Jared Diamond, *Collapse: How Societies Choose to Fail or Succeed*, Penguin Group (London), 2006, pp 79–119.
3 Reverend Thomas Malthus, *An Essay on the Principle of Population*, 1798.
4 Rachel Carson, Silent Spring, Houghton Mifflin, (New York), 1962.
5 DH Meadows, DL Meadows, J Randers and WW Behrens, *The Limits to Growth*, Universe Books (New York), 1972.
6 EF Schumacher, *Small Is Beautiful: A Study of Economics as if People Mattered*, Blond & Briggs (London), 1973.
7 International Union for the Conservation of Nature (IUCN), 1980.
8 United Nations World Commission on Environment and Development, *Our Common Future, Report of the World Commission on Environment and Development*, Oxford University Press (Oxford), 1987.
9 Geof Syphers, personal communication, 2009.
10 M Wackernagel and W Rees, *Our Ecological Footprint: Reducing Human Impact on the Earth*, New Society Publishers (Gabriola Island), 1996.
11 See www.footprintnetwork.org.
12 Food and Agriculture Organisation (FAO), *Global Forest Resource Assessment*, 2005.
13 United Nations Environment Programme (UNEP), 'Global Environment Outlook-4 (GEO-4)', 2007.
14 Live satellite interview, *Today Programme*, BBC Radio 4, August 2001.
15 Global Footprint Network, *Living Planet Report 2008*, WWF International (Gland, Switzerland), 2008.
16 'One Planet Living' is a term originally coined by environmental organisation BioRegional Development Group and is a registered trademark of BioRegional and WWF International.
17 P Desai and S Riddlestone, *BioRegional Solutions for Living on One Planet*, Schumacher Briefing No 8, Green Books Limited (Totnes), 2002.
18 Roger Wood, *Dongtan Eco-City*, ARUP (PowerPoint presentation), 2007.
19 John Barrett et al, *REAP*, Stockholm Environment Institute (SEI York), 2008.
20 UK Department for Environment, Food and Rural Affairs, *Sustainable Development Indicators in Your Pocket*, 2008.
21 P Desai and P King, *One Planet Living*, Alistair Sawday Publishing (Bristol), 2006.

Chapter 2

Think lifestyles — lessons from the BedZED eco-village

Though green buildings are part of creating a sustainable community, it is the whole lifestyle that a person adopts that determines overall ecological footprint. We have sometimes become too focused on energy-efficient buildings rather than looking at the bigger picture. We must grasp opportunities such as to reduce car dependence to bring large CO_2 savings as well as to create better places to live.

'Luck is when preparedness meets opportunity.'

Seneca the Younger[1]

Having drawn together the project, and lived and worked at Beddington Zero fossil Energy Development (BedZED) in south London, means that this is, inevitably, both a professional and personal account of the project. BedZED eco-village has been both a fantastic and a difficult learning experience for all involved and yielded much information for the wider industry. Not everything has worked, but lessons from its design, construction and ongoing monitoring remain influential, worldwide, to this day.

Set in an unremarkable and somewhat down-at-heel suburb of the otherwise leafy London Borough of Sutton, BedZED is a pioneering attempt to create a place where it is easy for people to reduce their environmental impact. Its colourful, photogenic wind cowls and green roofs have become internationally recognised as an icon of sustainable living. BedZED was arguably unique in its day in trying to create a whole sustainable lifestyle at a significant scale – with 100 homes plus 2,500m^2 of office and community space. There had been other green communities constructed in the UK, such as at Findhorn in Scotland and the Centre for Alternative Technology in Wales, but there was nothing at any scale aimed at the person in the street rather than the out-and-out green enthusiast.

This book is about creating sustainable communities. The word 'community' has numerous definitions, covering a wide spectrum from very close-knit groups of people living together and sharing common values, to virtual communities of people who may never meet except in cyberspace. In this book I use the term very loosely. I simply mean a group of people who are linked because of common location – neighbours for want of another term. In sharing a common location there is a shared interest at some level. At a most basic level it is simply to ensure civil relations. However, there are possible benefits in going further than this to secure better facilities, social interaction, solutions to problems or to create a positive common purpose. BedZED was never designed to be an 'intentional' community or commune, with adherents to a particular way of life. It was simply designed to be a greener place to live, fostering a higher quality of life and aiming to create a sense of community – where neighbours would feel sufficient connection to BedZED and their fellow residents to participate in its running and long-term future.

Figure 1
Beddington Zero (fossil) Energy Development (BedZED), Sutton, south London. Date of Completion – 2002.

The origins of BedZED

As with so many things, it was serendipity that brought BedZED to life. The project represents the coming together of a number of strands of work including that of architect Bill Dunster, engineer Chris Twinn, the London Borough of Sutton, the Peabody Trust, as well as the BioRegional Development Group, the organisation of which I am co-founder.

BioRegional's aim is to establish real-life, working examples of sustainable industries and ways of living based on using local renewable and recycled resources. By meeting more of our everyday needs in this way, we can reduce environmental impact and leave more space for wilderness and wildlife (in the final chapter of this book, we explore the possibility that leaving space for wilderness and wildlife is not just a nice thing to do, but may be essential for our planet to regulate the atmosphere). The approach draws inspiration from the philosophical and academic concept of bioregionalism, which looks at defining regions and meeting human needs based on natural boundaries rather than artificial political ones.[2] In the early years at BioRegional, we developed projects in sustainable forestry, recycling and eco-farming – more about the philosophy and practical application of bioregional development can be found in *BioRegional Solutions for Living on One Planet*.[3] We also started developing ideas for sustainable buildings and settlements set within a 'bioregional' context of meeting more of their needs from local renewable and recycled resources. Therefore, when in 1997 we needed new offices, BioRegional's co-founder, Sue Riddlestone, suggested we take the opportunity to express our commitment and ideas by building a green office.

BioRegional Development Group

BioRegional Development Group was established in 1994. Sue Riddlestone, BioRegional's co-founder, says: 'Our enterprise and science-based approach recognises the importance of the economy and the power of delivering change through products and services. At the same time we can create employment in green industries.'

BioRegional has worked in sustainable forestry, farming, recycling, technology development and eco-housing. Research into making best use of local wood resources led BioRegional to establish both a forestry management service reintroducing traditional practices to the woodlands in the southeast of England and a company supplying national retailers with local woodland products through a network of local producers – pioneering the concept of 'network production', marrying benefits of central coordination with decentralised supply. Work on a sustainable office paper cycle has led to 'The Laundry' paper recycling service in London as well as BioRegional MiniMills, which develops new clean technology for pulping non-wood fibres on a small scale, facilitating local paper supply. In bringing together the BedZED project and leading in monitoring it, BioRegional gained experience in design, construction and management of sustainable communities which supported the formation of a specialist zero carbon property development company, BioRegional Quintain Ltd, in which BioRegional Development Group has a shareholding and which is financially backed by London Stock Exchange listed company Quintain Estates and Development plc.

BioRegional Development Group originated the term 'One Planet Living' and led on creating the framework now being applied to projects as diverse as retailer B&Q's One Planet Home and the London 2012 Olympics. Headquartered at BedZED, BioRegional network is growing with offices in North America, South Africa and China.

BedZED comes to Sutton

At the time, BioRegional was based in the Ecology Centre, an educational centre run by the London Borough of Sutton. I was involved in the municipal authority's Local Agenda 21 process – a United Nations-inspired process requiring local authorities to create local sustainability plans. In one of these evening meetings in 1997, I asked one of Sutton's senior planners, Jeff Wilson, if he knew of any land on which we could build new offices. Sutton had been an early leader in adopting green policies so the idea was well received. He suggested a 1.2 hectares plot of land which the council was selling for residential development, but which he thought could incorporate office space as well. So the idea of a whole eco-village rather than simply an office building was born.

Previously I had been invited by Bill Dunster to give a lecture on 'permaculture', a green design philosophy, to his students at the Architectural Association.[4] Bill had designed his own solar house for his family incorporating a working studio, Hope House in Surrey (Figure 2). The detached house was self-built in 1995 on a plot of reclaimed land near Hampton Court Palace at the confluence of the rivers Mole and Ember, just before they enter the Thames. The home has a south-facing conservatory, photovoltaic panels and was later retrofitted with a wind turbine and wood-burning stove. Bill had been developing ideas for scaling up the concept, working with others including Chris Twinn at engineers Arup. With Bill and Chris, BioRegional started working to produce outline proposals for an eco-village for the land being put up for sale, which would include homes, offices and community space.

The coming together of the team and a touch of entrepreneurship turned out to be a good mix. A cost plan was drawn up with Gardiner & Theobald Quantity Surveyors, and BioRegional recruited an engineer, Nicole Lazarus, to start searching for a developer partner. Sue Riddlestone, with characteristic intuition, insisted we approach the Peabody Trust, a leading social housing provider in London who, under the leadership of director of development, Dickon Robinson, was a pioneer in design quality and innovation. A number of meetings followed with Peabody's development team, including one of its development managers, Malcolm Kirk, who ultimately came to project manage BedZED. Peabody recognised it would take a brave developer to take on the scheme, but agreed to work with BioRegional to submit a bid for the land.

Figure 2
Hope House, Surrey, 1995. The family home of BedZED architect Bill Dunster.

Initial design and aspiration

The design evolved over a number of months. Meetings took place with local residents and community groups and extensive discussions were held with the council. Bill Dunster had created a concept called 'Hope Town' which had taken Hope House as a building block for terraces of homes. Passive solar design was a key design driver. In the UK climate, homes generally have a net heating requirement so facing south allows them to gain heat from the sun. Modern offices with their computers and servers often have a net cooling requirement so facing north would help prevent overheating. Therefore terraces would be created, with homes facing south towards the sun and offices facing north. Skylights to the north would provide good lighting without glare to the office space. Having reduced energy loads, electricity would be provided by a biomass combined heat and power plant, with waste heat being piped via a district heating system to provide hot water and space heating. All roof surfaces would be used productively. All homes would have access to a private garden either at ground level or as roof terraces – so-called 'sky gardens' with some accessed via walkways. The very top surfaces would be green roofs covered in alpine flowers (sedum) to create a wildlife habitat. Car-parking spaces would be reduced from the usual requirement with the introduction of a green transport plan and car club. Provision would be made for electric vehicles with charging points fed by electricity, including from photovoltaic panels fitted to the buildings. Recycled and reclaimed materials would be used wherever possible, rainwater harvested and sewage treated on site with a 'Living Machine', an enhanced reed-bed system. To reduce waste, recycling facilities would be integrated into the design.

Figure 3
BedZED masterplan.

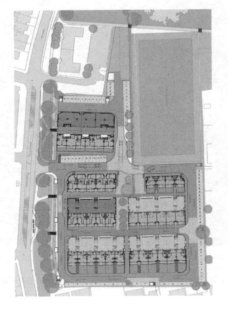

Securing the site

The bidding process for the land was hard fought against conventional developers. We were not the highest bidder. Difficult discussions took place within the council between those keen to support our bid and those who felt obliged to take the highest financial bid. BioRegional lobbied hard, saying that the council had made far-reaching commitments to the environment in various policy statements and that BedZED represented an opportunity to express that commitment. BioRegional sought clarification from central government on the legal position: local authorities were not bound to accept the highest bid, provided the bid they did accept offered best value, and permission was needed only from central government if the bid was not within 10 per cent of the highest financial offer. To further investigate the position, the council took the step of commissioning an independent report to place a financial value on the CO_2 savings.

It was close run by all accounts, but finally, in 1998, our bid was accepted – all credit to Sutton. The fact that the sale of the land incorporated a financial value for carbon savings was a first in the UK. As we worked through the process of winning planning consent with the local authority, we needed to continue to pioneer, altering convention on transport planning. We wanted to reduce car parking; however, planning policy stated a requirement for a minimum of 1.6 car parking spaces per dwelling built. We only wanted to build 100 spaces. When BedZED was granted planning permission in 1999 it included a requirement for a Green Transport Plan integrating a car club – another first in the UK.

Construction and early lessons

Work started on site in early 2000. It turned out to be a somewhat difficult time with staff shortages and cost inflation in the construction industry due to the number of large projects being built to commemorate the new millennium. Managing innovation and cost turned out to be a major issue – but this is easy to say with hindsight.

The first homes were completed at the end of 2001 with early residents moving in in spring 2002. BioRegional, as well as the BedZED architects, moved into the offices in the development in March of that year.

I had been the first to reserve an apartment and moved in in August 2002. This personal experience of living and working at BedZED has provided a privileged insight into how to build a sustainable community. There is nothing like first-hand experience to really understand what can and can't work. Published reports can never fully convey the subtleties of getting such a complex system as a community operating effectively – in practice it needs to be a coming together not only of technology, design and economics, but also of behaviour, convenience, interpersonal relationships, psychology, politics and culture.

Constructing BedZED was a challenging process because of the levels of innovation, but also because of inertia and a natural resistance to doing things differently. Development is a complex, integrated process and changing even one part of the process or system can result in a chain of challenges to overcome; for example, changing the specification of materials such as moving to reclaimed wood or steel can affect the professional indemnities of the design team, the warranties achievable, and therefore, ultimately, the mortgageability of the homes. Dealing with suppliers, contractors, planners, building control officers and the various organisations and companies involved in delivering a completed set of buildings while trying to keep to timescales and budgets can create a pressured environment. The project was not a success financially, which proved painful for the Peabody Trust; whose commitment requires special recognition for without it we would not have been able to learn the lessons to share with the industry more generally. The whole team on BedZED was committed to making the technical aspects widely available; a number of reports have been published and ongoing monitoring results are available.[5]

When BedZED was being designed, we, at BioRegional, were only just becoming aware of ecological footprinting as a methodology. We were thinking in more general terms about environmental impact and creating a place where it would be easy for people to lead a greener lifestyle. It was only after BedZED was complete, and when Sue Riddlestone and I were commissioned to write the book *BioRegional Solutions*, that we really started interpreting and communicating the strategies at BedZED more clearly in terms of ecological footprint. Nonetheless we knew that our impacts would come from energy, travel, food and waste, plus an increasing amount from overseas travel and holidays, which are all represented in Figure 4. BioRegional worked systematically with the design team and the Peabody Trust to try to make a whole sustainable lifestyle possible for residents.

Our three planet footprint

Figure 4
From the perspective of an individual, a three planet lifestyle can be represented as being made up of food, waste, transport, home energy and holiday components – varying person to person and location to location.

Saving energy, generating renewables and 'saving our planets'

The buildings at BedZED were of course designed to be exceptionally energy efficient. The masterplan was based on terraces of south-facing homes with offices and live-work units placed to the north (see Figure 5). High levels of insulation were installed – 300 millimetres of rock wool insulation giving U-values (insulation values) for walls of about 0.1 W (Watts)/m^2/K (compared with Building Regulations at the time of 0.45 W/m^2/K, presenting a 75 per cent increase in insulating performance). With south-facing sun-spaces, the homes were designed to reduce the need for space heating. The superinsulation was combined with careful detailing of the design to make the homes airtight to reduce heat losses via leakage and draughts. As explored later in this book, I personally am not convinced by the principle of orientating homes towards the south to maximise passive solar gain – at least not in the UK climate – but more about that in Chapter 4.

When building superinsulated, airtight homes, it is important to ensure good ventilation, but also to recover heat, or coolth in summer, from the outgoing air. This is usually done via a ventilation system incorporating a fan and heat exchanger, known as Mechanical Ventilation with Heat Recovery (MVHR). For BedZED, Bill Dunster and Chris Twinn proposed a passive ventilation with heat recovery system – the wind cowls for which BedZED is famous. These cowls are able to rotate, and a fin points them into the wind. Fresh air is forced into the homes via the aperture at the front of the cowl, while stale air is sucked out from the kitchens and toilets by the negative pressure created as wind flows over the rear aperture of the cowl. A heat exchanger between the incoming and exhaust flows of air enables heat recovery. The cowls, which have worked well, are certainly distinctive and have earned BedZED a few local nicknames.

Figure 5
Section through BedZED showing terraces with residential units with south-facing conservatories and office space to the north. Office roofs provide garden space for the residential units accessed via the bridges.

The homes were fitted with energy-efficient appliances – lighting and A-rated refrigerators and ovens. Water-efficient appliances such as spray taps and entrained air showerheads (which suck in air to 'bulk' out the water) were also fitted and save energy by reducing hot water use too.

Having reduced energy demand for space heating, hot water and electrical appliances, it was worth considering supplying all the energy from renewable sources. The target for BedZED was to generate the average annual energy demand for the buildings from renewable energy on site. The debate about on site versus off-site energy generation is a heated one and we return to it in Chapter 6. Nonetheless, at BedZED we did in the end try for all on site generation using local renewable fuel, and we learned some hard lessons in doing so.

A total of 777 square metres of electricity generating photovoltaic (PV) panels were fitted, generating a 109-kilowatt peak, the largest PV installation in the UK at the time (the energy could be used in buildings or used to power up to 40 electric vehicles). Some were integrated into the glazing of the south-facing conservatories, others were placed on the southerly aspect of the roofs. The main energy generation source planned for BedZED was a biomass-powered combined heat and power (CHP) plant. It was a new technology and we recognised it as a high-risk part of the project. The technology operates on woodchip, which we were providing by chipping local tree-surgery waste, diverting this material from landfill. The woodchip is converted to a gas which fuels an engine, generating electricity. Water is used to cool the engine, and this hot 'waste' water was piped to BedZED homes via a district heating system. Unfortunately, the technology did not work effectively and we have been unable to keep it operating long term. When it was working it did generate the majority of the energy to provide for our needs. (Small-scale biomass CHP systems are still some way off from being a practical technology, but reliable systems will emerge in future and they will have their place. Until then, they will need to be seen as experimental systems.)

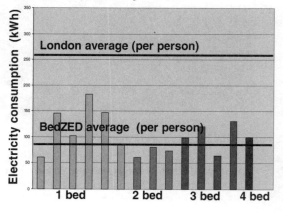

Figure 6

Example of data from monitoring of homes at BedZED demonstrates major energy savings over the London average. It is worth noting how the energy consumption between homes at BedZED varies considerably – almost threefold – depending on the person and his or her lifestyle.

BedZED electricity use

Renewable energy at BedZED and some lessons

Two sources of renewable energy were installed at BedZED – photovoltaics and a biomass combined heat and power (CHP) plant. The photovoltaic panels have successfully been generating up to 19 per cent of the total electricity consumption of the development (about 10 per cent of the total energy, as about half the demand is for electricity and half for hot water and space heating). Photovoltaics nonetheless remain expensive. We received a European Union grant to offset some of the costs. The simple pay-back periods remain in excess of 50 years. If the energy from photovoltaics is used to displace petrol in cars, then arguably pay-back periods come down to around seven years.

There are a number of different types of biomass combined heat and power plant. Some operate via a simple combustion process – for example, burning the wood to generate steam which powers a steam generator. These combustion-based systems are generally simple and reliable, but as with most technologies are usually more cost-effective at larger scales. The system we installed at BedZED was a gasification system. This operates by converting woodchip into a gas by heating it in a vessel with limited air supply, so it undergoes distillation rather than combustion. The wood gases generated are then used to fuel a converted diesel engine which in turns drives a dynamo, thereby generating electricity. We used the opportunity to supply the CHP as a way to create an 'urban forestry' programme, diverting tree-surgery waste in the neighbouring borough of Croydon from landfill to create a renewable energy fuel for BedZED.

The biomass CHP at BedZED was not successful. The gasification process turned out to be too hard to manage, probably not generating sufficiently stable high temperatures and with filters, for example, clogging with wood tars, possibly aggravated by turning the machine off every night, an operating condition agreed on as part of the planning permission. Gasification is much more easily controlled at larger scales with outputs of, say, 1 megawatt of electrical output rather than our 125-kilowatt plant. Larger-scale CHP plants are also likely to operate cost-effectively. New technologies must be supported, but there will always be risks and we learned that manufacturers' guarantees with technologies unproven in a real-life situation need to be treated with caution.

After three years of hard work by the gasifier suppliers, we had to accept defeat and install back-up gas boilers. With the Peabody Trust, BioRegional are now looking at installing wood-burning boilers which will mean we can generate about 50 per cent of our renewable energy on site.

Energy Saving

Figure 7
Making homes more thermally efficient, providing energy-efficient appliances and renewable energy reduces ecological footprint. This is achieved without decreasing quality of life, and in fact, improving it by increasing thermal comfort in the homes.

Although at BedZED we did not meet all our ambitions, we did make good progress. Monitoring has shown that average electricity consumption is 45 per cent lower than in the surrounding area of London and heating was 81 per cent less than the average. We have been generating at least a proportion of our energy from renewables via the photovoltaic panels.[6]

The idea behind this, however, is important. By saving energy and generating renewable energy, we are reducing our ecological footprint and 'saving our planets', as in Figure 7. When our CHP was working, residents at BedZED were saving up to 85 per cent of our ecological footprint associated with our energy supply. And this is without any decrease in quality of life or behaviour change by residents. In fact, arguably with well-insulated homes we are increasing quality of life by increasing comfort levels. Where residents also modify behaviour and save energy by switching off lights and appliances when not using them, a further 30 per cent reduction in energy consumption is possible. This gives us an overall reduction in ecological footprint associated with energy in buildings of 90 to 95 per cent. Therefore, in particular aspects of our lives, we can make massive footprint reductions – far more than the overall two-thirds reduction we need in the UK to move from a three planet lifestyle to one planet living.

Reducing car dependence and promoting sustainable transport

The car has possibly had a greater impact on shaping our communities than any other invention, as is explored in Chapter 9, bringing with it major environmental and social consequences. The internal combustion engine has been demonised by environmentalists, not without some justification.

Figure 8
The car club at BedZED –
a first for London.

At BedZED we reduced the parking provision from 160 spaces to 100. A number of these spaces are not full size, but 'smart car' spaces for micro-cars. Electric vehicle charging points were also installed. Unusual in a suburban area, residents are required to purchase a permit if they wish to keep a private car at BedZED, but permits are half price for smart cars and free for electric vehicles. However, our approach was not simply to make car ownership less attractive. It was to provide positive and better alternatives. A key part of our Green Transport Plan was to introduce the first car club to London. BioRegional did this by teaming up with the UK's first car club provider, Smartmoves, now called City Car Club.

The idea behind a car club is that it offers 'mobility insurance'. Even in areas where there is reasonable public transport, there are times when you need a car. You might be visiting someone and returning late; or picking up some eco-friendly shelving from B&Q (see Chapter 14). If, however, you have bought a car for these sorts of journeys, with your car conveniently sitting in your drive you end up using it for every journey – even those when you could have walked, cycled or used public transport. Car clubs are like car hire, but available for as little as an hour at a time – sometimes described as pay-as-you-go motoring. The car keys are left in the club cars. A smartcard lets you in and out of the cars, with a small on-board computer controlling the booking. Tapping in your personal identification number allows you to activate your booking and enables the car to be driven off. To ensure you can use a car when you need it, they can be booked over the internet or by telephone in a few seconds. Otherwise you can simply get into the car with your smartcard, let the on-board computer know when you intend to bring it back, and if no one else has booked it beforehand, it will create a booking for you.

The great advantage of car clubs is that you do have access to a car when you need one. However, because it is pay-as-you-go it makes you think before using it – so people walk, cycle and use public transport more (which is, of course, a good way to incorporate more exercise into our lives). The cars are serviced, insured, MOT-ed and valeted meaning that the inconveniences of car ownership are removed. The Royal Automobile Club (RAC) estimates that the average car in

Transport Saving

Figure 9

By introducing the car club, restricting parking and creating a better urban environment, we exceeded our target of reducing private car use. This reduces ecological footprint and saves our planet.

the UK costs £100 a week to run by the time all costs – maintenance, insurance, depreciation, road tax, fuel – are taken into consideration. The cost savings of being a car club member can be substantial. UK car club charity, Carplus, estimates that people driving fewer than 6,000 miles a year will save up to £3,500 a year by joining a car club.[7] From personal experience I estimate I save at around £2,000 by being a member, rather than owning a car for everyday use (more about my personal experience of giving up my car in Chapter 9).

We have three cars as part of the BedZED eco-village and we have achieved a 50 to 65 per cent reduction in car use. BedZED's car club was the first in London, but they are now widespread and growing very rapidly.

There is enormous potential for car clubs to be part of a fully integrated transport system. Although still emerging, they can grow to be extensive national and international networks coordinated with public transport. This is already starting to happen. It is now possible to programme your Oyster card (London's smartcard for bus and underground travel) to let you in and out of City Car Club cars. One day a single card could take you seamlessly via bus, train, underground, cycle hire and car club to wherever you wanted to go.

More sustainable food

Food comprises 25 per cent of our ecological footprint in the UK – not surprising when you consider the land and energy required for growing, processing, packaging, storage, distribution and cooking. Large areas of arable land are needed for crops for us and for animal feed. Then there is pasture for dairy and meat production and the energy required for cultivation and fertiliser.

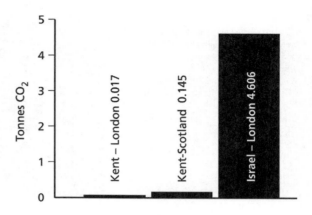

Figure 10

Work carried out by BioRegional quantified the CO$_2$ emissions from transporting a tonne of strawberries. When produced and distributed locally through the supermarket's regional distribution system, transporting strawberries releases 17 kilograms of CO$_2$. Flown from Israel and distributed out of season, transporting each tonne of strawberries releases almost 300 times as much CO$_2$.

Different diets have very different environmental impacts – intensively reared meat, for example, has a disproportionately large footprint (food footprints are examined in more detail in Chapter 7). Transport of food can also have a big environmental impact. Take, for example, a tonne of strawberries (Figure 10). When these are grown in, say, Kent (a rural area southeast of London known as the Garden of England) to be delivered to a supermarket in Kent or London via the normal supermarket regional distribution centres, transporting each tonne of strawberries releases 17 kilograms of CO$_2$. If the strawberries are grown in Scotland and distributed to London, each tonne of strawberries will have released 145 kilograms of CO$_2$. Out of season, when the strawberries are say flown in from Israel and distributed from Heathrow airport, each tonne of strawberries releases 4.6 tonnes of CO$_2$.[8]

Clearly there is a case for promoting more local and seasonal produce. This can also tie in with a higher-quality lifestyle – as endorsed by so many celebrity chefs, for example, who extol the virtues of seasonal produce in terms of taste and freshness. That is not to say that all our food should be local and seasonal. However, there is no reason why in the future we shouldn't aim to get, say, 50 per cent of our food locally or regionally – perhaps targeting a 50- to 100-kilometre radius.

At BedZED we have promoted more local, seasonal and organic produce. As residents moved in, we organised introductory evenings where we asked local organic box-scheme providers to come and talk to our residents. Many residents grow some vegetables or herbs in their gardens and roof gardens. We had also incorporated raised beds for growing food in an allotment area, although, being somewhat away from the buildings, these have suffered some vandalism from local teenagers and so are not as well used as they might be. More recently, a vegetable market has opened on Sundays at the BedZED community centre. Recognising the importance of food in new developments being built by BioRegional Quintain Ltd, for instance, we are doing a lot more to promote sustainable food – looking at farmers' markets, building rooftop allotments, incorporating urban agriculture and including vegetarian restaurants, making it easier and increasing the probability of people eating sustainable and healthier diets (see Chapter 8).

Figure 11
Links were made with local farmers able to make direct deliveries to BedZED.

Making recycling easy

Food Saving

Figure 12
Promoting local, organic seasonal food and diets high in vegetable protein rather than intensively reared meat reduces ecological footprint and helps to 'save our planets'.

Using recycled products and encouraging recycling

A large part of our ecological footprint is associated with consumer goods and waste – all the things that we end up throwing away, the majority of which still end up in landfill – but we can also add to this all the waste generated by companies providing us with various services and construction of the buildings and infrastructure we use.

We consume far more than is necessary, and certainly far more than we need to be happy, as we shall see in Chapter 8. For example, one TV programme showed how an ordinary family could save £1,400 a year simply by buying less of what we can do without – including clothes, books, newspapers and magazines. Of course, charity shops selling second-hand clothes and other goods are great for reducing footprint and some high-street clothes stores have even promoted student fashion shows based on remodelling clothes bought from charity shops. The more recent phenomena of the car boot sale and eBay are also making recycling easier and more of a leisure pursuit.

In the construction of BedZED, working with the Ellis & Moore Engineers, we tried to use reclaimed and recycled products where we could. These were reclaimed from the waste stream and used in, more or less, their original form. For example, most of the steel frame for the offices at BedZED is made of reclaimed steel beams and columns from the refurbishment of Brighton railway station. This reduced the environmental impact by saving 2,580 gigajoules (GJ) of embodied energy and 81.6 tonnes of CO_2 emissions. A large proportion of the studwork for the internal partitions was reclaimed timber. In other areas we were not successful; for example, in using reclaimed doors. It was just not possible on a scheme this size to secure a sufficient, reliable and timely supply. Overall a total of 14 per cent of materials by weight used at BedZED were reclaimed or recycled.[9] Learning from BedZED, for example, in new projects by BioRegional Quintain Ltd, we have increased this percentage to a target of 25 per cent.

At BedZED the aim was to make recycling easy. Unusual at the time, each home was fitted with segregated bins with four compartments – 'dry' recyclables (for paper, card, tins and plastics), green waste (compostable kitchen waste), glass and non-recyclable waste (mainly composite packaging such as bonded paper and plastics). These marry up to collection points around the estate, with a composting area near the allotments. Making recycling easy can greatly affect recycling rates. When one of my neighbours at BedZED was interviewed for the radio and asked, 'Are you an eco-warrior?', his reply was, 'No, I am a fireman, but I have started recycling because it is just as easy for me to put the rubbish in the segregated bins as it is for me to put it in one bin'.

Creating 'closed loops', where products are recycled for reuse, preferably locally, can greatly reduce ecological footprints. For example, at BedZED, recycling and reuse of office paper through the Local Paper for London scheme has been promoted. Bins are provided for white office paper. The paper is sent to the paper recycling plant in Sittingbourne in Kent some 50 kilometres away, and is then supplied back. The overall saving in ecological footprint of paper supply is a massive 85 per cent. More details are given in Chapter 7. Again we see that in particular areas of our lives, it is easy to exceed the overall two-thirds reduction needed in the UK to move from a three planet lifestyle to a one planet lifestyle.

Figure 13
Segregated bins make it easier and more convenient for people to recycle.

Waste Saving

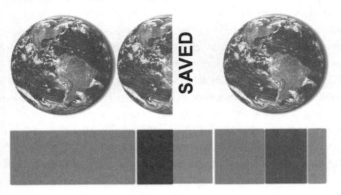

Figure 14
Making recycling easy and using recycled and reclaimed products can save our planets.

The rates of domestic recycling are not as high as we would have liked to achieve at BedZED, mainly because segregation by residents is not as good as it could be and composting of green waste is not offered by the municipal collection. Although approximately twice the rate of conventional apartment-type homes in the area, they are well below the 70 per cent recycling rates that should be achievable, as they are in countries like Switzerland and Austria. One lesson at BedZED is that long-term estates management and community engagement are as important as what is designed up front. At BedZED we spent a lot of time on design and not enough on long-term management. We are beginning to improve on these aspects, but it is easier if they are incorporated from the start – which is what we now do on all our schemes, spending as much time on long-term estates management as on initial design.

Water strategy at BedZED

To reduce water consumption, all homes were fitted with water-efficient appliances. These included spray taps and dual-flush 2-litre/4-litre toilets, considerably less than standard toilets with up to a 9-litre flush. We fitted aerated showerheads with a flow rate of 7 litres a minute – compared with a power shower of 14 litres per minute – which nonetheless give a good showering experience. Rainwater is collected off the green roofs and used for flushing toilets. The Living Machine did work effectively on a technical level (though for a period we had trouble with high bacterial counts probably due to chicken manure used to fertilise the green roofs), but the costs of ongoing maintenance were too high. The water system at BedZED has been taken over by Thames Water as a training facility for engineers and a membrane bioreactor. The 2007 BedZED monitoring report showed that BedZED residents were achieving consumption levels of 72 litres of mains water per day (less than half the local average) plus 15 litres of recycled and rainwater.

Figure 15
The Living Machine at BedZED worked well technically, but operating costs were too high because of its small scale.

Overall ecological footprint saving

Overall, living at BedZED it is possible for a resident, or you or me, to reduce ecological footprint by about one half – *should we choose to*. The caveat is important: analysis of the ecological footprints of people living at BedZED shows massive differences – Figures 17 and 18 compare two BedZED residents in 2006. This is because the overall ecological footprint is not just dependent on providing energy-efficient homes. The footprint is the sum of what is provided to people and their lifestyle choices. If people take three long-haul flights a year for holidays, then they will have a six or even eight planet lifestyle, regardless of whether or not they live in an energy-efficient home run by renewable energy. Because BedZED residents fly more than average, monitoring by BioRegional shows that the overall footprint saving at BedZED is only 11 per cent – demonstrating how personal choices are hugely important in determining ecological footprint. Nonetheless, it is easier for people to reduce their footprint at BedZED than living in a more conventional development, and even the housing estates just across the road from BedZED. BedZED residents will be saving CO_2 emissions from their homes because of the energy-efficient design and because they are fitted with energy-efficient appliances. They can easily relinquish private car ownership in favour of joining the car club if they choose to, because the car club cars are conveniently located on site. It is easy for people to recycle because the recycling facilities have been integrated into the design. Trying to do all this in a conventional development may not be easy.

Therefore, our aim in creating sustainable communities can be no more, or no less, than creating places where it is easy for people to reduce their ecological footprint *should they choose to*.[10] In Chapters 10 and 13, ways in which we can communicate the benefits of making the green choice are explored. Our key challenge as developers, architects or planners is to make the green choice easy, attractive and affordable for people; and at the same time to increase quality of life, health and the probability of our residents being happy – all of which we explore in later chapters. Ultimately our aim must be to achieve this within a fair share of the earth's resources.

Summary of BedZED monitoring 2007

Monitoring figures from 2007 showed that residents at BedZED were achieving a 45 per cent reduction in electricity consumption and an 81 per cent reduction in heating and hot water compared with homes in the surrounding area. Mains-water consumption has been reduced 58 per cent. Some of the north-facing units intended as live-work have been converted to residential units, and there is some evidence that these have ended up using more energy. In rating the thermal comfort of the homes, 84 per cent of residents found the homes comfortable in winter, but only 43 per cent in summer, with a majority finding it too warm. When asked about use of the sun-space, only 66 per cent said they used it for living space while 97 per cent said they used it for storage.

The survey showed that the overall rate of car ownership at BedZED is 0.6 cars per household, which is dramatically lower than the 1.6 cars per household for the wider area, not simply explained by having a high number of people on low incomes in the social housing. Some residents who own a car avoid the costs of a parking permit by choosing to park in neighbouring streets which has caused some friction. Private car mileage was estimated at 64 per cent lower than the UK national average.

A quarter of residents order an organic food box and, overall, residents estimate 25 per cent of food consumed by weight is organic, with individual household figures ranging from 0 to 85 per cent. Waste audits suggest recycling rates of 50 per cent compared with the area average of 21 per cent, but with particular scope to increase composting rates.

The average BedZED resident knew 20 neighbours by name with one person knowing 150 of her neighbours. In the area immediately surrounding BedZED, the average is eight people. Overall 65 per cent of BedZED residents said they knew more neighbours than where they previously lived, 18 per cent the same number, and 17 per cent knew fewer. The most cited reason for liking BedZED was the sense of community, with design, sustainability and sense of well-being in second, third and fourth places.

BedZED residents fly more than the UK average (true generally of Londoners). The overall ecological footprint of residents is 11 per cent lower than the surrounding area. Reducing flights and increasing sustainability of the municipality as a whole were identified as mechanisms to reduce the footprints to a one planet level.

Living at BedZED

Figure 16
Should they choose to, it is easy for a person to reduce their footprint by about one-half by living at BedZED.

Services 22%

Home 11%

Transport 23%

Food 31%

Goods 13%

Figure 17
Nicole's eco footprint is 1.2 planets and her carbon footprint is 4.4 tonnes a year.
She is a civil engineer and BioRegional employee working at BedZED. Nicole lives in a studio apartment, doesn't own a car and is a member of the car club. She travels by car and plane infrequently. She is very energy conscious and wastes little, recycling and composting everything she can. (*Footprint calculation based on Stepwise® software by Best Foot Forward.*)

Figure 18

Steve's eco-footprint is 2.3 planets and his carbon footprint is 7.6 tonnes a year.

He lives with his wife, Sue, in a three-bedroom maisonette at BedZED. Steve owns two cars (one of which is a smart car) and took an overseas holiday to Chicago in the year, a return distance of 12,700 kilometres – which is why travel is the largest part of his footprint. (*Footprint calculation based on Stepwise® software by Best Foot Forward.*)

Our Target

Figure 19

Our target – living on one planet.

Notes

1 Seneca the Younger, *Thyestes*, 1st century AD.
2 Kirkpatrick Sale, *Dwellers in the Land: The Bioregional Vision*, University of Georgia Press (Athens, GA), 1985.
3 P Desai and S Riddlestone, *BioRegional Solutions for Living on One Planet*, Schumacher Briefing No 8, Green Books (Totnes), 2002.
4 Bill Mollison, *Permaculture: A Designers' Manual*, Tagari Publications (Sisters Creek, FL), 1988.
5 An ongoing series of BedZED reports is available from www.bioregional.com.
6 Jess Hodge and Julia Haltrecht, *BedZED Monitoring Report 2007*, BioRegional Development Group, 2008.
7 www.carclubs.org.uk.
8 P Desai and S Riddlestone, *BioRegional Solutions for Living on One Planet*, Schumacher Briefing No 8, Green Books Limited (Totnes), 2002.
9 Nicole Lazarus, *BedZED Construction Materials Report – Toolkit for Carbon Neutral Developments Part 1*, BioRegional Development Group, 2002.
10 BioRegional Development Group and the Commission for Architecture and the Built Environment, *What Makes an EcoTown?*, 2008.

Chapter 3

Understanding CO_2, greenhouse gases and ecological footprint

We need to gain a good understanding of our environmental impacts in order to create truly sustainable communities and to focus on strategies bringing the greatest benefits most cost-effectively. CO_2 emissions are important, but we must understand them better. We should also not forget other greenhouse gases and the wider indicator of ecological footprint.

The previous chapter shows us clearly that, ultimately, it is the lifestyles that people adopt, or that are created for them, which are the main drivers for the environmental impact of their lives. What we build heavily influences lifestyle, but it is lifestyle rather than buildings that should be our main driver. Architecture and construction focus on the initial stages in a building's life, but what happens in the building long term is what really makes the difference (the role of long-term estates management in supporting sustainable lifestyle is explored in Chapter 12). We did not fully realise the extent to which this was true when we set out to design and build BedZED.

The development of sustainable communities is often dominated by green building design. We often hear statements along the lines of, 'Our buildings contribute nearly half of all our CO_2 emissions', and this sort of sentiment remains ingrained in organisations such as the Building Research Establishment and Green Building Councils. This is often followed by the assumption, explicit or implicit, that we will make large environmental gains by securing CO_2 savings by constructing buildings to high environmental standards. This thinking has led to an emphasis on very high-performance building envelopes and passive design for new buildings; for example, going well beyond other standards such as Building Regulations. The trouble is that the energy consumption in buildings is only partly due to what is built, and a significant amount of it is due to what people do in those buildings – the domestic, commercial and industrial appliances which are fitted. There is only limited value in considering this energy consumption as part of the building. We might use the following analogy: even though the majority of food is consumed in buildings, there is only a limited amount we can do in trying to drive sustainability of the food system through building design or standards. There is not much to be gained from saying buildings are responsible for 95 per cent of ecological impact associated with food! Although it is essential that we make our buildings more efficient, it won't actually reduce our overall environmental impact nearly as much as we might first assume.

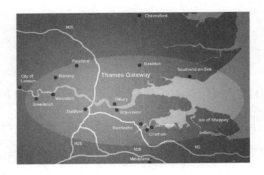

Figure 1
The Thames Gateway, the largest
regeneration area in Western Europe.

Some modelling gives us a surprise

Our first inkling that a 'green building' approach to sustainable communities had limitations was largely due to work done by my colleague, Nick James, when BioRegional was writing a report called *One Planet Living in the Thames Gateway*.[1] Some of the figures in this early report need to be considered in the light of more recent data on ecological footprinting, but the underlying pattern remains clear.

The Thames Gateway is the region east of London covering over 700 square kilometres including more than 1,000 hectares of brownfield (formerly industrial) land available for redevelopment. As the largest regeneration site in Western Europe, it has, since the 1970s, been proposed as an area in which to meet the forecast increase in housing required for London and the southeast of England. At various times some 160,000 to 200,000 new homes have been proposed for the region.

With our first residents starting to move into BedZED and spurred on by BioRegional's co-founder and London Sustainable Development Commissioner Sue Riddlestone, we started to model what might be the benefits of applying what we had done at BedZED to the regeneration of the whole Thames Gateway. At first we were stunned. Over a period of a few weeks of working and reworking data, a slow realisation started to dawn. Only a small proportion of CO_2 savings, and an even smaller proportion of ecological footprint, could be achieved by constructing very green buildings. It was the first time we had really started to tease apart in detail the relative savings from things like building fabric and insulation, from other interventions such as energy-efficient appliances, renewable energy supply, transport, food, waste and behavioural change.

One Planet Living in the Thames Gateway showed that simply building greener homes was not having as large an impact as we had anticipated. By targeting significant CO_2 and water savings in the home by building to BRE EcoHomes 'Very Good' standard (with high insulation standards and fitted with energy-efficient appliances and lighting) rather than simply meeting Building Regulations, we were able to get a 32 per cent reduction in CO_2 emissions from the homes in our model. This level of saving sounds good. However, it translates to an overall reduction in ecological footprint of only 4 per cent (we shall see why later in this chapter). It was only when we started to work the model hard by also reducing transport, waste and food impacts – and including behaviour change – that we really started to achieve some decent overall ecological footprint savings. In our best scenario, we were able to achieve a 40 per cent ecological footprint saving over the UK average. Greater footprint reductions would only be possible if central government spending on schools, hospitals, roads, etc was brought into the equation.

Rethinking the contribution of green building fabric

A few questions started rising in our minds. Just how big were the CO_2 savings from greater levels of insulation and solar design in the bigger scheme of things? We had spent a lot of money on the building fabric and form at BedZED, but how did this spending relate to the CO_2 and ecological footprint savings being achieved? Should we be taking a different approach in future? It was this line of investigation which led BioRegional to develop the One Planet framework that we describe in more detail in Chapter 10.

Table 1

Space-heating requirements for homes, collated from various sources. By the time we have reached a space-heating requirement of 40 kilowatt-hours per square metre per year ($KWh/m^2/yr$) we have saved between 75 and 80 per cent of space-heating energy in homes. From experience of trying to go beyond this, costs tend to rise significantly showing us that we are into diminishing returns. The One Brighton development is a case in point and is described in more detail in Chapter 10. It must be noted that *predictions* for space-heating requirements from homes can vary enormously from real-life monitoring data.

	Space heating kWh/m^2/yr
Existing housing stock	140–170
Victorian	164
1930s semi	113
Building Regs 2000	71
Building Regs 2002	59
Building Regs 2006	56
EcoHomes Very Good	44
Association of Environment Conscious Builders – Silver	40
CNBQ One Brighton development	23
BRE EcoHomes Excellent	23
BedZED	16
Code for Sustainable Homes Level 6	16
Passivhaus	15

Certainly new homes are becoming more efficient in terms of insulation standards, for example, as Building Regulations have improved over the years (see Table 1). Although we had been quoting 90 per cent space-heating savings at BedZED, it was in comparison to existing homes with the saving being far less when compared with meeting current Building Regulations. To get a clear perspective we are better considering the *marginal* or additional benefit of going beyond Building Regulations. In fact by the time we have reached a thermal performance for homes giving us a space-heating requirement of 40 kilowatt-hours per square metre per year, we have saved 75 to 80 per cent of heating load compared with existing housing stock. Going beyond this will save more energy, but costs also tend to rise substantially, an expression of the 80:20 rule. (It is worth mentioning that there is concern that many new homes are not meeting Building Regulations requirements, but this is the different issue of enforcement rather than the regulations in themselves.)

We must also separate the environmental impacts of the buildings per se from other impacts such as appliances which may be used in buildings. Whereas, for example, homes are becoming more thermally efficient, any savings in this area are being outweighed by increases in electricity consumption through the increasing number of household appliances and gadgets such as home computers and home entertainment systems. These increases are being paralleled in the commercial sector by the growing electrical consumption of IT equipment such as computer servers. We need to address the energy consumption of appliances separately, beyond considering them as part of the building. To reiterate the analogy: just because most food is consumed in buildings, it is not particularly useful to try to drive environmental savings associated with food through Building Regulations or green building standards.

An environmental and financial cost-benefit analysis

BioRegional's 2003 report on BedZED presented figures on CO_2 savings from improved energy performance and the costs associated with achieving them.[2] We can re-analyse these figures to understand 'green bang for green buck' from BedZED – the measures which gave the largest CO_2 savings for the capital invested – by dividing the CO_2 savings by the costs of achieving them. The costs were based on build cost excluding abnormal costs (such as special groundworks) and prototyping costs. We can start getting an interesting perspective on how best to invest to get maximum carbon savings. Capital expenditure is not the only indicator we should use in deciding where to put our money to achieve environmental savings as we must also look at indicators such as financial payback periods and life-cycle costs. Also we can consider purely environmental benefits, regardless of cost (it might even be logical at some level to say the dangers of climate change are so great we must save CO_2 emissions at any cost). However, capital expenditure remains an important factor in decision-making and does give us an interesting perspective.

The capital cost saving of 1 tonne of CO_2 per year varies between £265 for the green transport plan to £28,679 for the same savings from the building fabric (superinsulation and sun-spaces). Of course the figures are based on the BedZED context – a dense suburban area – where a Green

Transport Plan was moderately easy to introduce and the change in lifestyle resulting in reduced car use was not difficult to adopt. It might also be that the people attracted to live at BedZED are more willing than average to reduce car use. Nonetheless the lesson remains. It was approximately 100 times more expensive to save CO_2 by increasing the thermal performance of the building envelope than by introducing the Green Transport Plan. Energy-efficient appliances were approximately 10 times more cost-effective than the BedZED building fabric, although account needs to be taken of their lifespan of, say, five to 10 years compared with the predicted 20 to 120 years for the building envelope reflecting the lifespan of the glazing and masonry components respectively. Interestingly, though, 80 per cent of the extra cost for the building envelope was for the glazing for south-facing sun-spaces (£282,200 out of the £352,750 for the six-plot terrace) and therefore superinsulation was significantly more cost-effective than sun-spaces in reducing

Table 2
Cost-benefit analysis of different CO_2 saving measures at BedZED

	CO_2 savings per person per year (tonnes)	Additional capital cost per terrace (36 people)	Annual bill saving per person	Capex per tonne CO_2 saved per year
Building fabric total	0.34	£352,750	£19	£28,679
Superinsulation	0.27	£70,550	£15	£7,170
Sunspaces	0.07	£282,200	£4	£114,715
Energy saving from water-efficient appliances	0.17	£1,680	£9	£280
Energy-efficient appliances	0.17	£12,878	£27	£2,146
Green Transport Plan	1.3	£12,385	£500	£265
Wood-fired CHP	1.94	£77,022	-	£1,100
PV	0.17	£138,926	£80	£23,154

Most figures have been derived from the report 'BedZED Toolkit for Carbon Neutral Developments – Part II'. The building fabric costs were subdivided into superinsulation and sun-spaces, with sun-spaces making up 80 per cent of increased building fabric costs and representing 20 per cent of carbon saving. The bill savings from the biomass combined heat and power plant (CHP) are not included as the installation was not successful and no clear comment can be made about the price at which it could supply heat and power. Annual bill savings to residents from the Green Transport Plan are harder to quantify as they are dependent on many factors such as overall mileage and amount and type of public transport use. Monitoring showed average mileage at BedZED to be 3,317 kilometres per annum compared with the wider area average of 9,656 kilometres per annum. Very conservatively, it is estimated that the observed 65 per cent reduction in both car ownership levels and mileage at BedZED will save £1,000 per car per annum (or £500 per person per annum).

CO_2. Similar thermal performance savings at BedZED could have been achieved with extra insulation all around rather than incorporating the sun-spaces (indeed, our engineers at BedZED point out that sun-spaces should not be seen primarily as an energy-saving measure). However, overall the CO_2 and financial savings to residents in heating bills from both superinsulation and sun-spaces remains relatively small in comparison to the other measures. Arguably the sun-spaces can add sales value, but we will return to the pros and cons of sun-spaces and passive solar design in the next chapter. Photovoltaic panels, although technically successful, were also very expensive ways to reduce CO_2 emissions. Surprisingly perhaps, water-efficient appliances, by saving hot water, turn out to be a cost-effective energy-saving measure, on a par with energy-efficient appliances, to which we can add the advantages of water bill savings as well.

Stepping back, it came as a surprise that, although superinsulation and sun-spaces do save running costs, the savings are one to two orders of magnitude less than savings through services like the car club. Indeed, if we calculate the financial payback time for investing in a tonne of annual CO_2 saving (dividing capital cost per tonne CO_2 saved by bill saving for the 36 people in the terrace), it works out at almost 800 years for the sun-spaces, but only one week for the car club. Why is this? Well, it is because the marginal saving of very high-performance building fabric is relatively small, cars are very CO_2 intensive and the cost of motoring is extremely high (because of the fixed costs of car ownership and the high level of taxation on transport fuels). Therefore anything which reduces car use wins hands down on a 'cost of CO_2 reduction' basis. This doesn't mean that I am saying don't bother creating energy-efficient homes. What I am saying is that there is a point of emphasis and of diminishing returns with building fabric.

Developing a clearer appreciation of how impacts arise

Given that so much can be achieved without trying to get too much out of building fabric, why is it that so much of the industry has become so focused on green buildings as the key to constructing sustainable communities? One reason, as we have seen, is that we need to differentiate more clearly between new and existing buildings in terms of issues such as space heating. Another reason is that all of us in the industry need to develop a better appreciation of the relative contributions of building fabric versus appliances, food, transport, consumer goods, waste and the built environment more generally. The built-up space between buildings and the construction impacts of roads are often accounted for under the general category of buildings, but they are actually quite separate. More work needs to be done on this to get good data, but we can construct greener buildings without ever affecting the large impacts which arise from the spaces between them. Even more generally we need to understand the difference between various measures of impact such as direct CO_2 emissions, CO_2 footprint, greenhouse gas emissions and ecological footprint. Without this understanding we can become too heavily focused on aspects which will only bring small benefits. Fortunately, as we understand the bigger picture, it actually becomes easier in many ways to build a sustainable community – although it raises other challenges.

Figure 2
Often-quoted territorial CO_2 emissions figures exclude aviation.

Unpicking CO_2 and its relationship to ecological footprint

Let us try to start to unpick some of the confusion around CO_2 emissions figures and how they relate to other measures such as ecological footprint.

The most quoted government figures for CO_2 emissions are what we should really describe as 'direct CO_2 emissions' or 'territorial CO_2 emissions'. These figures represent the CO_2 directly emitted by any region or country from burning fossil fuels within its own territorial boundaries. This amounts to 8.8 tonnes of CO_2 per person per year for the UK as a whole.[3]

However, the territorial CO_2 emissions figures don't include international shipping or aviation. In the UK, these add a further 6.8 and 35.6 million tonnes of CO_2 per year respectively, or a total of 0.7 tonnes per person per year. Air travel may be the single largest part of a person's CO_2 emissions, so excluding these figures tends to mislead us (emissions from aviation, including nitrous oxides and vapour released at high altitude, have two to four times the global warming potential of the equivalent CO_2 released at sea level).[4]

Even when we take into account international shipping and aviation emissions, the figures still don't include CO_2 emissions associated with imported goods and services. For example, the CO_2 emissions used to make a television bought in the UK are usually attributed to the country in which it was manufactured, say China. Countries like the UK which are net consumers of manufactured goods are in effect net exporters of CO_2. We get a more honest idea of the CO_2 emissions we are responsible for by considering so-called 'CO_2 footprint' which includes CO_2 released anywhere in the world to meet a person's total consumption of products and services. The Stockholm Environment Institute estimates the CO_2 footprint of the average person in the UK to be 12.08 tonnes of CO_2 per person per year.[5]

We are getting there, but still have a way to go! If we stop at CO_2 footprint we are not getting a full indication of our contribution to global warming. Carbon dioxide per se is not the problem – the real issue is that it causes global warming. Global warming is caused by a range of gases which include methane and nitrous oxides as well as CO_2. We should really be considering greenhouse gas (GHG) emissions which are measured as tonnes of carbon dioxide equivalent (CO_2e). The largest man-made contributors to methane and nitrous oxide emissions are from agriculture –

Figure 3

Territorial CO_2 emissions figures also exclude the CO_2 released in other countries to manufacture imported goods. To get a good overview of impact, net importers such as the UK should include emissions associated, for example, with goods manufactured in China.

methane from cattle for milk and meat production, and nitrous oxides from nitrogen fertilisers. By the time we add in GHG emissions from agriculture and other sources, we find that the UK's GHG footprint is 16.34 tonnes of CO_2e per person per year.[5]

The GHG footprint of 16.34 tonnes is 86 per cent larger than the territorial CO_2 emissions figure of 8.8 tonnes. If we use territorial CO_2 emissions as our guide we underestimate the global-warming effect of emissions from imported goods and agriculture, and overestimate the importance of fossil fuels we burn directly ourselves, for example to power our buildings.

In fact, if we look at ecological footprinting as the main indicator, things look even more different as in the UK our CO_2 footprint accounts for only 65 per cent of our ecological footprint. So, for example, a person living in a home built to current Building Regulations in the UK might be releasing 1.5 tonnes of CO_2 to provide his or her heat and power. This equates to 17 per cent of territorial CO_2 emissions, 12 per cent of CO_2 footprint, 9 per cent of GHG footprint, but only about 6 per cent of ecological footprint. You can see how we might end up getting our emphasis wrong.

The clear lessons

Let us revisit the statement '50 per cent of CO_2 emissions come from buildings'. Taking into account that the difference between old and new buildings is often ignored, we can now read it as '50 per cent of territorial CO_2 emissions come from *all existing* buildings *and the built-up space between buildings*, not just buildings – and this statistic ignores CO_2 emissions from international transport, other greenhouse gas emissions such as from agriculture – which in sum total is only about 65 per cent of our ecological footprint.'

The big lesson to learn in terms of building new communities is that we may have been focusing a lot of attention in the wrong direction – but this in many ways makes things easier. We are probably making far more fuss than we need to in terms of green building design with complex and expensive-to-achieve (or even unworkable and counterproductive) standards such as outlined at the higher levels in the UK's Code for Sustainable Homes – at least in its current 2008 version.

Figure 4
A lot of CO_2 emissions attributed to 'buildings' more accurately should be attributed to the 'built environment' and all the infrastructure and space between buildings.

Using the 'big picture' approach makes it much simpler, for example, to build a green home: insulating it well, putting in good glazing and constructing it carefully so it is not leaky. In the UK, try to get under 40 $kWh/m^2/yr$ for space heating. Consider basic aspects of good energy-efficient building design such as opportunities for natural lighting and ventilation. Install energy-efficient appliances. There you go – you have a green home and can get on with concentrating on the other things like designing to reduce car dependence, sourcing renewable energy, increasing recycling, promoting local food and encouraging behaviour change. It really is not much more complicated than this. We don't need to be subject to what can sometimes seem like a tyranny of green architecture, or to be forced to perform engineering gymnastics, for the sake of green buildings – unless of course we want to.

What I am writing here will be seen as heresy in some quarters, but it is not meant to be a pointless undermining of attempts to create ultra-high-performance green buildings. It is just that it is useful to understand the cost-benefit associated with doing so – or more importantly the opportunity costs in time and money of focusing on creating a green building as opposed to a whole sustainable lifestyle. In the next chapter we explore in more detail some of the issues around green building design and how its very sincere origins may have led to an unconscious ideology which is worth questioning as we build the sustainable communities of the 21st century.

Notes

1 P Desai and N James, *One Planet Living in the Thames Gateway*, BioRegional Development Group, 2003.
2 Nicole Lazarus, *Beddington Zero (Fossil) Energy Development – Toolkit for Carbon Neutral Developments – Part 2*, BioRegional Development Group, 2003.
3 Department for Environment, Food and Rural Affairs, *Local Authority CO₂ Emissions Estimates 2006*.
4 IPCC, *Aviation and the Global Atmosphere: A Special Report of the Intergovernmental Panel on Climate Change*, Cambridge University Press (Cambridge), 1999.
5 Stockholm Environment Institute, *REAP v2*, 2008.

Chapter 4

From green buildings to sustainable infrastructure

Much of green building design has grown up from the concept of the autonomous house. However, we do have to be careful. We cannot assume that the excellent work on autonomous houses automatically scales up to building larger sustainable communities. At larger scales and higher densities, it is better to adopt an approach based on providing sustainable infrastructure.

> 'No man is an island, intire of itselfe; every man is a peece of the Continent,
> a part of the maine.'
>
> John Donne (1572–1631), Jacobean poet and preacher[1]

Modern green design traces its history back two generations. It finds its roots in the 1960s with the work of people including Buckminster Fuller, who popularised the concept of 'spaceship earth', and John and Nancy Todd, the New Alchemists, developing the concept of 'living machines'. The 1970s saw environmental concerns compounded by the energy crisis caused by an embargo of oil exports by Arab members of OPEC in response to Western support of Israel during the Yom Kippur War. The decade saw numerous examples of energy-efficient homes being built and the emergence of new thinking, such as the holistic design principles of 'permaculture' developed by Bill Mollison and David Holmgren – looking at building eco-systems around ourselves to provide food, energy, shelter and materials – a coming together of permanent (sustainable) agriculture and sustainable culture.

Much of green architecture today is heavily influenced, consciously or subconsciously, by the concept of the 'autonomous house' – a home which meets all its own energy needs, harvests rain, treats all its own waste and grows all its own food. It finds its first explicit expression in 1975, when architects and pioneers Professor Brenda Vale and Dr Robert Vale published the seminal volume *The Autonomous House*, in which they explain: 'The autonomous house on its site is defined as a house operating without any inputs except those of its immediate environment. The house is not linked to the mains services of gas, water, electricity or drainage, but instead uses the income-energy sources of sun, wind and rain to service itself and process its own wastes.'[2]

The approach contributes and derives a lot from the self-sufficiency movement of the 1970s – and the combination of shape, form and aesthetics of the autonomous house very clearly has these roots, not least in its choice of 'natural', often rough-hewn, materials such as local timber, adobe and, more recently, hemp and straw, complemented by reusing waste materials or those salvaged from demolition. It is in some respects a very romantic movement based on the return to the simple things in life, it is an urge that has always been with society in some shape or form, whether it be Lao Tse's Taoist teachings in the 6th century BC, the Arts and Crafts Movement of the late 19th century, or Mahatma Gandhi's Khadi in the 20th century.

One very influential expression of the autonomous house is the Earthship (see overleaf), originally conceived by Mike Reynolds in the 1970s. Inspired to use the earth's resources directly available on the site, key features of autonomous houses include:

- solar design with orientation towards the sun to collect its warmth for heating;
- 'thermally massive design' involving construction with large quantities of earth and stone to store heat and coolth to even out day and night temperature fluctuations;
- rainwater harvesting;
- waterless composting toilets which create nutrient-rich material for growing crops;
- on site treatment of grey water with growing plants; and
- on site electricity generation with photovoltaic panels and small wind turbines.

Other examples which draw to a greater or lesser extent on autonomous house philosophy include Ben Law's Woodland House and, at the scale of a cluster of homes, the Hockerton Housing Project and Great Bow Yard (see overleaf). BedZED, at the medium scale, also shares this heritage with its solar orientation and original aim to be self-sufficient in energy and treat black and grey water on site.

We have a lot to learn from the autonomous house philosophy – such as the focus on resource efficiency and making use of the natural resources we have to hand. Some of us may aspire to lead a more or less self-sufficient lifestyle in the 21st century and this forms the underlying basis for television programmes such as *It's Not Easy Being Green* (BBC 2). However, we also need to understand the limitations of the autonomous house approach, and think where, and where not, to apply its principles. Many of the features of the autonomous house appear time and again in green building designs and in many cases represent, or indeed are emblematic of, a lifestyle aspiration as much as a logical approach to sustainability. Most fundamentally, self-sufficiency is not necessarily the most efficient way to meet human needs, either environmentally, socially or economically. Although *technically* capable of being autonomous, many of the technologies are expensive and difficult to install and maintain at the small scale. Aiming to make homes or small estates autonomous, even when there are a few hundred homes, is not easy. Trying to do this – or setting standards to force developers to do this – has made delivery of sustainable communities more difficult than necessary.

The Earthship

Originally conceived by American Mike Reynolds, the passive solar homes can be constructed using recycled and local materials. Many earthships have been built using old tyres filled with rammed earth. Internal walls are often made from a honeycomb of recycled glass bottles or aluminium drink cans held together with cement.

The company behind these homes, Earthship Biotecture, offers systems to capture and treat rainwater, and gravel beds with growing plants to treat grey water from baths and sinks. Composting toilets or small anaerobic digesters enhanced with solar heat are promoted for converting sewage into compost. Photovoltaic panels or small wind turbines provide off-grid electricity which is stored in batteries.

In Taos in New Mexico, a whole community, the Greater World Community, is growing up, with all the buildings based on the earthship concept. A small cluster of earthships is also proposed for a site overlooking the marina in Brighton in the UK.

The Woodland House

Ben Law is a local hero in his neck of the woods: Prickly Nut Wood in Midhurst in West Sussex. Making a living by introducing traditional coppice management and running training courses, Ben has built his own house almost completely from materials from his wood or nearby farm. A green-oak frame supports a roof covered in chestnut shingles, with rendered straw bales forming the walls. The aesthetic qualities of the house, its genuine intent, plus the romantic notion of a woodsman building his own house captured the public's imagination when featured on the UK Channel 4 television series 'Grand Designs'. It was voted the favourite episode of the first 50 programmes.

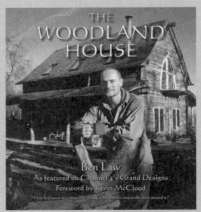

Hockerton Housing Project

Hockerton Housing Project was designed by Brenda and Robert Vale. Constructed by its residents and completed in 1998, the terrace of five houses in the Nottingham countryside faces the sun and is sheltered by earth. The soil-covered roofs mean that the houses blend into the landscape. There is no central heating; instead warmth is provided by the sun, body heat and waste heat, electricity is supplied via solar panels and a wind turbine, and waste water is treated on site. There are food-growing areas, livestock and honey production. Carp are raised in the pond and harvested for eating.

Great Bow Yard

Great Bow Yard in Langport, Somerset, is a hamlet of 12 eco-homes designed by Stride Treglown for developers South West Eco Homes. There are two terraces of houses and flats. Completed in 2005, all homes are built to the BRE EcoHomes Excellent rating, making use of passive solar and thermally massive design combined with lightweight timber-frame construction. Reclaimed bricks have been bound by lime mortar making them easier to reuse when the building reaches the end of its life. 'A'-rated energy-efficient electrical appliances have been fitted and a new wildlife habitat created.

So where then does the autonomous house approach have most relevance? It has its origins in single house schemes on good-sized plots and has been scaled up to small numbers of homes – it can add good value at this scale and density. At these low densities, the following main characteristics allow the autonomous house to work:

- There are few space constraints, so solar orientation can work regardless of other drivers for a masterplan such as successful street layout.
- Roof surfaces are large in relation to the number of people living there, so collecting solar energy and rainwater is more worthwhile.
- In some cases, connecting to centralised services such as sewerage systems, gas mains or even electricity grids may be unfeasible or very expensive, which tips things in favour of on site provision.

At medium and high densities, say over 30 homes per hectare, it is harder to hold on to autonomous house principles such as passive solar design.

Solar orientation
It is conventional green wisdom in the temperate climes of the northern hemisphere that homes should face south and we should place sun-spaces or conservatories on the south side to collect warmth – passive solar design. At higher densities this encourages masterplans with terraces running east to west so all the homes can face south.

BedZED works well as a masterplan on the scale at which it was constructed and it is a great place to live. However, there are things we should consider before automatically taking it as a template.

In practice it is arguable whether south-facing sun-spaces save energy. The warmth and the CO_2 savings they provide in winter are small, as we saw in the last chapter. The maximum benefit of solar gain is achieved on cold, clear, sunny winter days, but only by opening the doors to the sun-spaces at about 11am and closing them by about 3pm. Not many people are home at these times, or indeed use their homes in this way, so the benefit is not harvested. Privacy is another issue: large areas of glazing at higher densities lead to overlooking, and many sun-spaces end up with blinds or curtains kept closed year round. As soon as blinds or curtains are installed, solar gain is reduced, eliminated or even reversed – a sun-space with blinds can rapidly become a heat sink. Obvious in retrospect, sun-spaces generate most heat in high summer when it is not required, causing issues with overheating which become more significant as climate change creates warmer summers. Indeed, monitoring at BedZED shows most people find the homes too hot in summer. Cooling homes rather than heating them will increasingly be the issue in coming years as global warming kicks in.

Many residents at BedZED, however, say that they really appreciate the sun-spaces from a lifestyle perspective. For others they have simply become storage space. At 2 metres depth, the sun-spaces at BedZED are not living space like a full conservatory, but sitting space. If they are increased in size to become living space and a full conservatory, work by researchers such as Tadj Oreszczyn demonstrates that the majority of people (about 90 per cent) end up heating them in winter and increasingly cooling them using electric chillers in summer, so in reality, conservatories often substantially *increase* the energy consumption of the home rather than reducing it.[3] As we saw in Chapter 3, sun-spaces are also very expensive. If space and affordability are an issue they are certainly something that can be easily dropped without affecting (and even possibly improving) the thermal performance of the homes.

As soon as you drop an attachment to passive solar design, you are free to use it when it might work, but are not unnecessarily restricted by it. A whole new world opens up. Ironically sun-spaces cut down light into the main living areas. For quality of life, we might want to promote more east–west light. Indoor light quality is generally better from east and west windows, rather than south light which is harsh in summer. East- and west-facing windows are better suited to how people use their homes,

Reflections on BedZED – the engineer's perspective

It is now more than 10 years since BedZED was designed. Little did the team then realise that its underpinning carbon logic of efficiency step-change, including occupiers' energy use, plus the renewable generation capacity, would be adopted 10 years later by the UK government and embedded into regulations for all new-build.

But now is also the time for reflection because there is so much more that could be learnt from BedZED feedback to equip us for the rapid change times ahead.

My five big hitters are:

- Avoiding complexity: focus on passive measures, be it 300 millimetres of insulation, triple glazing, air-tightness or thermal bridging avoidance. Thermal mass as a heat- recovery mechanism is another intriguing aspect. Intuitive operation also comes high up the list. Interestingly, solar orientation becomes less of an issue if superinsulating on higher-density developments.
- Occupants: lifestyle choices can change energy/water use by a factor of four. Engagement, explaining and incentives are essential ingredients if sustainable 'enabled' buildings are to be used to their full potential.
- Costs: learning for the first time does cost extra, but this cost evaporates as the supply chain masters new ways of doing things. It is interesting that double glazing is now cheaper than single glazing; perhaps we can expect the same of triple glazing and solar collectors.
- Greenwash: beware of being sold the business-as-usual repackaged as sustainable. Sustainability requires a step-change in performance, not only in the components, and in the design predictions, but also all the way through site works to building operation actual performance.
- New-build is but the first step. Similar step changes are needed in transport, the existing building stock, goods/services provided from abroad, and community cohesion and governance.
- I look back at those inspirational times with Malcolm, Bill, Pooran, Lachlan and the team. It showed that a step change is possible and gave me the strength to push for more.

Reproduced by permission of Chris Twinn, Building Engineering Sustainability Group, Arup, 2009

particularly in the winter months – giving good morning and evening light which is most valuable when people are in their homes and not during the middle of the day when people are more likely to be out. Without worrying about solar terracing, we can free masterplans to address issues that make a greater contribution to social and, arguably, environmental, sustainability such as urban layout and community interaction. For example, making streets work by having shops facing each other, creating a vibrant local shopping area, will ultimately save a lot more CO_2 than passive solar design by reducing car use.

That is not to say we should ignore where the sun is coming from. If not orienting our homes south, it might be a very good idea to face roof surfaces south and angle them optimally to the sun, so that we can mount solar hot-water panels now, or perhaps retrofit photovoltaic panels in the future.

Solar orientation to guide design of the space between buildings

We can even turn conventional green solar design on its head. How about using solar orientation primarily to guide the design of the space between buildings? Good public space is essential for supporting neighbourliness and healthy living, as we shall see in Chapter 8, as well as creating a successful masterplan which can support eligible streets, squares, public spaces, shops and offices. When designing high-quality outdoor space for gardens and the public realm in a temperate climate, if anything it is preferable to have homes and terraces running north to south, allowing greater light access and creating sunny outdoor spaces – better for recreation, health, community interaction, and for growing plants and food. Indeed the extra growth rate of plants potentially offsets some or all of the CO_2 saved by space heating from passive solar design for the homes. However, for temperate climates such as in the UK, I am not advocating street or building layouts in any one orientation over another. Of course, in very hot climates the situation is reversed and orientation will be about creating shade as seen at Masdar City in Abu Dhabi, which is described in the next chapter. Therefore the particular priorities on the individual site should be used to guide the masterplan. However, good sustainable design is as much, if not more, about the space *between* buildings as the buildings themselves.

Figure 1
Should we be looking at solar orientation as a way to create good public spaces?

A balanced perspective on water: or the danger of throwing the baby out with the bath water

Just as with solar orientation, we should try to maintain a balanced perspective with water. Water is very much a local and regional issue and therefore approach to water management on any particular site needs to be directed by local factors. In some areas or parts of the world, water is a very precious resource and in these places it might be important to harvest as much rainwater and recycle as much waste water as possible on site. However, we should not automatically assume that this is the right environmental decision in all cases.

For example, in the UK, conventional sewage treatment happens to be a good environmental choice – it is, after all, based on natural bacterial action, and modern sewage works collect methane generated for electricity production so there is no great advantage per se in abandoning conventional municipal-scale sewerage systems in favour of on site water treatment. Indeed, if it were introduced as a new technology today it would be heralded as a great green innovation. In the UK, the energy used to purify water, deliver it through the mains and clean it via the sewerage system results in about 80 kilograms of CO_2 emissions per person – under 0.7 per cent of an average person's CO_2 footprint.[4] It is very hard to achieve as good an environmental performance trying to treat grey water (from sinks, baths and dishwashers) or black water (sewage) with smaller-scale systems for individual households or small communities.

Water availability – the ratio of water available locally to that being consumed – is a key determinant; it is true that even parts of the UK are becoming water stressed and subject to over-abstraction from aquifers, and climate change will exacerbate problems particularly in areas of high population density such as in the southeast of England. Water efficiency is, of course, the first thing to consider, and using water-efficient appliances (spray taps, aerated showerheads rather than power showers, and dual/low flush toilets) it is easy, without any reduction in quality of life, to reduce consumption from the average of around 150 litres per day to 100 litres per day. It is also usually worth collecting rainwater for irrigating the landscape using simple tanks and butts. In areas with moderate water stress, rainwater can be considered for flushing toilets if a decent amount can be collected for the number of toilets to be fed. This is dependent not only on the amount of rainfall, but also on the density of the development. At low densities the roof area over which rainwater can be collected is large compared with the number of toilets to be fed, so sufficient rainwater can be collected to be worthwhile. At high densities, the ratio of roof surface to number of toilets is low so it might not be worth fitting dual piping. Another factor is that it is generally not advisable to try to collect rainwater from roof terraces, gardens or green wildlife roofs for reuse in buildings because of the risk of contamination from bird droppings, for example. Depending on context, it might be better to use roof surfaces to meet social or biodiversity needs rather than rainwater collection.

Figure 2
Opportunities exist for reusing grey water such as integrating basins with toilets, collecting waste water for flushing.

Figure 3
Grey water from the bath and shower can be stored and reused for toilet flushing using the Ecoplay system, for example.

Before considering on site grey-water (or black-water) treatment, the benefits over municipal treatment should be carefully considered. The Centre for Alternative Technology, normally a great supporter of small-scale systems and self-sufficiency, describes the UK situation:

> Commercial grey water recycling systems use disinfectants that are often very energy intensive to produce ... All independent studies of systems that treat grey water for reuse in the home have found that their environmental impact outweighs any benefits, and that running costs are higher than mains water supply. Given the infrastructure and disinfectant doses needed, it is difficult to see these systems as environmentally friendly, especially for individual households.[5]

Grey water can sometimes be easily reused in the landscape with minimal filtration, although consideration needs to be given to fats from kitchens, soaps, detergents and bacteria from baths, and salts from dishwasher tablets, which can all cause problems. In certain situations such as commercial car-wash operations, grey-water recycling can be highly effective. In highly water- stressed areas, grey-water recycling can be considered either through household or community-scale systems such as the Ecoplay system or outdoor sand filters and reed beds. They all require maintenance and so should only be used on a domestic scale where this maintenance can be provided and afforded.

Now we come on to treating sewage or black water. Autonomous house philosophy tends to encourage us to consider on site black-water treatment – composting toilets and small on site anaerobic digesters allied to reed beds for water polishing. Composting toilets can be a good option if well maintained, but there are cultural barriers and maintenance issues to overcome. Small-scale digesters, though, do consume energy, and unless the methane is collected and used, say, for cooking, the balance of environmental benefit is less clear as methane is a potent greenhouse gas. However, efficient community-scale anaerobic digesters are emerging and, for larger communities, say 2,000 homes or more, may well start to become a viable option. Other technologies such as membrane bioreactors are available which use pressure to force water through a membrane with tiny pores which only allow water to pass. They have their place, but inevitably require more energy than conventional sewage treatment and are usually more energy- and labour-intensive to maintain. The level of water stress and access to municipal infrastructure will determine the best option.

As can be seen from the examples above, when deciding on the best water-recycling and/or treatment strategy, the local context and the relationship between water use in buildings and the landscape, as well as access to municipal water-treatment infrastructure need to be considered. In highly water-stressed areas, the additional energy costs of grey- or black-water treatment might well be justified. For example, in arid regions and deserts there may be little option and indeed it might be possible to generate the energy for this from solar power (see the Masdar City case study in the next chapter). As technologies change, so the environmental cost-benefit will change, but until then the approach we should take is to have *positive* reasons for on site water recycling or treatment before taking this option. Our default position should be to use municipal treatment.

Storm water

Another increasingly important issue relating to water and the landscape concerns the control of storm water. Highly built-up areas in particular are at increased risk from flash flooding if the ground cannot absorb water. Ways of soaking up this water and releasing it more slowly can be important. A set of strategies under the term 'Sustainable Urban Drainage Systems', or SUDS, can be applied, including porous surfaces for landscaping, enabling water to percolate into the soil below. Rainwater tanks can also mitigate against flash flooding as can green roofs which absorb water. Architect William McDonough proposed a 4-hectare 'living' roof for Ford's Dearborn truck plant in Michigan, US, which also formed part of the energy-efficient design of the building through its insulating properties. This green roof holds half the annual rainfall and its costs were offset by not having to construct storm-water drains. The roof has become a great wildlife habitat (see Figure 4).

From autonomous house to sustainable infrastructure

Living at BedZED, a medium-density development and successful in so many ways, in retrospect the value of the autonomous house approach is less obvious. It is useful in all sorts of areas to drop the assumption that it is generally best to try to make a house, or even a group of houses, self-sufficient. When considering the water strategy for a community, it is clear that the best environmental choice is selected by looking at supply and treatment at community and municipal scales rather than individual buildings. Water is one very clear example where we cannot scale-up directly from the autonomous house concept but need a paradigm shift in our thinking. In their book, the Vales state that the autonomous house: 'In some ways [...] resembles a land-based space station which is designed to provide an environment suitable to life but unconnected with the existing life-support structure of Earth'.[6]

Figure 4

The green roof at the Ford Dearborn truck plant in Michigan reduces storm-water run-off as well as creating a home for wildlife.

As thinking has evolved it seems strange now to try to disconnect homes from the life-support structure of earth when, as we shall see in the last chapter of this book, the self-regulating systems operating at a planetary scale are absolutely essential for our survival. Rather, we should make sure our homes are integrated and harmonised with wider natural systems. Indeed, just as the autonomous house approach cannot be scaled up for water, we find that neither can it be so for renewable energy, as is explored in the next chapter. Instead of trying to make buildings self-sufficient in energy, it is perhaps more useful to think in terms of taking a wider 'renewable energy infrastructure' approach.

To summarise, we should seek the best solution at whatever scale this might be. In some cases, self-sufficiency at the level of the house or community might be the right answer – in most cases it won't be. In Chapter 7, the benefits of promoting local and regional self-sufficiency – bioregionalism – as a guiding principle are outlined, but this is different from the autonomous house philosophy. Like all philosophies and approaches, we have to be careful to understand the limitations. It all too easily ends up as ideology.

Taking an infrastructure-led approach to creating sustainable communities does represent a paradigm shift in thinking. In the next two chapters, we explore how sustainable infrastructure can be used to create a zero carbon zero waste community – and how this sustainable infrastructure approach can help to make it easy for people to adopt more sustainable lifestyles. We will also see that by taking an infrastructure-led approach, we can free architectural expression as well.

Notes

1 John Donne, Meditation 17, Devotions Upon Emergent Occasions, 1642.
2 Brenda Vale and Robert Vale, *The Autonomous House*, Thames & Hudson (London), 1975, p 7.
3 A Pathan, A Summerfield, T Oreszczyn, R Lowe and A Young, *Trends in Conservatory Use*, Bartlett School of Graduate Studies, University College London. Report commissioned by the Building Research Establishment, 2007.
4 Judith Thornton, *The Water Book*, Centre for Alternative Technology (Machynlleth), 2005.
5 Centre for Alternative Technology, *Reusing Rainwater and Greywater*, Information Department, Centre for Alternative Technology, (Machynlleth), 2008, p 2.
6 Brenda Vale and Robert Vale, op cit, p 7.

Chapter 5

Zero carbon zero waste communities

We can think of communities as having a metabolism, taking in energy and nutrients and, in conventional communities, creating CO_2 and waste. By underpinning a community with sustainable energy, waste and water infrastructure, we can convert an unsustainable metabolism into a sustainable one. Taking this infrastructure-led approach enables sustainable communities to be built cost-effectively.

'How often I found where I should be going only by setting out for somewhere else.'
R Buckminster Fuller[1]

As we saw in the last chapter, there is a lot to learn from autonomous house thinking, but the approach may not necessarily suit us as we scale-up to medium- and high-density developments. What happens if we start with sustainable lifestyles as the driver, but support these with sustainable energy, waste, water, transport and food infrastructures at a community or municipal scale rather than the scale of a single house? If we provide this sustainable community infrastructure, can we more easily achieve our stated aim of helping people to lead happy and healthy lives within a fair share of the earth's resources?

Metabolism of communities

Communities can be described in terms of their inputs and outputs – sometimes described as their metabolism, much like a living organism – as they have been by thinkers such as Herbert Girardet.[2] Modern communities generally have a linear metabolism or flow of energy and nutrients – consuming food, fossil fuels and other natural resources, and producing CO_2 and waste, most of the latter ending up in landfill.

We need to transform our communities and cities into ones which recycle nutrients, waste and energy. Rather than a linear metabolism we should seek to create a circular one. This thinking led us to reanalyse the design of a community in terms of providing the infrastructure needed to support a circular metabolism, evolving the concept of the 'zero carbon zero waste' community – or 'Z-squared'.[3] What we might describe as an infrastructure-led approach to improving

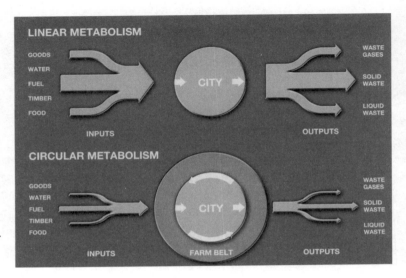

Figure 1
Most modern communities have a linear metabolism, sucking in energy and resources and spewing out CO_2 and waste which is sent to landfill.. We need to move to a circular metabolism.

sustainability underpins a number of developments such as the Western Harbour development in Malmö, Sweden, proposals for Dongtan Eco-City near Shanghai in China and for the 2012 Olympic Village in London.

Evolving the Z-squared concept

Building on work in the report *One Planet Living in the Thames Gateway*,[4] BioRegional drew together a team to create a concept for a zero carbon zero waste community to be designed taking a sustainable infrastructure approach. The team consisted of engineers, quantity surveyors and architects – KBR, Fulcrum Consulting, Cyril Sweett and Foster + Partners – coordinated by Jane Durney at BioRegional. We used the Thames Gateway regeneration area as the place where we would finally locate the concept.

Evolving Z-squared was not an easy process and took about a year. Part of the difficulty arose because we had to at least partly reverse the design process. Normally property developers take a site, decide on a schedule of accommodation (what to build based on the market and local needs) and ask the architects to draw up a masterplan. The engineers follow, almost 'retrofitting' the energy, water and waste services, with the quantity surveyors costing out the project in parallel. Of course, it is not as linear a process as this in reality, but it is the emphasis of the conventional process.

With Z-squared, we needed to take a different approach. We didn't start with a site. Instead we started with people – a community – thinking about what we would need to create a whole sustainable lifestyle. In terms of a schedule of accommodation, we wanted a mix of homes of varying sizes to attractive mixed-income and different age groups. We wanted offices, convenience retail, leisure and community facilities (as well as an ice-cream factory and microbrewery) all on site, within easy walking distance. We wanted to give priority to pedestrians and reduce cars and car parking. We wanted nurseries and a primary school so that parents could walk their children to school. If possible, and if there was wider need, we would incorporate a secondary school. It turned out that the size of our ideal community was governed by the catchment for a primary school – it takes about 2,000 homes, or a population of about 5,000 to support one. The schedule of accommodation we opted for is shown in Table 1.

Having decided on the schedule of accommodation, rather than looking to masterplan the community, we started to investigate its metabolism. We calculated the energy, water, materials, goods, services and food consumed by the community and the wastes produced – the community's metabolism. We also started to assess the ecological footprint of various possible

Table 1
Schedule of accommodation for idealised Z-squared concept.

Residential	Micro-flats/studios	100
	1-bedroom	700
	2-bedrooms	600
	3-bedrooms	250
	4-bedrooms	250
	5-bedrooms	100
	Total	**2,000 units**
Commercial and industrial	Supermarket	
	DIY store	
	Restaurants/cafés	
	Offices and workspaces	
	Business enterprise units	
	Ice-cream factory	
	Microbrewery	
	Hotel	
Community, education, health, leisure	Nursery and childcare	
	Primary school	
	Secondary school	
	Healthy-living centre	
	Leisure facilities	
	Swimming pool	
	One Planet Centre	

scenarios for how people might live at Z-squared – comparing 'normal' consumption (UK average) and consumption in our community on introducing energy and water efficiency, good recycling, sustainable food and reduced car dependence.

We started to identify flows of energy and wastes which were passing through and out of the community, but which we wanted to make use of ourselves to create a circular metabolism – for example we saw nutrients and energy leaving Z-squared in the sewage. Should we try to capture these nutrients and energy for reuse? Should we use composting toilets rather than flushing ones? If we did this, could we expect residents to accept them culturally? Could we also separate out other streams such as paper or green waste and process it with the sewage? Or should we process the streams separately? We realised we had to juggle environmental benefits, available technologies, technical practicalities, financial viability and behavioural and cultural issues to try to come to a resolution.

For a period we felt we were not getting anywhere, but going over old ground again and again. The number of possible options seemed too numerous and complex to get a handle on. We had dissected a complex working system and somehow had to find how it could all fit together with a new zero carbon zero waste metabolism. This sort of problem is not easily solved through a purely logical process.

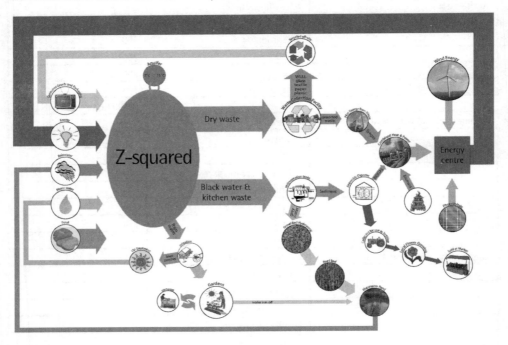

Figure 2
Metabolism: zero carbon zero waste.

It took a number of weeks, but one day, it all started to click into place (see Figure 2). A simple metabolic pathway emerged which in retrospect appears straightforward, if not obvious.

Zero carbon zero waste metabolism

In this metabolism, we see renewable electricity coming into site via an energy centre, primarily derived from large-scale wind turbines and a biomass combined heat and power plant (CHP) (with an order of magnitude larger than the one installed at BedZED, so with reduced technical and financial risk), but potentially supplemented by other sources such as photovoltaics. The waste stream is divided into two main flows: a wet and a dry recyclable stream. The majority of the dry waste can be segregated for recycling – paper, textiles, glass, plastics and waste electrical goods. Non-recyclable waste is gasified to produce 'syngas' and processed through a clean energy-from-waste plant, potentially even feeding the biomass CHP.

Z-squared is starting to get to the scale where we could perhaps consider on site black-water treatment. The solids from the wet waste would be separated out via a sedimentation tank and processed via an anaerobic digester. We suggested we could co-process black water (sewage) and kitchen waste, perhaps providing a macerator to each home. The biogas from the anaerobic digester can be fed into the CHP plant. The anaerobic digester yields a 'digestate' or compost which can be returned to the land. This could be used for food growing, growing biomass crops for the CHP or even growing flowers, replacing air-freighted ones. Waste water from the sedimentation tank is cleaned via gravel beds, polished through a reed bed and returned to the environment. Rainwater is collected for use in the landscape or treated simply with ultraviolet (UV) filters for use in the buildings.

The mix of technologies can change as can the location of processing sites

The Z-squared metabolic pathway is quite flexible. We can add or leave out technologies to adapt it to different local contexts. We can use different sources of renewable energy, both on and offsite, and change the mix of energy – for example, adding solar thermal panels or biomass heating rather than a biomass CHP plant. We could increase the efficiency of our community's metabolism by introducing aquifer thermal energy storage (ATES) systems (Figure 3). These use groundwater to cool buildings in summer, in effect extracting their heat, storing it underground in the aquifer and reversing the flow of water in winter to provide heating to buildings. We can adapt the waste flows. For example, the black water could be sent for conventional treatment and, instead of mixing food waste with sewage, we could easily compost these separately in an 'in-vessel' composter to create compost on site. We could augment our recycling facilities with a mini materials recycling facility (mini-MRF), which would allow us to process waste from the surrounding area, generating employment on site. If we can't introduce energy-from-waste on site, we could perhaps send non-recyclable waste to a municipal-wide energy-from-waste plant.

Aquifer Themal Energy Storage System

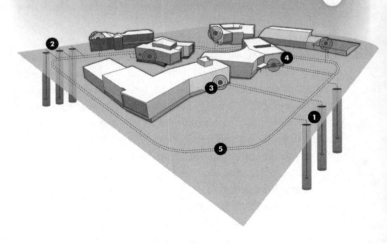

SUMMER

1. Charging of 'warm' bore hole with water warmed by cooling the building - stores heat for the following winter.

2. 'Cold' bore hole supplying cool water to buildings.

3. Water at around 10°C supplied to building at coefficient of performance (COP) of up to 25%.

4. Water at around 15°C discharged to 'warm' bore hole.

5. Distribution pipework carries warm and cold water around site between buildings and bore holes.

FULCRUMCONSULTING | © 2008

Aquifer Themal Energy Storage System

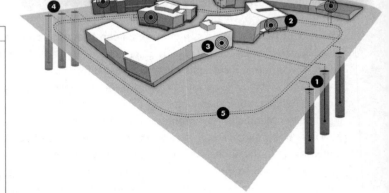

WINTER

1. 'Warm' bore hole, charged the previous summer, supplies warm water to the building at around 14°C.

2. Warm water from bore hole raised to 50°C by high coefficient of performance (COP) heat pump - which cools the water taken from the warm bore hole.

3. Water returned to charge 'cold' bore hole at around 8°C.

4. Water into 'cold' bore hole - charges cold store for the following summer.

5. Distribution pipework carries warm and cold water around site between buildings and bore holes.

FULCRUMCONSULTING | © 2008

Figure 3

Aquifer thermal energy storage (ATES) systems use groundwater to cool buildings in summer and, by reversing the flow, to heat buildings in winter.

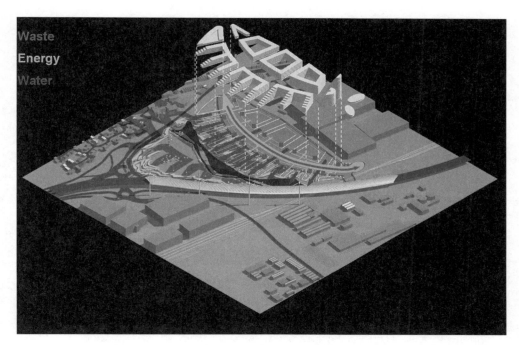

Figure 4
Energy, water and waste infrastructure flows through Z-squared.

Figure 5
Impression of Z-squared complete and functioning.

Water

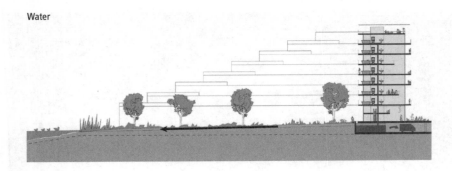

Waste

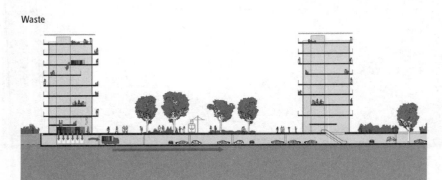

Energy

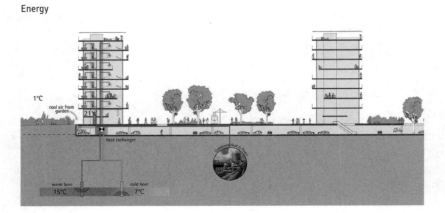

Figure 6
Z-squared: the street at podium level creates a void for sustainable infrastructure.

Landing Z-squared

To complete our Z-squared study we looked at the physical form it might take in the Thames Gateway. Working with the London Development Agency, a possible site in Dagenham was investigated. The 17-hectares, partly derelict former industrial site was assessed by architect Phil Smith and colleagues at Foster + Partners. A key aspect was to integrate the zero carbon zero waste services and other components of the sustainable infrastructure, at the same time as creating a masterplan which – on its own merits – would represent a great place to live. To enable the infrastructure to work effectively in a compact city design, a void was created under the buildings to simplify the delivery of energy and water, and make removal of wastes easier. The void could also serve as basement parking for cars (albeit with lower parking numbers) including car-club cars, creating a car-free, people-friendly street at podium level.

Costing out Z-squared

Quantity surveyors Cyril Sweett costed out the construction of Z-squared comparing it with a conventional base case. The findings are summarised in Table 2. We needed to invest an additional 6 per cent to install the on site energy, water and waste infrastructure; and spend 5 per cent more to upgrade the building fabric compared with UK 2002 Building Regulations. However, we were able to recoup 3 per cent of construction costs by reducing car parking and road infrastructure.

Overall, the difference was £47 million, or 8 per cent, additional capital cost. Since we completed the report in 2004, we now have 2006 Building Regulations, which means the additional cost in building fabric cost is reduced by 2 per cent, giving us a 6 per cent premium.

We were able to make four key observations:

- The additional premium is significant but not massive – not, say, 20 or 30 per cent, which would have been very difficult to engineer around financially. However, even 8 per cent on construction cost still plays havoc on a developer's return, viability calculations and financial indicators such as return on capital employed (ROCE); and reduced parking frees space for more development and increased margin.
- There is a long-term income stream associated with the provision of energy, water and waste services to the community. We could therefore remove these infrastructure costs from capital expenditure and include them as an investment in a utility services company. This has a financial advantage. The cost of financing property development is high, with speculative development (ie development without guaranteed sales) requiring an internal rate of return of, say, 15 to 20 per cent. Financing utility companies is usually lower, requiring an internal rate of return of only, say, 8 per cent, as the risks are usually considered lower. Thus there are ways in which the (small) premium of Z-squared can be reduced still further.
- There are avoided social and environmental costs in building Z-squared. For example, if we are diverting more from the waste stream which would otherwise be paid for by the local

authority, is there an argument that the local authority should co-invest in the utilities, or reduce local tax charges (such as Council Tax) to our residents? If we are saving CO_2 emissions, is there a benefit to society and can this be 'harvested' in some financial way, say through carbon credits? There are also health benefits for our residents through, for example, reduced car use; do these result in lower public health costs, which again could be harvested? Although in the short term, harvesting some of these avoided social and environmental costs may be difficult, in the longer term a strategy to gain financial benefit from them may well be possible. We return to the potential of such a strategy in the final chapter of this book.

- Being energy and water efficient, but more significantly creating financial savings through not having to own a car, the household expenditure for residents would be lower, saving them money. Only a small proportion of this would need to captured by the developer in order to completely offset the additional build cost.

The capital cost analysis of Z-squared gave us confidence that truly sustainable communities could be built cost-effectively and profitably even within a conventional economic context, albeit requiring a developer with a particular vision and commitment. Of course capital costs are not the only basis on which we can make financial decisions. If we move utility infrastructure costs into a services company, we need to have a workable business plan for that company. However, the Z-squared concept does start to show how an infrastructure-led approach gives us a simpler way to consider how to deliver sustainable communities. It is this approach which has informed, for example, BioRegional's work on One Planet Communities and the commercial operation of BioRegional Quintain Ltd. It has also been a key inspiration for globally significant projects such as the construction of Masdar City in Abu Dhabi (see overleaf).

Table 2
Z-squared estimated construction costs compared with a conventional base case.

	£	%
Base case	616 million	
Z-squared	663 million	
Difference comprising:	47 million	8%
Site-wide sustainable energy, waste and water infrastructure	35 million	6%
Build costs	26 million	5%
Reduction in car parking and road infrastructure	(17 million)	(3%)
Increased contingency (function of increased build cost)	3 million	-

Sustainable infrastructure as the engine for sustainable communities

By providing the local infrastructure for sustainable communities – energy, waste, water and, as we shall explore in more detail in Chapters 7 and 9, food and transport respectively – we can make it easier, more attractive and more affordable for people to lead a greener lifestyle. This infrastructure-led approach to creating sustainable communities is applicable more generally, and at different scales of development, than the autonomous house approach. We can apply it from whole cities down to a single house. In the latter case it might well be that we decide that the right solution is to build an autonomous house.

The infrastructure-led approach also frees up masterplanning and architecture. If we underpin sustainable communities with this infrastructure, we can, to a great extent, build anything we like on top. An analogy would be a modern car engine. One engine, perhaps with only minor modifications, can be used to power a number of very different-looking cars to meet different customer needs or aspirations. We can conceive of sustainable infrastructure in the same way – as a common engine that can power very different communities (see Figure 7).

Indeed, engineers conversant with sustainability will play a leading role in building sustainable communities. Brian Mark, a founding director of Fulcrum Consulting, puts the engineers first, but urges them to work with the whole team to create the desired (and desirable) outcome:

> Engineers must write the brief, before passing on to the other design professionals. And to the end, they must work collaboratively alongside others to help realise the vision – architects, project manager, or clients. Because a highly optimised building that is not loved by its users will never be truly sustainable.[5]

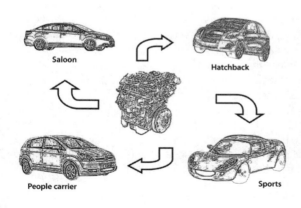

Saloon

Hatchback

People carrier

Sports

Figure 7
Toyota produce an engine which is used to power a range of vehicles from a people carrier to a sports car.

Is there one architectural language for sustainable communities?

Working on Z-squared raised the question of whether there is a particular architectural language that needs to be associated with sustainable communities. Green design and the autonomous house have created a particular aesthetic language for eco-buildings driven by solar design and the use of local natural and recycled materials. However, taking an infrastructure-led approach and provided we think about supporting sustainable lifestyles in the round, almost any architectural language can emerge from sustainability. Conversely, if we want to, we can start with any architecture language and underpin it with sustainable infrastructure. We do, however, genuinely need to think about good levels of energy efficiency and select materials which are of low embodied energy and low environmental impact. Green buildings do not need to look homespun unless we want them to. We can have sustainable buildings that look Modern, Mock Tudor, International, Postmodern, Neoclassical or Islamic Revival. Some architectural languages might be harder to make truly green – the metal and glass box, for example, though in theory it could be done with 100 per cent recycled aluminium, ultra-high performance glazing and photovoltaic shading.

Masdar – zero carbon zero waste comes to life

The Z-squared concept was the source of inspiration for Masdar City in Abu Dhabi (UAE) which carries 'Zero Carbon Zero Waste' as its epithet. Masterplanned by Foster + Partners, the Z-squared concept has here been adapted to suit the different climate and cultural context. Solar energy, rather than wind and biomass, is the main source of energy. The traditional Arab city masterplan has informed the layout of the narrow streets so that the buildings create shade for each other

Masdar City – zero carbon zero waste comes to life

In September 2008, building began on the world's greenest city, Masdar City, a zero carbon zero waste and car-free community in Abu Dhabi. Designed with the principles of a traditional Arabic walled city, this high-density, mixed-use development will house approximately 50,000 people and up to 1,500 businesses focusing on sustainable products and services.

The city is being developed by Mubadala and masterplanned by Foster + Partners. It will include a university, innovation centres and manufacturing facilities for sustainable technologies and renewable energy supply. BioRegional led the team developing the One Planet Sustainability Action Plan for the city.

Energy will be supplied from a concentrated solar power plant and photovoltaic panels. No more than 1 per cent of waste will be sent to landfill, the vast majority will be recycled, with residual waste being converted to clean energy through a plasma gasification process. Water consumption will be reduced by 50 per cent, ultimately with almost all non-potable water supplied from recycled water, with treated waste water returned to replenish groundwater. The much reduced fresh water requirement will be supplied by a solar desalination plant.

With a maximum distance of 200 metres at any time from transport links and amenities, zero CO_2 emissions from transport within the city walls will be achieved by encouraging walking and cycling through the shaded narrow streets in the context of Abu Dhabi's extreme climate and by providing easy access to public transport facilities and the solar electric Personal Rapid Transit network. The need for residents of Masdar to travel will be reduced due to the provision of facilities on site, such as food retail and deliveries, workplace and leisure facilities. Targets also include 50 per cent of journeys to and from Masdar to be made by public transport by 2020, and monitoring of air travel.

Even before the first buildings have been completed, a 10-megawatt array of photovoltaic panels has been installed, generating energy and offsetting carbon emissions from construction.

Figure 8
Computer generated image of the Masdar City.

and public spaces. Some design features from Z-squared have directly transferred across, such as raising the street to podium level, creating a services void. The void has been augmented to create space for a Personal Rapid Transit system of guided pods running on solar energy to underpin the smooth functioning of the city.

A simple approach to zero carbon and zero waste

The infrastructure-led approach certainly gives us a much simpler way to deliver sustainable communities. It puts engineers and infrastructure companies in a leading role implementing the nuts and bolts of sustainability, freeing up the architects to concentrate on design to support community interaction, healthy living, beauty and simply creating a great place to live, work and play.

BioRegional started using the term 'zero carbon' for the Z-squared concept, specifically following our experience of BedZED and our feeling that we should not be trying to generate all renewable energy on site. We wanted zero carbon to be used for buildings running more or less completely from renewable energy (we do sometimes need fossil fuels for back-up), but through a combination of off-site, as well as on site, renewable energy generation. As a term, 'zero carbon' is catchy and has been picked up widely and redefined in all sorts of different ways, often pushing the definition back to a presumption of 100 per cent on site renewable energy generation. The effect of this is to make zero carbon hard to achieve again. As the aspirations of zero carbon, as well as zero waste, are so important for sustainable communities, it is worth exploring how these might be achieved. We will look at the issues in more detail in the next chapter.

Notes
1 R Buckminster Fuller, architect (1895–1983), unsourced.
2 Herbert Girardet, 'The Metabolism of Cities', *Creating Sustainable Cities*, Schumacher Briefing No 2, Green Books (Totnes), 1999.
3 J Durney and P Desai, *Z-squared: Enabling One Planet Living in the Thames Gateway*, BioRegional Development Group 2004.
4 P Desai and N James, *One Planet Living in the Thames Gateway*, BioRegional Development Group, 2003.
5 Brian Mark, personal communication, 2009.

Chapter 6

A closer look at zero carbon and zero waste

The aspiration of zero carbon and zero waste will be central to the design and operation of sustainable communities. Increasing efforts are being made to try to define the terms, sometimes making them far more complicated than they need to be. As a global society we are currently so far from zero carbon and zero waste that we have huge opportunities to take great strides forward in these areas without needing to argue too much about the details of definitions.

'A designer knows he has achieved perfection not when there is nothing left to add, but when there is nothing left to take away.'

Antoine de Saint-Exupéry[1]

Zero carbon buildings

Scientists are now saying that we are already exceeding safe limits of CO_2 in the atmosphere – see Chapter 15. Therefore we do need to make sure, as soon as possible, that our buildings are running more or less completely from renewable energy. To achieve this we need to:

- ensure our buildings are designed or retrofitted to be energy efficient;
- ensure that any energy-management systems are operating well;
- encourage people using the buildings not to be unnecessarily wasteful;
- consider opportunities for generation of renewable energy on site; and
- work at regional, national and international levels to develop our electricity grid so it is fed by electricity generated from renewables rather than fossil fuels.

The first thing to do is to make sure that our buildings are energy efficient. We don't need to try to save every last bit of energy, which can be expensive and sometimes even counterproductive. For example, trying to reduce the use of artificial lighting by increasing window size may create glare on computer screens which means blinds are drawn all the time, increasing electricity consumption. However, we must take a committed and sensible approach to building fabric and energy-efficient appliances. Any energy-management systems operating in the building need to be regularly checked and well maintained – from thermostats and light sensors, to air-conditioning controls and whole building-control systems. Users need to be aware how best to use the building. There are very simple things that make a lot of difference – for example, which windows to open to ensure a good level of cross-ventilation during the day or to deliver cooling at night. Ideally this information should be in every resident's welcome pack, building handbook or new office worker's staff induction.

Having done our best to reasonably reduce energy demand, we can think about renewable energy supply – both generated on site or fed via a wider 'green' electricity grid.

Sources of renewable energy

Renewables come from three ultimate sources:

- Sun   solar energy, biomass from plants, wind, hydro and wave power all ultimately created or driven by the sun
- Moon   tidal power
- Earth geothermal from heat in the earth's core originating from the time of creation of the planet itself

Key renewable energy technologies are shown in Table 1. The table does not include nuclear fission energy as the radioactive fuel is a finite resource, though nuclear power is going to be a major plank in a low-carbon future. There are sufficient known reserves of uranium to fuel reactors for about 100 years at current rates of use.[2] However, nuclear energy only supplies about 6 per cent of total world energy requirement[3] so any major increase in the number of nuclear reactors running on uranium will greatly reduce the lifespan of this source. But, if thorium and fast breeder reactors are introduced, the quantity of nuclear energy which could be generated would increase over a hundredfold.[4]

Nuclear fusion technology, long heralded as an abundant and cheap future energy source created by combining hydrogen atoms to form helium, to all intents and purposes would be renewable given the abundance of hydrogen relative to how much we might consume, but engineers remain a long way from an operational fusion reactor.

Renewable sources are not always automatically 'good' – for example, there has been a lot of debate on biofuels which take crops out of the food chain (eg diverting maize to alcohol production), valuable land out of food production (eg rape oil), or require huge amounts of pesticides and fertilisers to grow. We saw in Chapters 1 and 3 that we must not only consider CO_2 emissions, but also ecological footprint, ie the availability of productive land or sea required to produce the resource. For biomass to be good it must not only come from a sustainably managed source, but also be derived without unduly increasing ecological footprint – for example, by using agricultural residues or crops grown on marginal land so as not to take land out of food production. The sustainability of biofuels is such a big issue that a Roundtable on Sustainable Biofuels has been set up in 2007 and hosted by the Ecole Polytechnique Fédérale de Lausanne, Switzerland, to establish standards and criteria for eco-labelling of biofuels.

Renewable energy can also be generated from industrial, domestic and municipal waste through various processes including incineration, anaerobic digestion, pyrolysis and gasification. The extent

Table 1
Key renewable technologies.

Wind turbines	Small and large (up to 10 MW each and growing). Building mounted, on-shore and offshore. Vertical and horizontal axes (the former less efficient but better suited to turbulent conditions).
Solar thermal (hot water)	Cheaper flat plate collectors and more expensive efficient evacuated tubes.
Photovoltaic (electricity)	Cheap polycrystalline and more expensive monocrystalline panels. Emerging thin film technology.
Dual solar	Hybrid solar thermal and photovoltaic system.
Hydropower	Large and small scale – large-scale schemes requiring large dams to be constructed can cause environmental problems.
Solid biomass and liquid biofuels	Solar energy stored by photosynthesis as plant material. Includes wood, crops and agricultural wastes used in wood fires, stoves, pellets, charcoal, biomass CHP, biofuels including bio-alcohols and bio-diesels.
Energy-from-waste	Incinerators, landfill gas, anaerobic digestion, pyrolysers, gasifiers, syngas.
Anaerobic digestion	Natural bacterial decomposition of organic wastes including sewage and food, producing biogas which can be collected for heating or electricity production.
Geothermal	Water can be heated from deep underground to provide heat or steam for electricity generation.
Air-source and ground-source heat pumps	Not strictly a renewable energy technology, but in certain circumstances can be an efficient way to generate heat or cooling from renewable electricity.
Tidal barrages and lagoons	Systems to collect energy from the rise and fall of the tides with very large barrages proposed for river estuaries such the Severn where tidal flows are considerable.
Wave and marine currents	Emerging technologies to harvest energy from waves or turbines to collect energy from underwater currents.
Hydrogen	Not a renewable energy source but an energy *carrier*, particularly being promoted for fuel cells. Can be generated using renewable energy to split water into component hydrogen and oxygen.

to which energy-from-waste is renewable is dependent on the origin of the waste. If the waste is composed of material such as paper or food waste then it can be renewable. We should consider, though, the origin of the waste material – for it to be truly renewable, the waste itself should be traceable back to a sustainably managed source such as sustainable forestry or sustainable farming. Waste streams such as plastics derived from fossil fuels when burned cannot be considered renewable.

Potentially we could meet all our energy needs from renewables. Thousands of times more solar energy reaches the earth than we need and we can harvest it directly, or via biomass or wind and wave power (see final chapter).

Economic reasons are often cited as a barrier to growth in renewable energy. However, with volatile oil and gas prices, trying to predict with any accuracy the financial viability of different technologies is difficult. On balance a reasonable position is that we have reached 'peak oil', that oil supply has reached a plateau, but that demand will continue to increase. Peak oil is also known as 'Hubbert's Peak', after Shell geologist M King Hubbert, who in 1956 predicted that global production would peak around the year 2000. Hubbert was not far wrong. If we haven't already reached peak supply, then we will do before 2015. After that we will still see global oil demand rising but supply falling, causing an underlying rise in price of oil, particularly if the economy grows significantly again.

More of a threat to renewables is coal of which there are much larger reserves than for oil. Coal can be converted to a liquid fuel to replace oil. We will be in a lot of trouble if we continue to burn coal in the way we have been doing to date. However, there are some interesting possibilities such as the widespread use of carbon capture and storage (CCS) either by, for instance, pumping it into deep aquifers or getting vats of algae to soak it up.[5] Theoretically, if we were to burn fossil fuels but capture the CO_2 released and store it, then we could think of fossil fuels as low-carbon energy sources.

The carbon footprint of renewable energy

Sometimes people ask the question whether it has taken more fossil fuel energy to manufacture renewable energy systems than the renewable energy they generate during their lifetime – which would be terrible. Fortunately the evidence is in our favour.

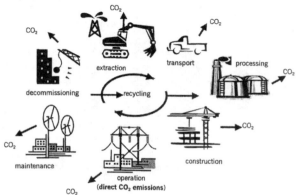

Figure 1
Life-cycle greenhouse gas emissions for electricity generation technologies.

All power generation systems have a CO_2 footprint arising at some point during their manufacture, operation, maintenance or decommissioning. Life cycle assessment (LCA) can be used to compare the footprint for each kilowatt-hour of electricity from different forms of generation and these have been reported, for example, by the UK's Parliamentary Office of Science and Technology.[6]

The CO_2 footprint of electricity from coal-fired power stations is about 1,000 grams of CO_2 per kilowatt-hour (gCO_2/kWh), whereas gas-fired power stations generate electricity with a footprint of 650 gCO_2/kWh. Reassuringly, renewable energy technologies all come out very well from this analysis. Biomass electricity has a footprint of 25–93 gCO_2/kWh. Photovoltaic panels do take a lot of energy to manufacture but over their lifespan, the electricity they generate, solar electricity, has a footprint of only around 58 gCO_2/kWh in the UK, which is much better than coal or gas. In sunnier countries where their energy output is greater, the footprint is even lower at about 35 gCO_2/kWh. Wind generation turns out to be the best. On-shore and offshore generation comes in at around 5 gCO_2/kWh (offshore is slightly less efficient because of the larger foundations required). Nuclear energy is also carbon efficient at around 5 gCO_2/kWh, but as high-grade uranium ore deposits are depleted, the CO_2 will increase as we shift to lower-grade ores which take more energy to extract. By using low-carbon manufacturing and maintenance (eg factories themselves running on renewable and using low-carbon construction techniques such as low-carbon cement for wind-turbine foundations), the CO_2 footprint of electricity generation can be reduced further. In the case of biomass, if we incorporate some form of CCS, we can create an energy-generation system with a negative CO_2 footprint yielding electricity at -410 gCO_2/kWh. This means at the same time as generating electricity we can be actively pumping CO_2 out of the atmosphere and potentially reducing the effect of climate change. We explore one way this might play out in future in the final chapter of this book.

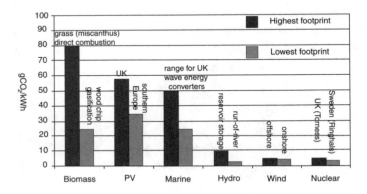

Figure 2
Range of CO_2 footprints for UK and European low-carbon technologies.

Should we push for on-site generation?

There is major debate in the industry about the relative merits of on-site ('microgeneration' or 'building integrated generation') versus off-site generation, the latter generally being large-scale projects such as big wind farms and solar arrays. Some argue that we should only use the term 'zero carbon' for buildings which generate all their electricity on site – and we should aim for all buildings to be power stations. However, matching on-site generation with demand is not easy as demand is very variable, depending on when people are in the buildings and what appliances are being used. In particular, peaks in demand are not easy to meet. Many forms of renewable generation are also intermittent – solar energy is only generated when the sun is out or it is at least sufficiently bright. In trying to overcome peaks and intermittency we can end up installing excessive amounts of on-site generation or resort to storing energy in batteries which is expensive and not necessarily environmentally friendly (hydrogen fuel cells may serve the function of batteries, but are still some way off commercialisation for widespread use). Intermittency and storage are more easily and efficiently dealt with at the level of the national grid where peaks tend to even out compared with individual buildings and energy can be stored, for example, by pumping water into elevated reservoirs during off-peak demand, and electricity regenerated via hydro-electric power.

Others have proposed that we need to introduce a concept of buildings meeting their 'net annual demand' from on-site generation – where electricity is supplied to the grid when more is generated than required and drawn off the grid when demand exceeds generation, but overall giving a net balance of zero. However, this concept remains completely arbitrary – is there an *a priori* reason why a building should generate all its own power? This idea of a self-sustaining building or home might well be a ghost of the autonomous house ideology that we explored in Chapter 4. But it is worth exploring in more detail why there remains such a strong drive for on-site generation. The arguments generally used in favour of on-site generation include:

- we avoid loss of energy in transmitting electricity through the high-voltage grid transmission system;
- conventional power stations are often inefficient because heat generated as a by-product is not used, but just wasted; and
- the challenge of climate change is so great that we need to generate as much renewable energy as possible, so all new buildings at least should generate their own power.

We do need to examine these arguments in turn, as although there is value in some cases for on-site generation, it is in very many cases proving counterproductive.

First is the issue of electricity losses in high-voltage transmission and distribution. These, however, are not as large as people might assume. UK government figures show them to be in the region of 7.5 to 9 per cent.[7] This is not something to be ignored, but integrating renewable energy generation into buildings is often not efficient – in fact it can be many times less efficient than generating electricity remotely and transmitting it, even given grid losses. One very clear example is attempting to generate electricity from wind turbines mounted on buildings. Evidence in situ shows that turbines mounted in this way suffer from the slower and more turbulent wind flow around buildings which greatly reduces their performance. As energy generated from wind increases with the square of the radius of the turbine blades and with the cube of wind speed, putting a turbine twice as large in a location twice as windy generates 64 times (6,400 per cent) the electricity.[8] In addition, buildings often have to be structurally reinforced to carry the turbines, vibration is a serious issue and there must be easy access to the roof to allow for maintenance. By the time all of this is considered, a 9 per cent loss in transmission can be a very small price to pay. Transmission losses per se are not sufficient to argue for on-site electricity generation.

A second reason given for encouraging on-site generation arises from one area of major inefficiency in large-scale generation: the waste heat in combustion-based generation – such as large-scale coal- and gas-fired power stations. Although improved in efficiency, the most efficient electricity generation that can be achieved is about 60 per cent for 'combined cycle' plants which use waste heat to generate steam which is used to generate more electricity.[9] The heat produced by combustion processes is often completely wasted – although there are more schemes now looking at using this waste heat for horticultural food growing, industrial processes, piping the heat to homes or for leisure uses such as swimming pools. Even large-scale renewable systems such as large-scale wood-fired power stations which don't use this heat are very wasteful.

The waste of heat energy in large-scale combustion power generation is the reason why many favour a move towards on-site combined heat and power (CHP), where the otherwise waste heat can be pumped or piped as hot water or steam to provide heat for buildings or industrial processes. Community and municipal scale gas-fired CHP is common and used extensively, notably in countries like Denmark. While not renewable, CHP plants running on natural gas do have an important place in reducing CO_2 emissions. Although some people are proposing micro-CHP systems which can run on gas in individual homes, they are not currently cost-effective, so CHP remains a community- or municipal-scale solution. Community and municipal CHP systems can run on renewable fuel sources such as biogas from waste farm animal slurry, organic municipal wastes, landfill gas and biomass including woodchip.

A third argument used to push for on-site generation is that we need to generate as much renewable energy as possible and so we must generate as much on site as possible. Some argue that if new buildings don't generate their own electricity, they are 'stealing' renewable energy from existing buildings. Although we can generate electricity on site, the technologies generally remain expensive (note renewable heat is much easier to generate cost-effectively on site, for example, via solar thermal and wood heating systems). The issue with on-site electricity generation is the cost of forcing it – that same money, time and energy could be spent generating far more renewable energy offsite. We are also starting to see cases where on-site generation has been forced through mechanisms such as planning requirements, but maintenance costs and technical issues mean that the systems are not maintained. In the final analysis, if on-site renewable electricity generation is too hard or too expensive to maintain, there is no benefit in installing it. Some argue the cost-effectiveness of on-site generation will increase as the market for it grows and so unit costs come down. However, for every increase in efficiency for on-site renewable generation, we are getting parallel increases in efficiency for off-site generation, so the differential continues.

I have no particular axe to grind with respect to on-site or off-site electricity generation. Our challenge with global warming is great, with many demands on our time and money. Therefore I think we should do whatever is easiest, most cost-effective and will bring the greatest environmental benefits. In this context, forcing on-site electricity generation, which has been a trend, for example, in the UK through planning policies and the Code for Sustainable Homes, has not been helpful. There are cases where, for instance, wind turbines have been installed where it was known that they would be unlikely to generate much power because of the poor wind flow caused by surrounding buildings. When selling a building or a home, why should we have regulations requiring that they generate some or all of their own energy? An analogy might be with buying any product which uses electricity. If we don't expect to buy a refrigerator or computer which generates some or all of its own power, why should it be expected of a building or a home? It may be best to think of electricity as a pooled resource shared via national and international grids and if we want it to reduce CO_2, we should as a society make the whole grid green as soon as possible. If we want to encourage on-site generation, this is better done through incentives such as tax breaks, feed-in tariffs (paying more for renewable energy whether generated on- or off-site) and grants, rather than forcing it bluntly through building or planning regulations − although in my view it is always better wherever possible to create a level playing field between on-site and off-site generation.

The pertinent question therefore might be: When should we generate renewable energy on-site? It must be when it is the right thing to do environmentally, economically and practically − taking into account all the issues around long-term maintenance. Photovoltaics are easy to install and maintain but remain very expensive, and in the short term it might be best to deploy them in countries with a lot of sun for maximum benefit. Building-mounted wind turbines are proving ineffective in practice. Biomass CHP is hard to operate on a small scale. Key on-site technologies we are left with are simple, related to renewable heat rather than electricity and with a long track record − such as solar thermal systems and wood heating systems (log, woodchip and wood pellet stoves and boilers) which are easy to operate at individual house and community scales. Renewable heat production is therefore something which should be seriously considered for on-site renewables.

In future, as technologies change and improve, there might be a greater role for on-site electricity generation. When on-site generation is competitive with generation offsite we will see people starting to adopt it more freely anyway. If 'smart grids' emerge, which enable computer-assisted balancing of power generation and power demand, as promoted by leading thinkers such as Amory Lovins of the Rocky Mountain Institute,[10] then certainly the real benefits of more on-site generation become apparent. It is conceivable that energy companies might in future offer to lease and maintain on-site generation systems for individual buildings or homes. However, it might be that individual home-owners are not best placed to become power generators.

A green grid

If we are not, in the near future, going to be generating renewable electricity on site in any great quantity, how can we run our buildings on renewable energy? The answer will be to rapidly increase the amount of renewable energy supplied into our electric grid as a whole – supplying green electricity to both new and existing buildings and industries. Studies by the Centre for Alternative Technology, for example, have shown how the UK can be run completely from fossil fuels – though requiring complete government commitment combined with a major push for energy efficiency – by as early as 2027.[11] Renewable energy generation should very much be part of national government energy policy, rather than trying to make it part of building or planning regulations.

BedZED architect sticks to his guns

When Ryan Air is folk history, car pools are everywhere, and we visit vegetarian greasy spoons in our lunch hour, the UK will have to run itself on the limited stocks of renewable energy available within its national boundaries. If every green grid off-site generation device ever dreamt up by an infrastructure engineer was built – with offshore turbines at minimum spacings over the entire Continental shelf – we would still struggle to meet much more than 25 per cent of our current national energy demand.

All of the off-site generating capacity would be needed for our stock of much-loved, but inefficient historic buildings. In fact we have about 500 dry kilograms of biomass allocated/per capita if we harvest woodland sustainably and compress agricultural waste without losing food production – leaving about 250 kilograms per capita to run a household. This tiny amount is what is needed for top-up winter domestic hot water in a superinsulated ZED home built to zero space heating specifications and with solar thermal providing hot water all summer.

Put monocrystalline photovoltaics on the half of the roof facing south, and enough electricity is generated to meet annual electric demand up to densities of 50 homes per hectare, with a summer surplus to cope with reduced outputs from offshore wind. This density band represents 70 per cent of all the homes in the UK. Higher-density urban developments can run off biomass CHP using similar fuel quotas, but only if BedZED fabric standards are achieved. This suggests that it is not realistic or sensible to claim limited renewable off-site generation capacity for new buildings, as this is effectively stealing an existing community's rights to a future powered by renewable energy. It is important that we all understand the future shortage of national and international renewable energy supplies today, because we need to apply every renewable harvesting opportunity, both on- and off-site, if we are to achieve an equitable democratic future and a workable long-term urban fabric.'

Bill Dunster, Principal, Zedfactory and co-author, The ZED Book, Taylor & Francis, 2007

Green tariffs and carbon trading

In the short term, as consumers if we want to encourage more green generation, we can switch to so-called 'green tariffs'. However, the nature of green tariffs varies enormously – from not much better than buying standard electricity, to offsetting emissions by tree planting, to something closer to the real McCoy, electricity guaranteed as coming from a green source such as wind turbines.[12]

Carbon offsetting and trading are other approaches, enabling people to emit CO_2 themselves but pay in some way to reduce CO_2 somewhere else – by planting trees, increasing energy efficiency in developing countries, or investing in renewable generation. Offsetting and trading have their place, but ultimately we have to stop building up CO_2 in the atmosphere as we are doing at the moment. There are numerous loopholes in trading and offsetting which make them hard and very expensive to police, particularly because of their international nature. At a fundamental level, they also hold the seed of moral jeopardy. If we accept that releasing CO_2 is a bad thing, it is hard to make this OK by paying for reductions somewhere else if we do nothing else. Witness a couple of other examples of offsetting. At BioRegional Quintain's office we started a saturated-fat offset scheme. If someone wanted a full English breakfast of fried sausages and bacon, they had to pay someone else to eat a bowl of cholesterol-busting porridge. Similarly, www.cheatneutral.com enables people to cheat on their partner but offset it by paying for someone else to remain celibate – so that there is no overall increase in cheating.

A workable definition of zero carbon for buildings – 'zero carbon ready'

As described in the last chapter, BioRegional started using the term 'zero carbon' as part of the zero carbon zero waste community concept. We specifically wanted to use a term for buildings run completely on renewable energy from a combination of on site and off-site sources.

How then might we look at zero carbon? A good starting point might be to think of electricity as a common or pooled resource, shared through the grid system. Rather than trying to make individual buildings or a set of buildings self-sufficient, the best way to supply renewable electricity is for the grid as a whole to become green – and for the government to set the regulatory and incentive frameworks to enable a rapid shift to a zero (or very low) carbon electricity grid. As technologies are changing and emerging all the time, we should not unduly promote on- or off-site renewable electricity generation ahead of the other, but allow a practical and economic solution to emerge.

What should we be building today to ensure a zero carbon future? First, we can make sure buildings are designed to be energy efficient – as we have seen, not necessarily trying to save every last bit of energy, but setting good standards. This can be controlled by *simple* regulation such as setting energy limits for space heating, cooling, lighting and ventilation – the parts of a building's energy consumption which are *directly* affected by building design. Second, we can avoid installing any heating, cooling or electricity-generating capacity which directly runs on fossil fuels (except for back-up), perhaps setting a limit for fossil fuel back-up of, say, no more than 10 per cent of annual demand. Third, we can consider installing renewable energy generation on site systems where we can justify it (particularly renewable heat, but also renewable electricity where capital and maintenance costs are acceptable) – but this must not be forced. If we want to encourage on site generation we should do it by positive incentives such as grants, reduced taxes or enhanced tax allowances, feed-in tariffs (preferential rates for generating electricity) or other financial credits. Fourth, any energy not generated on site needs to be supplied via grid electricity, preferably through good-quality guaranteed green tariffs to stimulate further demand for green electricity generation. As the grid becomes green, the buildings are 'zero carbon ready'. This strategy does not place unhelpful burdens on new buildings to generate their own renewable energy. However it does depend on us collectively, as the electorate, giving government the mandate to show leadership in energy policy to allow a rapid shift to a green grid – which regardless needs to happen if we are to avert catastrophic climate change.

Zero waste in more detail

We know that we are reaching peak oil, but we also have to be careful with other resources and need to be aware of 'peak uranium and peak phosphorus', for instance.[13] Creating a circular metabolism will help us to reduce our dependence on finite resources. In the 20th century we thought we had the freedom to be wasteful without consequence – we just dug more holes and filled them at increasing rates with our waste. The 21st century will be different. We might even start regularly mining our landfill sites for the resources held within them – particularly metals like aluminium which can occur at higher concentrations in landfill than bauxite ores and gold from dumped electronic circuit boards.

Ultimately we can envisage a society which recycles all its waste. Today, given the composition of our waste stream and technologies available, we can recycle at least 70 per cent of domestic waste. A further 28 per cent of the waste stream can be used for energy-from-waste, which means even today we could set a target to send no more than 2 per cent of our waste stream to landfill (the UK currently achieves a recycling rate of about 30 per cent, so there is great scope for improvement). OK, this is not quite zero because of such things as residual toxic materials including heavy metals, but it is a massive improvement on the current situation. If products are re-engineered in future to remove the amount of toxic materials in them, or we incorporate greater recovery processes for them, then this figure would be reduced further to maybe 1 per cent or even zero.

As well as enhancing our capacity to process materials for recycling, we should make segregation of waste as easy as possible. Recycling is often prevented by poor separation and so segregation for easy recycling should be encouraged. We can do this by providing segregated bins within homes and workplaces, positioning recycling bins in convenient places or using efficient collection systems such as Envac which sucks waste to collection points (see box overleaf). Recycling, however, is also prevented by composite materials – such as packaging made from paper bonded with plastics, each individually recyclable, but prevented by being made into a composite. Over time, reducing the percentage of composite materials can enable greater recycling rates to be achieved.

Life-cycle assessment shows that for most materials, recycling, where it can be well organised, is a better option than energy-from-waste. For example, a report by the Technical University of Denmark summarising life cycle assessment studies concluded: 'The results are clear. Across the board, most studies show that recycling offers more environmental benefits and lower environmental impacts than other waste management options'.[14]

Therefore our aim should generally be to recycle as much as possible. However, energy-from-waste for non-recyclable fractions does have its place. There are four main types of energy-from-waste technologies: incinerators, anaerobic digesters, gasifiers and pyrolysers. Incinerators have had

KISS zero carbon – keep it simple and sustainable

Principles which could form the basis for a zero carbon strategy for buildings:

1 Always be informed first about how to create a whole sustainable and ultimately zero carbon lifestyle.
2 Ensure all new buildings are designed to be energy efficient – not necessarily trying to save every last bit of energy, but setting very good standards as a minimum. We can always push further through experimental projects, but most of the savings will come from getting the basic building fabric right in terms of decent insulation, glazing and air-tightness (while ensuring good indoor air quality). In the UK, Code 4 and AECB Silver are good benchmarks to start with.
3 Introduce a requirement for all homes to have data on energy consumption collected for three years, so that it can inform delivery and future standards.
4 Accelerate the rate at which the grid becomes green through a coherent national renewable energy policy, but create a level playing field between on- and off-site renewable energy solutions; and introduce incentives for renewable heat, increasing on- and off-site renewable heat solutions.
5 Manage electricity and heat demand, for example through national energy pricing, simple regulation on energy efficiency of appliances and by promoting positive behaviour change.
6 Provide incentives such as zero VAT on renewable energy and energy-efficiency technologies and products (making them budget neutral by increasing VAT on non-renewable technologies and products).
7 Where it is deemed important to encourage research and development in on site and off-site renewables, use the tried- and- tested method of targeted grant programmes rather than prematurely introducing prescriptive national policy and using the wider industry and public as guinea pigs.
8 Fix a date by which time new homes and other buildings cannot be constructed to receive fossil fuel supply directly (eg, natural gas and coal) except for back-up (this date could be 2016). All these homes will then automatically become zero carbon homes as soon as the grid is green – they are therefore 'zero carbon ready'.
9 Create a positive culture of sustainability in the industry – for example, by introducing simple, short but compulsory sustainability training for building professionals including all site workers to bring about a change of culture (much as has been done for health and safety).
10 Over time, based on practical experience, introduce higher levels of building standards.

bad press from environmentalists because of toxic emissions such as dioxins (from plastics) and mercury, but also because they can reduce the incentive to recycle as waste is needed to feed 'hungry' incinerators. Modern, well-run incinerators though can be clean and do have their place. Anaerobic digesters use bacterial action to convert organic wastes (food, paper, etc) within a general waste stream into biogas which can be used for energy as well as generating a digestate which can be used as fertiliser. This leaves other waste like plastics which can be treated in another way or sent to landfill (inert materials such as plastics are not necessarily a problem in landfill – at one level we can think of it as returning oil back underground, locking up the CO_2). Anaerobic digestion is often part of a series of waste treatment processes for a waste stream – often called mechanical biological treatment (MBT). Gasifiers and pyrolysers treat waste at a high temperature in the absence of oxygen, to create a gas or liquid fuel which can be used to power a generator. It is feasible for gas produced in this way to be mixed with natural gas and distributed via the natural gas mains.

Envac Waste Collection
The Envac waste collection system comprises underground pipes which suck waste to a collection point. Removing bins from the street enhances the streetscape and reduces the need for noisy waste collection vehicles. The system has been installed at Wembley City, the development around Wembley Stadium.

1 Residents sort their waste in the kitchen and deposit it in the relevant inlet.
2 Computer-controlled emptying takes the waste away twice a day, one waste stream at a time.
3 Waste is sucked through the underground network of pipes at 70 kilometres per hour, to the waste collection station.
4 The fans that create the vacuum are situated here in the waste collection station. When the waste arrives it is diverted into the correct container.
5 The air is cleaned by filters before it is released.
6 The waste collection contractor collects the waste and recyclables, and only has to visit the central station.

The overall energy balance for the vacuum system compares very favourably with use of waste collection vehicles, and experience shows recycling rates are improved.

Some interesting possibilities may reveal themselves in time. Packaging, particularly food packaging, makes up over 30 per cent of the domestic waste stream.[15] If more of our food packaging is made from agricultural and forestry wastes rather than fossil sources – for instance bioplastic films and straw food trays – it wouldn't take much to ensure that these were a clean renewable biomass fuel, so that when buying your food, you were also buying renewable energy.

Reclaiming and 'up-cycling' rather than recycling

Even better than recycling is reclaiming. Recycling is taking a waste product and reprocessing it – for example, taking waste wood, chipping it and binding it with resins to form chipboard. Reclaiming means taking material out of the waste stream and using it again more or less unprocessed. Charity shops which sell clothes are one example, or recycling products through eBay is another more contemporary route for that matter. In certain circumstances we can reuse building materials by reclaiming them. For example, steel joists can easily be reused, as was done at BedZED, by cutting to size, sandblasting and repainting. Reclaiming can be far more energy efficient than recycling. Reclaimed steel, therefore, is more eco-friendly than recycled steel (waste steel melted down and reformed) which itself is more energy efficient than making virgin steel from mining iron ore.[16]

Reclaiming is not always practical and depends on numerous factors. For example, reclaiming bricks can be difficult depending on the type of mortar used in the building process (lime mortars are far easier to reclaim than cement mortars, although the former are more expensive and a bit more difficult to use). Demolition and new construction may not be going on at the same time, or materials from one might not match the needs of the other. Therefore, for effective reclaiming, reclamation yards need to be set up so materials can be stored and delivered when needed. This storage and double handling of materials can make it uneconomic, although the economics do start improving as energy prices and landfill taxes increase.

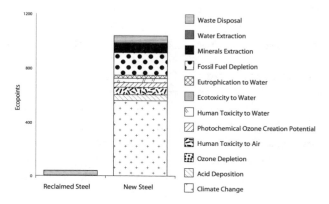

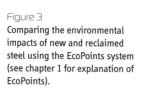

Figure 3
Comparing the environmental impacts of new and reclaimed steel using the EcoPoints system (see chapter 1 for explanation of EcoPoints).

Eliminating the concept of waste – Hempcrete

Hempcrete is a hemp and lime building technology, created through a partnership with Lhoist UK, Castle Cement and agricultural merchants Hemcore. It has been developed as a low-carbon alternative to traditional brick-wall construction. It can be ploughed in at end of life as fertiliser to grow the next generation of buildings.

Each cubic metre (35.5 cubic feet) of hempcrete locks up 110 kilograms of CO_2 due to the CO_2 absorbed during the growing of the hemp plant. The material has good insulation properties and supports good levels of airtightness while enabling the wall to breathe. In addition to walls, Hempcrete has been used for floor slabs, roof insulation and plasters.

Hempcrete was used in the construction of the distribution centre for Adnams Brewery in Suffolk in the east of England. Its thermal properties also meant that it removed the need for a cooling system, saving on the original cost estimates.

Recycling itself is sometimes divided into 'up-cycling' and 'down-cycling' depending on whether the new use is higher or lower value than the waste. Most recycling is down-cycling, for example grinding up waste green glass bottles for sand. Wherever we can up-cycle this is to be favoured. A well-known example of up-cycling is taking waste plastic bottles and converting them into clothes such as fleeces. Another example is taking broken glass and converting it into high-quality kitchen work surfaces as is done by companies such as GlassEco.

Beyond waste: 'Cradle to Cradle'

If in our society all waste becomes an input for another process, we will have no waste. Ultimately in the 21st century this should be our goal. If we design products in such a way that at the end of their life they can be reborn (through reuse or recycling) to provide another function, in effect we eliminate waste, and indeed eliminate the concept of waste.

This has been most clearly and eloquently expressed by McDonough and Braungart in the book *Cradle to Cradle* which describes how products can and should be designed and made from materials to become part of a long-term cycle of human use.[17]

A strategy for zero waste

We have often heard the 'Reduce, Reuse, Recycle' mantra. We can refine this to create a strategy for zero waste in the following way:

- Reduce the amount of waste generated by reducing wasteful consumption.
- Eliminate the concept of waste – design products to be reused or to yield materials for reuse.
- Reclaim or up-cycle – salvage materials from the waste stream to be reused or made into higher value products.
- Recycle – reprocess waste in new products, preferably locally.
- Design products to be a renewable energy fuel at the end of their life.
- Generate energy cleanly from waste

We should not be overly strict about what to do with any particular waste, but should consider the best option in any particular case. The 'right' end for the waste might be very different depending on the product, the location of recycling, reclaiming or reprocessing facilities, whether it is mixed with other waste or contaminated, and the economics. And, of course, we must remain alive to the possibilities that new products and new technologies will change the mix and balance of options over time.

Notes

1 Antoine de Saint-Exupery, *Terre des Hommes*, Chapter 3, Gallimard, (Paris), 1939, p 60.
2 OECD Nuclear Energy Agency and the International Atomic Energy Agency, *Uranium 2007: Resources, Production and Demand*, OECD (Paris), 2008.
3 G Boyle, *Renewable Energy*, Oxford University Press (Oxford), 2004.
4 American Nuclear Society, *Fast Reactor Technology: A Path to Long-Term Energy Sustainability*, November 2005.
5 C Goodall, *Ten Technologies to Save the Planet*, Profile Books (London), 2008.
6 Parliamentary Office of Science and Technology, *Carbon Footprint of Electricity Generation*, Postnote Number 268, October 2006.
7 UK Government Department for Business, Enterprise and Regulatory Reform, *Digest of United Kingdom Energy Statistics*, A National Statistics Publication, 2007.
8 G Boyle, op cit.
9 www.gepower.com.
10 www.rmi.org.
11 P Allen, J Bull and T Helweg-Larsen, *Zero Carbon Britain*, Centre for Alternative Technology, 2007.
12 V Graham, *Green Tariffs for Domestic Consumers: Reality or Rhetoric?*, National Consumer Council, 2006.
13 Richard Heinberg, *Peak Everything: Waking Up to the Century of Declines*, New Society Publishers (Gabriola Island, BC), 2007.
14 Technical University of Denmark, 'An International Review of Life Cycle Comparisons for Key Materials in the UK Recycling Sector', WRAP, 2006.
15 E Graf et al, *Food Product Development: From Concept to the Marketplace*, Springer (New York), 1991.
16 N Lazarus, *Toolkit for Carbon Neutral Developments Part 1:The BedZED Construction Materials Report*, BioRegional Development Group, 2002.
17 W McDonough and M Braungart, *Cradle to Cradle: Remaking the Way We Make Things*, Rodale Press (Ashford), 2003.

Chapter 7

Connect your community locally

Just as we aim to ensure that a community has a sustainable metabolism, so we can knit the community into its hinterland and region through the infrastructure and services we design. We can think of this approach as creating a local eco-system and a mutually beneficial relationship between urban centres and rural areas, where they are supporting each other with jobs by trading energy, food and services such as recycling and recreation. This is called 'bioregional development'. Trading locally is important to reduce CO_2 emissions from freight transport, to create communities which are more resilient to spikes in oil prices and global economic swings, to facilitate 'industrial symbiosis' and to foster a healthy, diverse and vibrant economy.

Each time we construct a building or group of buildings we have an opportunity to think about what sort of future we will be supporting. We can think of it as a privilege and responsibility. The infrastructure and services we incorporate – for energy, food, recycling and transport – can be selected to support local, long-term, green jobs. In this chapter we explore how we can build communities to support economic and environmental health at a regional level, particularly looking at food systems which are an important part of our ecological footprint.

Think global, act local – regions as eco-systems

'Think globally, act locally' has been a green mantra and guiding principle since the 1970s. We can apply the principle at two levels – first at a resource level (ie, local food, local materials and, in many cases, local energy), and second at an economic level (creating local jobs to supply green products and services).

In Chapter 4 we discussed the important contribution made by the autonomous house concept, but also the limitations of trying to be self-sufficient at the level of the individual home or building. However, there is clearer and wider value in being more self-sufficient at the level of the community and region. One name for this approach is 'bioregional development'.[1]

Why is promoting greater local and regional sufficiency a good thing? The main reasons are:

- Transporting goods (food, paper, construction materials, etc) results in CO_2 emissions. As a general principle, if we reduce transport distances we can reduce environmental impact.

- In reducing transport we can reduce our need to invest in transport infrastructure which saves money and reduces ecological footprint.
- In trading goods and services more locally we can promote healthy local economic development.
- Local trading allows us to make recycling environmentally and financially cost-effective. If we have to transport waste great distances for recycling, the benefits are lost.
- Local economic development allows us to support greater numbers of small businesses which enable us to create mixed-use development which has multiple benefits for the environment, quality of life and health (as we will see in later chapters).

In creating a sustainable future, it is vital that our economy and systems of trading are integrated into, and supportive of, natural systems. Indeed 'ecology' and 'economy' share the same etymological root – 'oikos' – which means 'home'. We must take the opportunity to align both ecology and economy when creating a place to live.

There is a lot we can and must learn from nature and the functioning of natural systems. We are all familiar with the basic functioning of eco-systems. Eco-systems, for example, are heavily based on recycling nutrients and energy locally. A bird might eat fruit from a tree, burning the sugars in its muscles to generate the energy to fly. In so doing it will also consume oxygen and release CO_2. The tree will absorb sunlight and the CO_2 released by the bird and, through the process of photosynthesis, produce sugars and oxygen. The bird will also deposit droppings containing seeds. Both the tree and its seeds will use nutrients in the bird's droppings to assist their growth. It is a self-sustaining, mutually supportive cycle ultimately powered by energy from the sun.

Just as in Chapter 5 we conceived of a community as having its own metabolism, so we can conceive of a sustainable region as an ecosystem, developing a close and mutually dependent relationship between urban areas and the rural hinterland. As we shall see in Chapters 8 and 9, in creating a sustainable 21st century, communities will emerge as walkable and cyclable compact urban areas and cities. They will also meet more of their needs from within their own boundaries through processes such as urban forestry and urban farming, but be supported by a hinterland producing much of their food and energy and recycling their wastes. We will start to knit back communities into the land and local environment, supporting local zero carbon and zero waste cycles. We see this regional eco-system illustrated in Figure 1, which very much parallels and builds on the metabolism of the zero carbon zero waste community in Chapter 5.

The benefits of local economic development are not just environmental, but also social. A bioregional form of development generates a diversity of jobs – in farming, manufacturing, service industries, etc – rather than for just one sector which, for example, gives young people an opportunity to choose a range of careers to suit their aptitudes. Long-standing UK government policy has favoured service and financial sectors over farming and manufacturing, but not everyone finds it fulfilling to work in front of a computer screen and push money around for a living. A healthy economy is a diverse one with a high local component. Such an economy is also

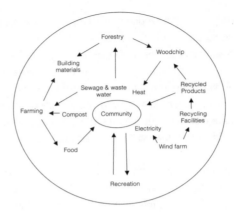

Figure 1
A regional eco-system –
an expression of
bioregional development.

more resilient than one too heavily dependent on specialisation and global trade. When designing or building a community we can think about the opportunities for supporting local green employment – creating jobs at the same time as improving environmental performance. For example, designing a drop-off point for local organic food in a residential building, or incorporating a farmers' market into a masterplan, can increase the proportion of local food consumed, support local sustainable farming and offer a lifestyle benefit. Designing recycling facilities and including local 'zero waste' office paper recycling in estates management, can support local jobs in recycling and help companies with their corporate social responsibility targets. Biomass energy boilers can be linked to local forestry and even targeted to particular woodlands to restore traditional management such as coppicing, again supporting jobs and having a positive impact on biodiversity. We look in a little more detail at some of these examples later in this chapter.

The need for a balanced, less oil-dependent economy

There has been a long-standing debate on the relative merits of globalisation of the economy (both through international finance and international trade) and local economic development. Having made billions of dollars from international financial speculation, financier, philanthropist and thinker George Soros, in the 1990s, described the global financial markets as a 'wrecking ball'[2] – with finance moving between countries with no commitment to people or place and poorly regulated. The validity of his view of the shortcomings of international financial markets became very apparent as the global financial crisis took hold in 2007 and 2008. Indeed there has been a loss of faith in the international financial structures we have built up. However, international finance is not the only problem. We should also be wary of the risks of relying on global trade, partly because global trade and global finance are closely linked, but also because global trade is often unaccountable, hard to police and prone to geopolitical instability. Global trade is not immune to rises in the price of oil which lead to increased costs in manufacturing and transport.

For example, in 2008, the spike in oil prices was a body blow to global trade and helped precipitate the severe economic downturn. Future spiking of oil prices is inevitable given that oil supply has reached a peak (for example, oil supply has been unable to increase since 2005 even though there was growing demand as the economy expanded through to 2007) and relatively small mismatches between supply and demand have had enormous effects on traded oil prices.[3]

Because moving things around the world uses oil, global trade is very vulnerable to volatility in oil prices. In turn, this dependence on oil contributes to a sense of unease, geopolitical tension and outright war. The Western world does not feel comfortable being on the end of an oil supply chain from the Middle East, any more than it does being on the end of a gas pipeline originating in Russia or Algeria, and this distorts foreign policy. With rising global population and consumption, tension around oil and gas is not going to reduce. With the huge challenge we face as a global society to avert climate change and the focus we will need to reorientate away from a dependence on fossil fuels, we simply cannot afford to be fighting over resources. The move away from an ideological focus on global trade to local economic development will require a paradigm shift in thinking. We can move towards it willingly now, or ultimately it will probably be forced on us more painfully at a later date anyway, when we won't have oil to move products around the world.

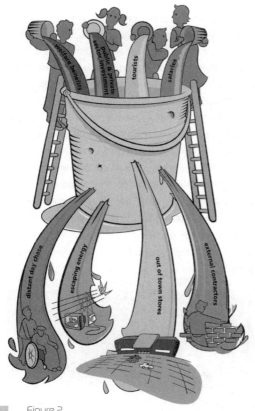

Figure 2
The New Economics Foundation makes an analogy between the local economy and a leaky bucket. There are numerous opportunities for local entrepreneurs to plug the leaks and make a community more resilient and self-supporting.

The value to local economic development

If we can foster locally self-supporting bioregional communities we have the opportunity to reduce oil dependence as well as to reduce CO_2 emissions. At the same time we can also increase employment. One case study is that of 'Local Paper for London' where by creating a more or less closed loop, the local zero waste cycle for office paper, major transport and ecological footprint savings has been achieved and jobs supported.

The social and environmental case for local and regional economic development has been convincingly made by leading economists including EF Schumacher[4] and Professor Richard Douthwaite.[5] A key advantage of local economic development is called the 'local multiplier'. The benefit to any economy is the number of times money gets spent within it before the money leaves the economy. The UK Sustainable Development Commission reports that each £10 spent on local organic produce generates £25 for the local economy through this 'recycling' of money, whereas the same £10 spent in a supermarket generates only £14.[6] The New Economics Foundation (NEF) uses the analogy of a leaky bucket.[7] Money flows into a community through salaries, tourism and welfare benefits. It then flows out through external contractors, out-of-town retailers, taxes, wasted energy and waste to landfill. To create a healthy economy, the NEF works with communities to identify opportunities to plug the leaks and encourage a local entrepreneurial spirit.

Local economic development also allows us to remain responsive to local context, the natural and social heritage of the area and to maintain or create local distinctiveness. Globalisation tends to create more monotonous, standardised and less locally responsive structures. We can learn from traditional practices in the area – indigenous knowledge – often developed over hundreds of years of trial and error and so often embodying considerable wisdom. For instance, many traditional farming and forestry practices were sustainable because they were developed before we had access to cheap oil, artificial pesticides, herbicides and fertilisers. It might be that we can support or even revive some of these traditional industries to great benefit. For example, traditional coppice management of UK woodlands can yield a sustainable harvest of wood and creates an open woodland structure which supports fast declining species such as woodland butterflies. In the UK most of these woodlands have fallen into neglect. There is great scope to revive them by creating a steady market for harvested wood (such as by installing biomass boilers) and by reintroducing management, thus creating rewarding jobs particularly for young people. Being responsive to culture and heritage also enriches sustainability, enabling us to engage more widely and deeply with people and, indeed, ourselves.

Figure 3
A coppiced woodland which generates a renewable harvest of wood, unique habitats for wildlife and places for people to enjoy.

Local recycling can reduce CO$_2$ emissions and support local jobs

Approximately one-third of paper is printing and writing paper – high-quality white paper – and over 50 per cent of that still goes to landfill. Instead it could be recycled back into high-quality paper.

In central London, BioRegional has worked in partnership with London Recycling to create a door-to-door collection of waste office paper under the name of The Laundry. The idea is that 'we collect your dirty paper, clean it and give it back to you'. The waste office paper is taken for 'cleaning' at the recycling mill in Kent, creating a local zero waste closed-loop cycle and making large ecological footprint savings. Using imported recycled paper reduces footprint by about two-thirds over virgin paper, even if the virgin paper comes from sustainably managed forests. Using locally recycled paper, whereby the distances the waste and recycled product travel are reduced, further decreases ecological footprint – by some 85 per cent over virgin paper. Even greater benefits are possible: behaviour change such as printing double-sided can easily reduce overall paper use by 30 per cent. So when use of locally recycled paper is accompanied by some behaviour change, a massive 90 to 95 per cent reduction in ecological footprint is achievable.

Moreover, large paper pulp mills for virgin paper support relatively few jobs and a large percentage of the income is used to pay back bank loans. The nature of recycling is that it is generally more labour intensive. A 2005 European Commission report, *Taking Sustainable Use of Resources Forward: A Thematic Strategy on the Prevention and Recycling of Waste*, states that recycling creates 25 times as many waste industry jobs as landfill, and eight times as many as incineration, with net job creation over using virgin materials.

But aren't developing countries dependent on international trade?

One point usually raised when talking about promoting local economic development, is that this prevents poorer countries trading their way out of poverty. There are a number of points on this,[8] but a summary of the main arguments is given here.

Promoting local economic development doesn't mean stopping international trade; it is just about the balance between international and local trade and the types of products and services we might trade in. Of course, a lot of international trade simply doesn't contribute to international development. For example, when trading many food products between European countries we export the same products as we import, simply swapping food between countries where there is no net benefit to development – see Table 1.[9]

Table 1

A lot of food moves between European countries for no obvious benefit yet contributes to CO_2 emissions.

	UK imports per annum from the Netherlands	UK exports per annum to the Netherlands
Poultry	61,400 tonnes	33,400 tonnes
Pork	240,000 tonnes	195,000 tonnes
Lamb	125,000 tonnes	102,000 tonnes
Milk	126 million litres	270 million litres

Where we do trade with poorer countries it is often not on good terms. The poorest countries haven't yet developed the institutional or social infrastructure to trade effectively, so it is on a very uneven basis. There remains major exploitation, and much international trade still supports child and indentured labour, with a few relatively rich merchants in these countries making some money. Like it or not, the reality is the (ruthless) commodity trader in a New York skyscraper dealing with a product grown by a cocoa farmer living in a hut in West Africa. More recently, successful countries like Malaysia, India and China have built up internal markets first – having protectionist policies in the early days to allow their infant industries to grow – *before* being exposed to the rigours and vagaries of international markets.[10] Many countries in Africa have suffered as they have borrowed money to switch to cash crops for export – for example, Tanzania in its switch to cotton, but whose revenue from selling cotton doesn't buy the food that could have grown on the same area.[11] There are many people and NGOs from these least developed countries who promote a more self-sufficient route to development rather than trying to trade internationally.

Ultimately we must not forget that international trade creates CO_2 emissions from transport and it is going to be some of the poorest countries that are first affected by climate change – whether it be low-lying Bangladesh vulnerable to sea-level rise, or Mozambique subject to increasing drought. However, not all international trade is equally damaging. In *BioRegional Solutions* we proposed an international sustainable trade index called FEET (Foreign Exchange Earned per Tonne of transport carbon dioxide emissions). We can see what the FEET index is for a number of products from South Africa. The higher the FEET score the better in terms of sustainable trade, indicating that South Africa is earning more money for lower CO_2 emissions.

The FEET index for tourism was based on the average spending by a UK tourist to South Africa divided by CO_2 emissions from a London to Cape Town return flight. Software development in South Africa gave a very large FEET score which couldn't be calculated as the income was large and the CO_2 emissions from supplying the software were very small. The figures show that, for the same amount of CO_2 released into the atmosphere, South Africa earns almost 20 times as much from exporting wine by sea as exporting grapes by air. In retrospect, the conclusion is obvious – that

Table 2

Dividing foreign exchange earned by the amount of CO_2 released in transport gives us an indication of sustainability (the FEET index) of different forms of international trade. FEET figures for South Africa are presented below.

Product	Export price	Rand/ tonne product	Mode of transport	Transport CO_2 per tonne product	FEET index (Rand per tonne CO_2)	FEET rating
charcoal	£319/tonne	5,740	road-sea	0.33	17,390	low
apples	£554/tonne	9,970	road-sea	0.30	33.233	medium
grapes	£2.80/kg	50,400	road-air	6.00	8,400	very low
good quality wine	£3/bottle	45,000	road-sea	0.30	150,000	high
Baygen radios	360 rand/radio	163,800	road-sea	0.30	546,000	very high
tourism	see text	see text	return air	see text	6,720	very low
software	see text	see text	electronic	see text	extremely high	extremely high

countries earn more with less damage to the environment from exporting higher value-added products and that we should favour sea freighting and avoid air freighting. Therefore, where we do trade internationally, we should steer it towards high-value FEET products. And when trading with developing countries, we must make sure it is done on a fair-trade basis to avoid human exploitation.

On the basis of FEET, unfortunately tourism did not turn out well – South Africa does not earn a huge amount compared with the CO_2 emitted. Of course tourism and eco-tourism may be justified on other bases including generation of income to protect natural habitats. There is one lesson though: if going on holiday, spend as much money as possible in the local economy (preferably on eco-friendly products and services) to increase the FEET rating, and don't haggle prices down in markets and bazaars. Salve your conscience by leaving behind as much money as possible.

Local economic development increases opportunities for industrial ecology

Local economic development also increases opportunities for industrial ecology. Industrial ecology is a powerful idea paralleling bioregional development and based on the recurring theme of 'closing the loops'. Industrial ecology seeks to shift industry away from being organised on linear, open-loop processes where resources, energy and capital investments flow through the economy becoming waste, to closed-loop processes where wastes become inputs for new processes.

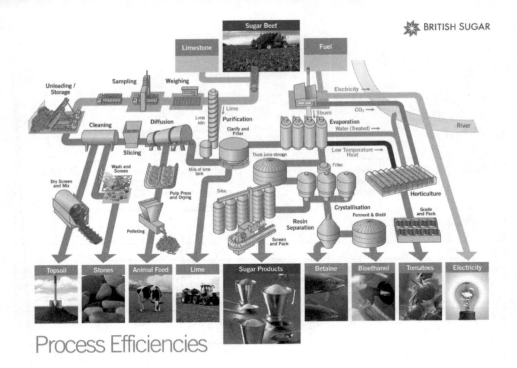

Process Efficiencies

Figure 4
Industrial symbiosis.

Related to industrial ecology is the concept of industrial symbiosis – where we start seeing clusters of industries emerging, each using the waste (or by-product) of the other. One good example of industrial symbiosis is operated with British Sugar at its heart which results in the production of a range of products including sugar, electricity, tomatoes, animal feed and topsoil. Co-locating industries is an important aspect of industrial symbiosis to enable by-products to be supplied on to the next user cost-effectively by reducing transport costs. This has also led to the idea of eco-industrial parks which could be important features to support bioregional development. (Note – it would be even better if eco-industrial parks were themselves conceived as clean, green mixed-use communities with the multiple benefits of mixing employment and residential areas.)

Future Food

In the UK Cabinet Office report *Food Matters: Towards a Strategy for the 21st Century*, even the government recognises that radical changes are required if our food system is to meet the demands of the coming years – in environmental, economic and health terms.[12]

As we saw in Chapter 3, food has not always been given the attention it deserves as it represents only 7 per cent of our direct CO_2 emissions. However, it contributes around 25 per cent of our ecological footprint[13] and is equal to the footprint associated with energy use in our homes.

As we improve the efficiency of our homes, for example through better levels of insulation, then the ecological footprint of food becomes much more significant. As well as having a massive land take, farming is also responsible for emissions of the major greenhouse gases (GHGs) methane and nitrous oxides. Surrey University figures suggest that the food system as a whole ends up accounting for about 19 per cent[14] with about half of these GHGs arising from agriculture and about half from food manufacturing, retailing, transport, catering and domestic cooking.

Possibly more so than in any other part of our lives, it is the food *system* as a whole – production through to retailing – which determines the overall environmental impact. Design, estates management, governance and culture will all need to be brought to bear to support the emergence of a sustainable food system. The difference in emissions and the investment in infrastructure needed between the extremes of a food supply system are enormous. Compare the ecological footprint of a green bean grown and packaged in Kenya – air freighted 7,000 kilometres, refrigerated and distributed by road to a supermarket regional distribution centre, then on to a supermarket, driven home in a car – with a bean grown on an allotment, or even in a garden and carried home less that 10 metres.

Of course things are not always as clear cut as at the extremes. Various studies have compared local versus imported foodstuffs. For example, a study on imported Spanish tomatoes grown with little or no artificial heating and lighting released less in the way of GHGs than UK tomatoes grown in heated and lit glasshouses.[15] However, in some cases UK glasshouses are heated by waste heat from power stations or industrial processes – so how should we account for the GHGs in this case? Things can get complex when looking at the detail. Another case is local food distributed in small quantities by relatively inefficient vans compared with food distributed in bulk by relatively efficient lorries. Bean for bean, more CO_2 may be released by transporting locally in small vans. A study by BioRegional showed the most efficient food system would be one (say for the southeast of England) where food was collected and distributed in large lorries *regionally* rather than nationally or internationally – what we might call a bioregional distribution system.[16]

Hidden costs of our international food system

When exports involve live animals there are welfare issues to consider too. Moving food around the world also has potentially enormous problems with the spread of disease. For example, take foot-and-mouth disease (FMD). In 1967, there was an outbreak of FMD in the UK but as our food system was more localised at the time, the disease was contained in only a relatively small area in Cumbria and Lancashire. The 2001 FMD outbreak spread rapidly from Sunderland to affect most of the country, as livestock movements were much greater and over longer distances. The spread of a disease, and with it the difficulty of controlling it, increases with the square of the distance travelled. Transport meat or livestock twice as far and it is four times as difficult to control the spread of distance. The 2001 outbreak was probably caused by meat coming from Thailand; transport meat 10,000 kilometres rather than eating meat produced within 10 kilometres – ie, move it a thousand times as far – and it is one million times as hard to control the spread of disease. It cost the UK an estimated £9 billion,

Figure 5
Food and Mouth Disease devastated the UK livestock industry. International trade in meat and livestock greatly increases the risk of the spread of disease and makes outbreaks much harder to contain.

approximately the total income from all meat production in the UK in one year. The FMD outbreak in 2007 was much more controlled, but only after the implementation of expensive monitoring and, regardless, movement of livestock was banned or restricted for a five-month period at great cost to farmers.[17] The UK government aims to charge farmers for costs of disease control, but this will only make UK meat less competitive, increase imports and increase risk of disease! And FMD is just one disease. The UK is now also at risk from other diseases such as bluetongue, first identified in South Africa, but which spread to southern Europe on to the UK, probably assisted by climate change. Promoting local food is a much better way to reduce the risk of diseases spreading and avoids us having to create such bureaucracies and red tape for our farmers, reducing their competitiveness. Taking this approach will require us to develop a more mature approach to dealing with risk – which is something we will have to do at all sorts of levels in our society.

Creating a more 'bioregional' food system can have other benefits. The countryside we love in the UK and which has such recreational value, has been created by it being a working farming landscape. Supporting local food production can have the advantage of maintaining our countryside heritage, or as the UK Countryside Commission used to say, we can 'eat the view'.

A one planet diet

So what does a sustainable diet and food supply system look like and how can those of us involved in the planning and development industries support a move towards it? Analysis suggests that in the UK we can achieve a 50 per cent reduction in the ecological footprint of food through four key interventions, in order of importance:[18]

- Changing to a diet lower in meat and dairy products (which can also be healthier).
- Reducing food wastage.
- Decreasing transport.
- Increasing the percentage of food produced using low impact farming such as organic.

Through promoting bioregional development, we have seen earlier in this chapter how we can reduce transport impacts. Although reducing food miles will help, especially those associated with air freighting, the largest footprint saving will come from reducing the amount of intensively produced and processed meat and dairy products in our diet.

Meat and dairy products constitute a disproportionately large part of our ecological footprint. Globally, livestock account for 18 per cent of total global greenhouse gas emissions.[19] Huge areas of the precious productive surface area of the planet are required not only for pasture, but also for growing crops for raising livestock. For example, it takes 7 kilograms of grain to produce 1 kilogram of beef.[20] Some of the world's most destructive processes are related to meat production – such as clearance of Amazonian rainforest for growing soya for raising beef in intensive food lots in the US. In rich countries we eat more meat, particularly red meat, than is healthy anyway. Sustainable diets will contain less animal protein and more vegetable proteins. The opportunity in sustainable communities might be to introduce codes of practice to promote sustainability in food retail and catering; or to create a lifestyle offer which incorporates healthier eating such as a good selection of vegetarian options or outlets.

Food waste is another big impact and the amount of food we waste has increased. The UK government-funded Waste & Resources Action Programme (WRAP) estimates that we now throw away 30 per cent of the food we buy.[21] This has been exacerbated by supermarket promotions such as 'Buy One Get One Free', encouraging people to take more than they need, a lot of which ends up in the bin. We do need to promote a more thoughtful retail culture. Again codes of conduct or targets in leases to food retail operators might be one way forward. From a resident perspective, a culture of not wasting can also be nurtured through the general governance, estates management and community engagement structures which are discussed more in Chapter 12.

Finally, increasing the amount of food produced through low-impact farming will reduce ecological footprint. Conventional agriculture has driven up yields by using fossil fuels and energy-intensive processes to create artificial fertilisers and pesticides. There is considerable debate about the environmental benefits of low-input agriculture such as organic agriculture, which sometimes has lower yields per hectare, for example with cereals. However, evidence suggests overall crops grown organically are less greenhouse gas intensive than conventional crops.[22] In the report, *Eating Oil*, Sustain and the Elm Farm Research Centre quote reductions in energy use of between 20 and 80 per cent for organic produce over conventional agriculture.[23] Other low-input farming techniques such as integrated pest management, Conservation Grade and LEAF can also be considered as well as formally certified organic standards. Leading environmentalists such as James Ephraim Lovelock believe that how we farm the land may be more important than CO_2 emissions in a sustainable future,[24] and so it is an area ripe for reinvention and transformation.

The urban environment as a source of food and other natural and renewable resources
As well as getting more of our food locally from the hinterland, there is great potential to increase food production in urban areas. In the context of a society which has traditionally valued food quality and freshness, many large cities in China have retained food growing as they have spread,

enclosing extensive areas of urban agriculture. In the next chapter, we will look at other examples and opportunities as part of a wider exploration of the possible benefits to physical and psychological health of linking more closely people and food growing.

In addition to food growing, we can look to the urban environment as a source of other renewable resources. For example, Croydon Council (the borough adjacent to BedZED) and BioRegional have worked together to stimulate 'urban forestry'. Forestry practices were introduced in the management of street and park trees gaining recognition to international Forestry Stewardship Council standards for sustainable management. The project showed that it is possible to process tree surgery waste for woodchip to supply heating and CHP plants, albeit those not sensitive to woodchip quality. It is one good example of how we can use urban areas to generate more of our needs and in this case turning what was previously a waste into a renewable resource.

Knitting sustainable communities into biodiversity

This chapter has been about thinking of ways to create an eco-system to support sustainable communities with their needs for food and other resources. But we can also look at ways we can construct sustainable communities to support natural habitats and wildlife. Built-up areas, roads and other infrastructure can fragment natural eco-systems. Even if they don't destroy habitats, they can prevent movement of species, creating small isolated populations which are not viable long term because of in-breeding – sometimes referred to as the 'living dead' by naturalists. It is of course important to protect habitats, actively recreate them or allow them to develop naturally simply by leaving space. However, as important is to ensure that there are corridors between the habitats, linking them to allow species to move through and between them. One excellent example where this is being done is at the Mata de Sesimbra project just south of Lisbon, where natural wildlife corridors are being protected, but where development is creating the incentive and finance to enhance the corridors and to restore traditional cork oak forest.

Mata de Sesimbra

Developer Pelicano has proposed a major 5,000 home and resort complex on 5,000 hectares of degraded land south of Lisbon, Portugal. The area has been subject to illegal sand quarrying and the traditional cork forest had been replaced by exotic pines which have suffered from nematode infestation. Remnants of traditional forest remain, especially alongside the streams flowing through the site. Aggregating the development rights of landowners enabled a coherent site-wide approach to be taken.

Pelicano commissioned extensive mapping of the biodiversity left on site. Working with foresters and ecologists, a comprehensive plan to protect and enhance the remaining wildlife areas, with major cork oak and umbrella pine restoration, has been proposed, funded in part by the construction of six compact villages built on the most degraded parts of the site. By masterplanning around wildlife corridors and creating new ones, the economic benefits of development have been harnessed to bring biodiversity value. Long term, residents and businesses within the scheme will pay a small 'green tax' which will support forest management. Restoring the natural landscape and unique ecology associated with the traditional cork industry will enhance development value as well.

Protected area

Ecological corridors

Development areas

Sustainable communities can support bioregional development

I hope in this chapter I have managed to convey that every time we work with a community we have an opportunity to nurture an eco-system to support it. We should think of any building or group of buildings as a whole system – economic, social and environmental – and think how we use the opportunity to support bioregional development, industrial ecology and the local economy. We can think about integrating recycling and buy-back schemes. We can think about food, energy and transport services – designing in products and services which make it *easy* for the people to adopt a green lifestyle. Figure 6 demonstrates how this approach has informed development of the One Brighton scheme on the south coast of England, which is a key case study for Chapters 10, 11 and 12.

In the next chapter we approach sustainability from a different, more personal angle. We will look at health and happiness and how emerging scientific data in this area can help us to create places where people are likely to be healthier and happier.

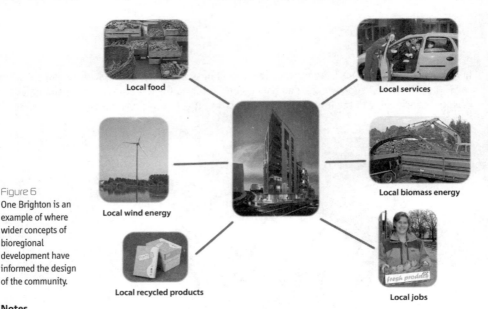

Local food

Local services

Local wind energy

Local biomass energy

Local recycled products

Local jobs

Figure 6

One Brighton is an example of where wider concepts of bioregional development have informed the design of the community.

Notes

1 P Desai and S Riddlestone, *BioRegional Solutions for Living on One Planet* Schumacher Briefing No 8, Green Books (Totnes), 2002.

2 George Soros, *The Crisis of Global Capitalism: Open Society Endangered*, Little, Brown (London), 1998.

3 Richard Douthwaite, personal communication.

4 EF Schumacher, *Small is Beautiful: A Study of Economics as if People Mattered*, Blond & Briggs (London), 1973.

5 Richard Douthwaite, *The Ecology of Money*, Schumacher Briefing No 4, Green Books (Totnes), 2000.

6 UK Sustainable Development Commission, 'Healthy Futures: Food and Sustainable Development', 2004.

7 www.pluggingtheleaks.org.

8 P Desai and S Riddlestone, *op cit.*

9 Caroline Lucas, *Stopping the Great Food Swap – Relocalising Europe's Food Supply*, The Greens/European Free Alliance, The European Parliament (Brussels), 2001.

10 H-J Chang, 'Protecting the Global Poor', *Prospect Magazine*, Issue 136, July 2007.

11 P Desai and S Riddlestone, op cit.

12 UK Cabinet Office, *Food Matters: Towards a Strategy for the 21st Century*, 2008.

13 J Barrett and S Frey, Stockholm Environment Institute, *Our Health, Our Environment*, Paper for the International Footprint Conference, Cardiff, 2007.

14 Tara Garnett, *Cooking up a Storm*, Food Climate Research Network, Centre for Environmental Strategy, University of Surrey, 2008.

15 S Sim, *Sustainable Food Supply Chains*, Portfolio submitted for the degree of Engineering Doctorate in Environmental Technology, University of Surrey, 2006.

16 N Davies and P Desai, *BioRegional Food Networks*, BioRegional Development Group, 2001.

17 Iain Anderson, *Foot and Mouth Disease 2007: A Review and Lessons Learned*, Report for the Prime Minister and Secretary of State for Environment, Food and Rural Affairs, The Stationery Office, 2008.

18 Ben Gill, *The Impact of Food – Providing Sustainable Diets in the Thames Gateway*, BioRegional Development Group, 2005.

19 Food and Agriculture Organisation, *Livestock's Long Shadow*, December 2006.

20 *Environmental Health Perspectives*, Vol 110, No 5, May 2002, pp 445–56.

21 WRAP, *The Food We Waste*, Project Code RBA 405–0010, Banbury, 2008.

22 AG Williams, E Audsley and DL Sandars, *Determining the Environmental Burdens and Resource Use in the Production of Agricultural and Horticultural Commodities*, Cranfield University and Defra, 2006.

23 Sustain and Elm Farm Research Centre, *Eating Oil – Food Supply in a Changing Climate*, 2001.

24 J Lovelock, *The Vanishing Face of Gaia*, Allen Lane, Penguin Books (London), 2009.

Chapter 8

Health, happiness and multiple benefits of green space

We can use science to help us create better places where we can increase the probability of people living happy, healthy and more environmentally sustainable lives. Scientific evidence tells us that the consumerism which has increased our ecological footprint is not making us happier. It also tells us that physical and psychological health is increased in walkable, cyclable and more neighbourly communities where there is access to greenery and green space. When we link all this together with healthier eating, food growing and creating space for wildlife, we start to create positive feedback loops and also increase property values.

'We shape our buildings then they shape us.'

Winston Churchill[1]

Aiming for zero carbon and zero waste, together with ecological footprint targets, gives us an insight into how technically we may create sustainable communities. However, technical solutions by themselves will not deliver sustainability. We also need to address the human dimension and engage with people at a very personal level.

So, taking a different tack, where might our greatest hope in creating sustainable communities lie? It might be in this simple observation: our ecological footprint has grown enormously in the past 50 years, yet if anything, we are slightly less happy.

The study of happiness is now a science, according to Lord Layard, happiness advisor to the UK government.[2] Happiness is a surprisingly measurable and reproducible metric. Ask people how happy they are on a scale from one to five, and you can get a reliable measure over time and between people. Thus we can measure it and analyse what is likely to make us more or less happy. It has given rise to a whole branch of psychology which Dr Martin Seligman of Pennsylvania State University has called 'positive psychology'. It has also led to the founding of interdisciplinary research teams such as at the Well-Being Institute at the University of Cambridge. All this research means we can start taking a scientific approach to creating happier people and places.

In the UK our ecological footprint has increased 70 per cent since 1960.[3] This increase in footprint has been accompanied by an approximate doubling in wealth, but we are no happier than in the 1950s and, if anything, we are slightly less happy.[4] Figures from the New Economics Foundation show a decoupling of GDP and life satisfaction in the UK since the 1970s (Figure 1).[5] We all know it deep down – keeping up with the Joneses fuels status anxiety, increases consumption, promotes environmental damage and reduces happiness. Overall happiness does not correlate well to ecological footprint – the US and Costa Rica have similar levels of life satisfaction, but the US has 4.5 times the ecological footprint of Costa Rica.[6] Once basic material needs have been met, happiness does not increase as we get more materially rich, particularly if our neighbours and peers are even richer than us. So for example, as Layard quotes, after unification the standard of living went up in East Germany but happiness levels decreased. It is not only the poor, but also the rich who are unhappier in less equitable communities. This leads us to the conclusion that more materially equitable societies, where the difference between rich and poor is less marked such as in Scandinavia, are those which will be happier. This does turn out to be the case with studies, for example, which show Denmark ranked as the happiest country in a list of 178, compared with the less equitable UK coming in at 41.[7] As we shall see in this chapter, Scandinavia is often cited as a leader in creating a happier and healthier society.

If increasing material wealth does not necessarily make us happy, what does? Things like good relationships, security in employment, our attitude to life, our levels of trust and good health all make us measurably happier. People are happier if they are thankful, compassionate and if they socialise more.[8, 9] Not surprisingly, people are also happier if they are healthier. Health improves happiness and happiness improves health – supported with evidence that happier people live longer.[10]

Can we use these scientific findings to guide us in creating happier communities? There are two main areas we can consider:

- Increasing physical health through good levels of exercise and better diets.
- Increasing psychological well-being through promoting trust, improving mental health and promoting material equity.

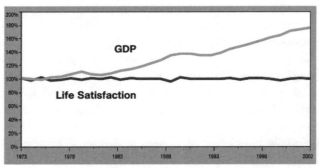

Figure 1
There has been a decoupling of increasing material wealth and life satisfaction in the UK. There is now an opportunity for us to rethink our goals in the 21st century.

Increasing physical health – air quality, exercise and diet

Physical health and happiness are closely linked. Whereas in the last century, the major progress in health was due to improvements in sanitation, nutrition and immunisation,[11] the major determinants of health in the rich countries are now lack of exercise and over-eating. Whereas we still look to doctors to deal with health by treating disease, physician Dr Robin Stott calls for a more balanced view of health, stating: 'We have not invested sufficiently in the social and environmental factors that underpin true health.'[12]

Emissions from cars are a major contributor to respiratory ill-health, particularly in children. A high proportion of children in the UK suffer from respiratory problems, and nitrous oxides and other pollutants from cars are a contributing factor. Creating communities with fewer cars and car-free areas which are pedestrian friendly and where children can play will reduce air pollution and have a positive impact on respiratory health.[13]

Figure 2

Building sprawling, car-based suburbs as in many US cities, we create a different shaped person to when we build compact cities with good walking and cycling facilities, as in Copenhagen, Denmark. We shape our buildings and inevitably they shape us.

Lack of exercise is a major concern with our modern sedentary lifestyles. Many of us only walk a few metres a day – from home, to car, to the seat at the office computer. A 2005 UK time-use survey found that we spend on average 10 minutes a day on sports and over two and a half hours watching TV, DVDs or listening to music.[14] Levels of obesity and diabetes are at epidemic levels with the World Health Organization estimating that obesity is killing about 550,000 people a year in North America and Western Europe.[15] Obese people die on average nine years earlier than those with a healthy weight.[16] The average distance people walk has fallen by a third over the last 20 years[17] and an estimated £1 billion is spent by the National Health Service in the UK on ill-health related to physical inactivity.[18] The statistics and trends in children and young people are looking worse. In the UK in 2002, 22 per cent of boys and 28 per cent of girls aged two to 15 years were overweight or obese, predisposing them to diabetes, heart disease, low self-esteem and depression.[19] Even 15 minutes of exercise a day, say just walking to and from school, greatly reduces the incidence of children being overweight. To see what the UK might look like in a few years, we might visit Florida, where it is common to see people so obese that they travel on electric buggies, unable to walk. It is almost surreal to think that we can eat so much that we disable ourselves.

Creating communities where it is pleasant safe and convenient to get to school or the office by walking and cycling, not only reduces CO_2 emissions, but can also greatly improve health. Indeed in the UK an estimated 41 per cent of all journeys are less than 3.2 kilometres, a distance easily cycled in 15 minutes, and 35 per cent of the population agree they could just as easily walk or cycle many of the short journeys they now make by car.[20] However, traffic and concomitant safety fears prevent this from happening. Therefore, the way we plan and design our suburbs and cities greatly influences how much exercise we get. Professor Philip James, Chair of the International Obesity Task Force, calls for towns and cities to be radically redesigned as planning around the car is one of the worst contributors to obesity. He highlights Scandinavian cities as 'slim cities' because they are designed to encourage cycling and walking.[21]

Cycling charity aims to reduce costs of healthcare

Cycling charity Sustrans estimates that every £1 spent on cycling could save the UK National Health Service £20 in treating conditions linked to sedentary lifestyles, by encouraging children to cycle and making towns safer places to ride bicycles. Its work is backed up by experience in France, where 10 towns have reduced the proportion of overweight 7 to 12-year-olds from 10 per cent to 7 per cent for girls and 19 per cent to 10 per cent for boys by promoting cycling. Sustrans has recently launched similar projects in the UK, encouraging children to cycle to school. With one in five cars on the road at 8.50am on the school run, it says its scheme will also cut spiralling emissions from transport.

www.sustrans.org.uk

Increasing psychological health

An interesting phenomenon in countries like the UK is the increase in fear of crime, although overall underlying levels of crime have probably not increased. Why might this be so?

A major determinant of happiness is the levels of trust we have in our fellow human beings – and this has decreased markedly in countries like the UK.[22] This has paralleled our creation of more mobile and anonymous communities. Researchers Dr Stephen Farrall from Sheffield University and Dr Jonathan Jackson of the London School of Economics found that, 'People did not neatly separate out the issue of crime from general unease towards social stability and the pace and direction of our changing society … both fear of crime and anxiety about crime distilled popular concerns about neighbourhood breakdown.'[22]

Mobility and the car have had a huge impact on shaping our interpersonal and community relationships. For example, cars might help connect people over greater distances, but at the same time they distance people from their immediate neighbours: there is clear evidence of how roads disrupt communities and local social networks (Figure 3).[22]

Neighbourliness is an important factor in creating a sense of trust. Many people say they aspire to living in a village with neighbourliness and community spirit a key factor. The mobility and anonymity of modern communities mean we often don't know our neighbours. We tend to fear what we don't know. If we don't know our neighbours we are more likely to fear them. How our communities are masterplanned and how they operate, therefore, can have a huge bearing on levels of trust created. To nurture trust, we should shift from communities based around the car to those designed around pedestrians and child-friendly public space, creating places where neighbours can meet and mingle.

At BedZED we have evidence of how this works in the context of building a sustainable community. Car-free public space has been created at the heart of the eco-village, a safe place enjoyed by children and neighbours. As we saw in Chapter 2, a survey in summer 2007 showed that a BedZED resident on average knows 20 of his/her neighbours by name while the average in the surrounding area is eight, and the UK average closer to three. Seventy per cent of BedZED

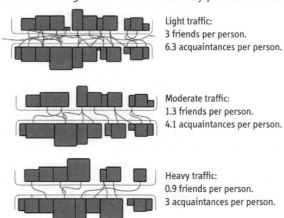

Light traffic:
3 friends per person.
6.3 acquaintances per person.

Moderate traffic:
1.3 friends per person.
4.1 acquaintances per person.

Figure 3
Traffic destroys social fabric.

Heavy traffic:
0.9 friends per person.
3 acquaintances per person.

residents also report an improved quality of life over where they used to live. However, knowing your neighbours does have costs – it can take me an hour to do my recycling at the weekend as I pass my neighbours and end up chatting to them. But this is the sort of interaction that is essential for a happy community long term. As Jane Jacobs has said: 'Sidewalk contacts are the small change from which a city's wealth of public life may grow.'[25] Small problems are picked up, such as discontent over a noisy child, or problems with the grounds maintenance, when they are likely to be easier to solve and before they have the chance to escalate into bigger problems. People are naturally sociable animals and we are designed to work out problems in this way. This natural policing is enormously effective and cost-effective. If our communities don't manage themselves in this way we end up paying for it through taxes for social services, policemen or, when they cause stress and ill-health, through the health service. In this context it is not surprising that people often talk about wanting to live somewhere with a greater sense of community such as in a village.

The structure of our communities also has a bearing on mental health. As our demographics change and more people are living alone, and as community fabric and neighbourliness has decreased, more people are being tipped into clinical depression and anxiety states needing medical treatment. Of course genetic factors are important – but so are environmental and social factors. We can think of ways of creating places where the probability of good mental health is increased. Neighbourliness – encouraged by good public space – can offer some protection against isolation which is a predisposing factor to mental ill health.[26] Exercise too affects our mental health, so communities which encourage walking and cycling can have positive benefits. As the UK's Chief Medical Officer stated in 2004: 'Physical activity is effective in the treatment of clinical depression and can be as successful as psychotherapy or medication.'

More general social issues such as social equity have a bearing on psychological health with both the rich and poor less happy in less equitable societies. Although social equity will have its origins in culture and politics, it is physically expressed, for example, in good social housing and the avoidance of gated or economically segregated communities – something which the Danes and Swiss have been generally better at than the UK and which is reflected in greater levels of happiness in their countries.[27] Scientific evidence therefore tells us that social equity, putting aside any moral stance, is a driver for building happier communities.

The role of mixed-use developments in happiness and reducing crime

Mixed-use planning – where we integrate homes, offices, schools, retail, etc – has multiple benefits for sustainability, including, as we shall see, in promoting happiness and reducing crime. Lord Layard states that 'commuting is the single activity which people report as causing the greatest reduction of happiness'.[28] Where mixed-use communities enable people to live closer to work, and with less time spent commuting, more time is freed for socialising and the family – activities which are enjoyable in themselves but also increase happiness through reinforcing community ties and providing informal moral guidance to children.

Should every building become an eco-village?
Every time we think about constructing or refurbishing a building we can use the opportunity to consider how it can contribute to community life and sustainability. Given the benefits of mixed-use development, could a building currently with a single use, say either office or residential, be converted into a mixed-use building and become an eco-village? Could an office introduce a car club available to the wider community? Could the building support local convenience retail, or become a drop-off point for local organic produce? Could open space, even a car park, host a weekly farmers' market? We should seize joyfully these myriad opportunities to support a happier society.

With respect to crime, one feature of mixed-use communities is that they are naturally policed night and day reducing opportunities for criminal or unsociable activities. Whereas neighbouring suburban developments are purely residential, BedZED has been conceived as a village with a mix of uses. While the surrounding area is troubled by petty crime such as graffiti, BedZED itself has remained more or less graffiti free. If we are to believe Alice Coleman's proposition that social malaise can be measured indirectly by looking at markers such as vandalism and litter, then BedZED has little social malaise.[29] On the other hand, development with separate dormitory suburbs and business districts builds the infrastructure for crime, with the former deserted during the day and the latter at night.

Greenery, health and property values
There is mounting evidence linking the way our built environment is constructed with health and well-being, as we have seen already. The planning and development industry can go further and positively engage with, or even lead on, the health agenda. 'Health professionals have no more levers to pull', states Dr William Bird, GP and senior lecturer at Peninsula Medical School. However, Dr Bird is working with planners to promote increased access to green space as a cost-effective way to increase health. There is clear and growing evidence now that green space boosts health by increasing physical exercise, increasing social inclusion and reducing air pollution – which combined reduce anxiety and depression, diabetes, cancer, cardiovascular disease and lung disease. For example, there is an inverse relationship between the amount of greenery in an area and obesity (see Figure 4).[30]

As well as improving physical health, green space also increases psychological and social health. Frances Kuo and colleagues' classic study on the deprived Robert Taylor Homes public housing development in Chicago compared residents, in the same development, living adjacent to squares with greenery, with those without grass and trees. They found that 'the more vegetation in a common space, the stronger the neighborhood ties near that space – compared to residents living adjacent to relatively barren spaces, individuals living adjacent to greener common spaces had more social activities and more visitors, knew more of their neighbors, reported their neighbors were more concerned with helping and supporting one another, and had stronger

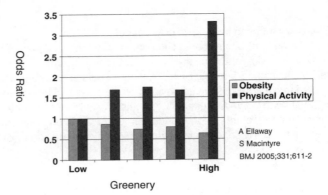

A Ellaway
S Macintyre
BMJ 2005;331;611-2

Figure 4
There is an inverse relationship between green space and obesity. High levels of greenery are associated with higher levels of physical activity and lower levels of obesity.

feelings of belonging.'[31] Kuo describes these neighbourhood ties as the glue which makes a collection of unrelated neighbours into a real community providing social support, a sense of belonging and a mechanism to defend against crime. Later studies have shown very specific psychological benefits, for example that single mothers are significantly better able to cope with major life issues if they have access to green space.[32]

From a developer's point of view, the creation of good green space, free of traffic and noise, can easily be paid for by reducing car-based infrastructure such as roads and car parks – often leaving money to spare. From home owners' or property investors' perspectives, there is clear evidence to show that trees and greenery increase property values.[33] However, the benefits can be much wider than simply a question of aesthetics. For instance, green space creates a more comfortable microclimate and reduces storm-water run-off. Figures from the Center for Urban Forest Research suggest that street trees in Minneapolis saved $6.8 million in energy costs, $9.1 million in storm-water treatment, as well as increasing property values by $7.1 million.[34]

Maximising the value of green space to people and the planet

Through a drive for improved health and well-being, we might choose to introduce more and better green space as we design new communities, or perhaps even go as far as to dig up roads or car parks to create it in existing communities. We could take the opportunity to maximise the benefits of green space to sustainability – for example, wildlife and food growing. Every time we create green space for people, we also have the opportunity to create habitats for wildlife or space for food production – or indeed we could integrate all three by planting community orchards and vineyards as, for example, has been done with great success at Village Homes in Davis, California. Much has been written about attracting wildlife into urban areas so I will not dwell on this. However, there has until recently been less focus on urban food production. As food is such a big part of our ecological footprint and the planet has limited land, we might well see food production in cities increase rapidly in this century. Some of the opportunities for this are worth exploring in a little more detail.

Planning for happy, healthy and sustainable eating

We saw in Chapter 1 that food supply and what we choose to eat will be as important as energy, waste and transport in sustainable communities. At the same time, doctors and nutritionists are telling us to eat more fresh fruit and vegetables and reduce the amount of saturated fats, especially from red meat which, as we saw in the last chapter, is consistent with a more environmentally sustainable diet.

As planners, architects and developers, how might we support healthier and more sustainable eating? We might create space for farmers' markets and drop-off points for local food. Public spaces could be planted with food-growing plants – so-called edible landscaping.[35]

We might also be able to promote urban agriculture which, as we saw in Chapter 7, remains important in China, but has also grown up in Cuba because of limited access to oil. We could integrate vegetarian restaurants into developments and introduce green leases requiring operators like hotels to provide healthier, more sustainable food. When selling homes we could provide information on healthier eating or design kitchens for ease of storage and preparation of fresh vegetables.

Can we go further and positively create places where we can, through food, improve happiness? Psychologist Professor Richard Stevens, as part of a televised experiment, *Making Slough Happy*, (BBC 2) proposed a 10-point plan for happiness. One recommendation was 'plant something and nurture it' and another to 'get physical – exercise for half an hour three times a week'. We can combine the two by growing more of our own food, increasing happiness and sustainability. We could therefore think about creating more opportunities for this – integrating allotments, community gardens and orchards into masterplans and herb boxes and rooftop mini-allotments into architecture.

Figure 5
Beautiful and dramatic edible landscaping outside the restaurant at the Eden Project in Cornwall in the west of England.

Figure 6
Urban agriculture in China.

Urban agriculture

Following the collapse of its trade partner the Soviet Union in the early 1990s, and the US trade embargo, Cuba was forced by necessity to become more self-sufficient for food, fuel and other raw materials. Due to extremely limited access to fossil fuels, machinery and artificial fertilisers, Cuba established food production systems with the minimum need for transport and chemical inputs. Urban agriculture is very widespread, supported by the Urban Agriculture department of the Ministry of Agriculture, which supplies seeds, tools and advice to new urban gardeners and training by outreach workers. Formerly vacant lots, balconies, rooftops and backyards in cities across Cuba have been converted to cultivation, resulting in fresh produce available from private stands throughout urban areas.

Kitchen gardens known as *huertos* are run by individuals, families or institutions such as daycare centres and schools, and range in size from a few square metres to one or two hectares. Other units, known as *auto-consumos*, are attached to colleges, hospitals and factories with the objective of

producing food for the students' and workers' lunches. Raised beds filled with mulch (known as *organopónicos* as they were originally converted from hydroponic units) are also common, as they can be built on any waste land including old car parks and building sites.

Eco-friendly practices such as the use of earthworm composting, animal and green manures and crop rotations result in an estimated 90 per cent of Havana's fresh produce – including fruit, vegetables, eggs, meat, rice and medicinal plants – coming from local urban farms and gardens.

Should developers, planners and architects really take on the happiness agenda?

It might seem like social engineering to take a deliberate approach to creating places where we try systematically to reduce car dependence, increase the probability of knowing your neighbours, increase the amount of local food consumed, and try to influence the health and happiness of residents. However, social engineering is, like it or not, what planners, architects and developers do. We might as well do it in a considered and positive way. Is it really any more social engineering than when we build roads, which inevitably destroy local social fabric and neighbourliness, or build out-of-town supermarkets which provide us with carbon-intensive food and undermine town centres, or create sprawling suburbs which force car dependence and promote obesity?

Planners have a long history of considering wider social benefits. Architects and masterplanners too are taught to consider the creation of delight in the design of buildings and places – something which supports happiness. However, private developers have a reputation, often with good reason, of being mercenary in their approach and thinking. Generally they are seen as having an interest in promoting health and happiness only at a most superficial level and only where this can help to sell properties. In the development world, any agenda on health and happiness therefore has been driven by social housing providers and philanthropic developers, notably by Victorian industrialists such as William Hesketh Lever's Port Sunlight and Cadbury's Bournville model village. There is an opportunity now to take as much a scientific as an altruistic approach, and perhaps every developer should consider formally creating a health and happiness plan. This is, for example, what BioRegional Quintain Ltd does for every scheme in which we are involved. That is not to say that we can guarantee or force people to be happy, but we can maximise the probability of happiness being an outcome.

What we design and build has such a bearing on health and happiness, might we one day see Happiness Regulations sitting alongside Planning Regulations and Building Regulations? I hope not. But as responsible professionals we must start applying the lessons. More generally, governments too could seek to use happiness as a driver for policy rather than being fixated on economic growth, following the lead of the King of Bhutan whose long-stated aim is to increase Gross National Happiness rather than Gross National Product.

Suburban village concept – Nightingale Orchards
This concept masterplan for a suburban village is conceived as a community set in an orchard, and was competition winner for an eco-community flagship scheme in Surrey. Southern Housing Group and BioRegional Quintain with Feilden Clegg Bradley Studios, Place Landscape Architects, NBT Consult and Ellis & Moore Consulting Engineers. (See Chapter 14 on retrofitting suburbia.)

A new frontline in health promotion?

The 20th century was about improving material well-being and lifting many people out of abject poverty, and this remains the case in a good number of developing countries. In rich countries, increasing wealth did improve health and happiness in the first part of the century, but in the second half of the 20th century and into the 21st century, ever-increasing consumption has diminished health, failed to increase happiness and is driving environmental destruction. Might we in the 21st century shift our focus in rich countries from the pursuit of materialistic concerns and consumerism to well-being, health and happiness? Sustainable communities will be central to this shift. Creating more sustainable communities promotes places with fewer cars which will encourage walking, cycling and growing local food – exactly what scientific evidence tells us will make people healthier and happier. It does mean that planners, architects and developers should positively take up the challenge and become a new

The philanthropic developer's view of BedZED

Looking back to the inception of BedZED, to the demanding and stressful years spent on construction, to managing the risks entailed in selling and letting the homes, and to the grind of sorting out the inevitable teething problems, I doubt if any of us realised quite how influential it would turn out to be. While we had high hopes that it would be a ground-breaking development, I don't think any of those involved expected it to become government policy that all new homes built in England should be zero carbon by 2016. To me it is inconceivable that this would have happened without the existence and example of BedZED. And yet surprisingly I have found even greater awareness and enthusiasm for BedZED abroad than at home. No other UK housing project since the era of the postwar New Towns has achieved the same level of global recognition.

It is deeply important that the greatest success of BedZED has been to foster a successful and resilient sense of community in its residents. No amount of technical accomplishment would have compensated for failure in this key aspect. So it is possible to take a more sanguine stance when contemplating the failure (so far!) of the wood-burning CHP and the local sewage processing capability of the Living Machine. I am sure that the technology will catch up with our aspirations sooner or later. In this regard we can recognise that BedZED is action research of the most important kind, with a committed cross-section of residents establishing what works for ordinary people and gently pushing forward the boundaries of what is possible in our crucial search for sustainable lifestyles.

The Peabody Trust took responsibility for building BedZED, and did so because we argued that poorer people are the section of society that will suffer first and foremost if our society fails to find a more sustainable way of life. Everything that we have learned about climate changes in the 10 years since that decision was taken has reinforced that analysis. BedZED is a living test-bed from which a huge amount has been learned, and is still being gleaned. It is most encouraging that other developers and house builders are absorbing those lessons and are rising to the challenge of pushing out the boundaries to reach beyond BedZED.

Dickon Robinson, former Director of Development, The Peabody Trust

frontline in health promotion. Indeed happiness can be a *strategy* to achieve sustainability. It might even be that promoting health and happiness will turn out to be the most important strategy for sustainability – perhaps even more far-reaching and powerful than the calls to reduce CO_2 emissions.

Notes

1 Winston Churchill, speech to the House of Commons, 28 October, 1943.

2 Richard Layard, *Happiness: Lessons from a New Science*, Allen Lane (London), 2005.

3 Global Footprint Network, *United Kingdom's Footprint 1961–2003*, 2008; see www.globalfootprintnetwork.org.

4 Professor Richard Douthwaite, personal communication based on draft essay, 'Why cap and share is needed for an international recovery', March 2009.

5 N Marks and H Shah, *A Well-Being Manifesto for a Flourishing Society*, New Economics Foundation (London), 2004.

6 N Marks, S Abdallah, A Simms and S Thompson, *The Happy Planet Index*, New Economics Foundation (London), 2006.

7 Ibid.

8 E Dunn, L Aknin and M Norton, 'Spending Money on Others Promotes Happiness', *Science*, Vol 319, 2008.

9 D Kahneman, E Diener and N Schwarz, *Well-being: The Foundations of Hedonic Psychology*, Russell Sage Foundation (New York), 1999.

10 D Danner et al, 'Positive Emotions in Early Life and Longevity', *Journal of Personality and Social Psychology*, Vol 80, 2001.

11 Graham Scambler and Donald Patrick, *Sociology as Applied to Medicine*, Baillière Tindall (Oxford), 1986.

12 Robin Stott, *The Ecology of Health*, Schumacher Briefing No 3, Green Books (Totnes), 2000.

13 National Air Quality Strategy (1997).

14 Office for National Statistics, *Time Use Survey*, HMSO (London), 2006.

15 World Health Organization, *The World Health Report 2002: Reducing Risks, Promoting Healthy Life*, 2002.

16 KR Fontaine et al, 'Years of Life Lost Due to Obesity', *Journal of the American Medical Association*, 289, 2003, pp 187–93.

17 UK Department for Transport, *Transport Trends 2007*.

18 S Allender, C Foster, P Scarborough and M Rayner, 'The Burden of Physical Activity Related Ill Health in the UK', *Journal of Epidemiology and Community Health*, 61(4), 2007, p 344.

19 British Medical Association Board of Science, *Preventing Childhood Obesity*, 2005.

20 UK Department for Transport, *A Sustainable Future for Cycling*, 2008.

21 Philip James, address to the American Association for the Advancement of Science, Boston, reported in *The Times*, 18 February 2008.

22 Hall World Values Survey, 1999.

23 Economic & Social Research Council, *Society Today*, Press Release, May 2008.

24 R Rogers, *Cities for a Small Planet*, Faber and Faber (London), 1997.

25 Jane Jacobs, *The Death and Life of Great American Cities*, Random House (New York), 1961.

26 David Goldberg and Ian Goodyer, *The Origins and Course of Common Mental Disorders*, Taylor and Francis (London), 2005.

27 New Economics Foundation, *The European Happy Planet Index*, 2007.

28 Richard Layard, op cit.

29 Alice Coleman, *Vision and Reality in Planned Housing*, Hilary Shipman (London), 1985.

30 A Ellaway and S MacIntyre, 'Graffiti, greenery and obesity in adults', *British Medical Journal*, 331, 2005, pp 611–12.

31 Frances Kuo et al, 'Fertile Ground for Community: Inner-City Neighborhood Common Spaces', *American Journal of Community Psychology*, Vol 26, No 6, 1998, pp 823–49.

32 Frances Kuo, 'Coping with Poverty: Impacts of Environment and Attention in the Inner City', *Environment and Behavior*, Vol 33:1, 2001.

33 L Anderson and H Cordell, 'Influence of Trees on Residential Property Values in Athens, Georgia: a Survey based on Actual Sales Prices', *Landscape and Urban Planning*, Vol 15, 1988.

34 Linda Mcintyre, 'Treeconomics: Interview with Greg McPherson at the Center for Urban Forest Research', *Landscape Architecture*, February 2008.

35 R Kourik, *Designing and Maintaining your Edible Landscape Naturally*, Permanent Publications (East Meon), 2004.

Chapter 9

Compact and car-free — simply a better city

Communities with fewer cars and car-free communities bring multiple benefits. As well as reducing CO_2 emissions, we can create places which promote well-being by encouraging walking, cycling, neighbourliness and better, safer, quieter, cleaner public space. Building communities based around people rather than the car is also cheaper and saves residents money long term.

'Some day all cities will be built this way.'

Dr Sultan Al Jaber, CEO, Masdar

Imagine streets and squares where you hear the sound of children playing freely and the tranquillity of old people sitting out under the shade of a spreading tree ... where during the day the air is filled with chatter of business people on their mobile phones and in the evenings with laughter from numerous café tables ... where you can hear buskers playing in an adjacent square alongside birdsong from somewhere overhead ...

Would this scene be improved by the presence of cars and traffic? If nothing else, the quality of public spaces is improved enormously when they are not dominated by the car.

Environmentalists have long demonised the car. Cars, lorries and vans release 21 per cent of UK CO_2 emissions, which is 10 per cent higher than in 1990.[2] To many cars represent freedom and convenience. They connect people and places. For many people it is inconceivable that they could lead their lives, or that society could function, without them. However, probably nothing has undermined our health and communities more than the automobile. Physical and mental health have both been affected, as we saw in the previous chapter.

Of course, we should not be anti-car for the sake of it. They have their place and there is huge investment in creating cars that run on renewable energy – although whether the planet can support a heavily car-dependent global population is questionable given the resources and land needed for making and running cars and the road infrastructure, even if they are run on renewable energy. Rural communities especially need some form of independent transport because public transport is not sufficiently frequent or convenient. In urban and suburban areas, however, we have a good opportunity to reduce car dependence – not just to reduce CO_2

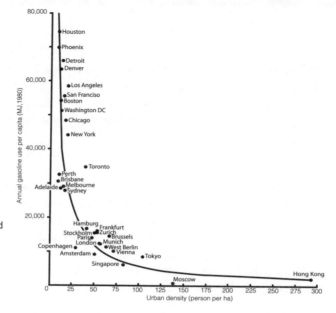

Figure 1
Petrol consumption is clearly correlated to population density.

emissions, but because it creates better places where there is a greater probability of people leading happier and healthier lives. Renewably powered cars don't alter the positive benefits to health and happiness of low-car and car-free communities.

How we plan our cities and suburbs has important outcomes. Density, for example, is a key determinant of CO_2 emissions. For example, petrol consumption per capita is clearly related to population density (Figure 1).[3] The grouping of cities is absolutely clear. Low-density American cities with a population below 50 people per hectare have a high per capita petrol consumption. Australian cities form a second cluster. European cities with population densities between 50 and 150 people per hectare form a third cluster. Very high-density cities in the Far East have very low per capita petrol consumption. The relationship between density and petrol consumption was one reason for Richard Rogers' promotion of the Compact City idea in his book *Cities for a Small Planet*.[4]

Figure 2
Venice – the best city in the world? Is it simply coincidence that it is free of cars?

Reducing car dependence and promoting five-minute living

Reducing car dependence can be viewed as a game of probabilities – taking a host of measures, each of which systematically makes it slightly more convenient and cheaper to walk or cycle than to drive, slowly tipping things in our favour. These measures can include:

- Increasing density so more facilities are within walking and cycling distance.
- Limiting car parking to homes and reducing road infrastructure.
- Making it more convenient to walk, cycle or use public transport than drive – eg, by not building out-of-town-style retail centres or multistorey parking in city centres.
- Introducing services such as car clubs and selling them as convenient, cost-effective and attractive – particularly to reduce the need for second and third cars in households.
- Charging for car parking (except perhaps disabled parking) even in residential areas and using the proceeds to support public transport.
- Introducing schemes such as congestion charging.

To create walkable and cyclable communities, we should ensure that facilities such as shops, schools, offices and public transport are within 500 metres of homes creating compact communities sometimes described as 'five-minute living'. The resulting increase in density also helps reduce land take, important at a global level as sprawling cities eat into farmland and space for wildlife. It also allows us to reduce the cost of road infrastructure which is a great way of saving money for the developer or municipality in capital cost and also for the residents in the reduction of taxes paying for its construction and maintenance.

It is important to recognise a tipping point in our strategy to reduce car dependence. If at all possible we should create a context where people don't make that *critical* decision to buy a car. Once someone has bought a car, paid its fixed costs and it is sitting in their drive, then it *is* cheaper and more convenient to use it rather than walk, cycle or use public transport. A lot of the battle to reduce car mileage has been lost – in the case of cars, possession is nine-tenths of the problem. If we can avoid the car being purchased, or we can persuade people to sell them, for example when they buy a home in a new development designed with a car club, we are in a much stronger position. A member of a car club has not paid the fixed costs of car ownership, and motoring is on a 'pay as you go' basis which means there is a higher probability that people will think twice before taking out a car.

Again some critics might say that taking a systematic approach to reducing car ownership does not offer people choice but is, more or less, crude social engineering. However, as suggested in the last chapter, it really is no more social engineering than building sprawling suburbs where people can only live decent lives if they *do* own a car. And we mustn't forget that the car-centred social engineering of the past 40 years has left us with a legacy of environmental degradation, societal disintegration and epidemic levels of obesity and diabetes. This is no exaggeration.

Rather than reducing choice, a holistic approach to reducing car dependence actually *increases* choice. Services like car clubs usually have a range of different-sized vehicles so users can select the one suited to their particular journey: small hatchback for local shopping, large hatchback or saloon for a family day out. UK operator Street Car also offers vans. Certainly the interest in car clubs in the UK has grown rapidly. According to car club charity Carplus, by 2008 there were over 50,000 people using 1,500 car-club cars. The majority of members were still based in London where 70 per cent of the cars were located, though membership was growing steadily in other large cities in the UK.

The world's largest car club is Zipcar in the US which operates in major cities including New York, Seattle, Washington and San Francisco where they are also spreading rapidly at university campuses. Zipcar's line-up includes more than 50 makes and models from the cute to the swanky: Minis, smart cars, BMWs, Mustang convertibles, Toyota Hybrids and electric cars. Car clubs could evolve in time to have a complete range of vehicles incorporating people carriers, vans, motorhomes, electric vehicles, mopeds, sports cars and even boats. They could become total mobility clubs. They might also assist in allowing renewably fuelled vehicles to penetrate the market earlier than they otherwise might. You have to be a very keen environmentalist to accept the limitations of electric vehicles given their limited range, but a car club offers the flexibility to use the electric vehicle for the short journeys and a fossil-fuelled (or preferably biodiesel) vehicle for longer ones.

Tipping things in favour of being car-free is helped by sticks as well as carrots. Although often controversial, introducing charging for permits to park does help, especially if the proceeds are used to support public transport or a local green transport plan. Congestion charging in town and city centres is also an option, although it adds bureaucracy and complication and might be avoided through other measures.

Planning to favour public transport, walking and cycling

There are numerous examples around the world where public transport and walking and cycling have been favoured over use of the private car. One often-quoted example is Curitiba in Brazil (see box overleaf). In town planning, we can ensure that pedestrians and cyclists are consciously prioritised. Even when walking and cycling comprise a significant proportion of total journeys, there is evidence that this is not given sufficient weight with a bias, generally unconscious, towards car travellers in transport planning practice.[5] It is possible to actively challenge this bias. For example, in 1990 York Council in the north of England formally introduced a road-user hierarchy to guide implementation of its transport policy.[6] This gave priority to road users in the order:

1   Pedestrians.
2   Drivers with disabilities.
3   Cyclists.
4   Public transport passengers.
5   Commercial/business vehicles requiring access.

6 Coach-borne shoppers.

7 Coach-borne visitors.

8 Car-borne long-stay commuters and visitors.

Shifting car dependence can seem a tough job, but when done systematically over a number of years it ends up going hand in hand with a change in lifestyle and a change in the way people organise their lives. Sometimes we can start from scratch and build a car-free city, as is being done at Masdar City in Abu Dhabi, as we saw in Chapter 5, and this hopefully will become far more common in the coming years. Even when it might not be right or possible to go as far as building a car-free city or community, we can certainly introduce a range of strategies to reduce our dependence on cars which at the same time will improve the public realm, public health and quality of life.

Curitiba – an example of a city that has prioritised public transport
'Bus rapid transit' is now widely accepted as a good way to protect against gridlock as cities grow. One of the earliest and most successful examples is the system introduced in Curitiba. Under the strong leadership of architect and Mayor, Jaime Lerner, Curitiba in southern Brazil has pioneered on a number of environmental fronts and is considered one of the best examples of urban planning. This includes an integrated transport system with lanes radiating from the centre devoted to a bus rapid transit system. Transport has been addressed in an integrated way to avoid urban sprawl. Bi-articulated buses with capacity of up to 270 passengers are used for a central express service operating much like a subway. This connects with feeder lines from outlying neighbourhoods and inter-district routes. Used by an estimated 85 per cent of the population, the buses use a simple automated payment system so that the same fare is paid regardless of the length of journey into or out of the city, meaning that people living on the outskirts of the city are not disadvantaged.

By focusing high-density development along five structural arteries, low congestion in other parts of the city centre has allowed a large pedestrian zone to thrive.

It is interesting to note that Curitiba has embraced sustainability issues more widely, for example offering reward points for recycling which can be used on buses during off-peak times – using spare public transport capacity to fund recycling and a cleaner city. Brilliant.

Compact masterplans save costs to invest in better buildings – a South African case study

There are not just environmental, social and health benefits in building compact and car-free communities. There are major financial advantages as well. Compact communities are cheaper to build than sprawling ones. We often overlook the enormous financial costs of building the infrastructure for sprawling cities and suburbs. The costs for roads and utility distribution for water, sewerage and energy are hidden – often paid for or subsidised by government and therefore not met, or only met in part by the private developer. We saw in the Z-squared case study in Chapter 5 that reductions in parking and road infrastructure yielded cost savings which could be invested in renewable energy and better buildings. Although this is a case study from an industrialised country, the same holds true in emerging economies.

BioRegional has been working with Johannesburg EcoCity Trust in South Africa since 2001, when it was led by Annie Sugrue. Johannesburg EcoCity is an NGO supporting a number of green social enterprises including recycling companies and bicycle repair schemes within the Ivory Park township close to Johannesburg. The 2002 World Summit on Sustainable Development (WSSD), also known as the Earth Summit, was being held in Johannesburg, so BioRegional supported EcoCity in showcasing some eco-housing and building an eco-community centre in Ivory Park. Working with Bill Dunster Architects, local architect Ken Stucke and Arup Africa, a terrace of three homes and an earth-sheltered community centre were proposed. After some sessions and consultation with the residents, the proposals were accepted by the Ivory Park community. The timetable was tight and although we didn't manage to complete the buildings in time for the summit, those under construction proved a popular attraction when combined with the other eco-activities in the township. As an experiment with the homes, we created external insulating blocks using waste polystyrene packaging from white goods such as fridges. The polystyrene was hand-shredded to create chips which were incorporated into a block using cement as a binder. These 'eco-blocks' were pinned to the external walls and then rendered. Like BedZED, in retrospect the build costs were too high, but the buildings did perform very well – being warm in winter and cool in summer – and remain very popular with the users. Although the buildings could not be replicated easily because of build cost, we were able to start engaging with mainstream construction companies to start exploring what might be possible.

Figure 3
Construction of eco-homes and a community centre in Ivory Park township, Johannesburg, 2002.

After decades of oppression under the apartheid regime, the South African government has been investing heavily in moving people from so-called informal settlements (shanty towns) to low-cost permanent settlements. Although this is good and admirable on many levels, it is being done by building hundreds of hectares of suburbs on a low-density grid pattern, with small individual homes on individual plots, with space to park a car, even though future residents are unlikely to own one. Often there is little or no community focus, facilities or space to establish businesses on site. The majority of jobs are in the city centre and so people have to commute, adding to the misery of congestion on the roads and draining money from household budgets. Although perhaps usefully addressing short-term aspirations, there is no doubt that these new suburbs are creating problems for the medium- to long-term future.

Could we develop a different model at no extra cost which could start to create a sustainable community rather than a dormitory suburb? Jobs are as important as homes, so promoting mixed-use development is essential, incorporating workshops, offices, shops and space for market gardens. Mixing income groups is important to prevent the creation of poor ghettos and this has started to happen, for example at Cosmo City, a development of 12,500 homes on a total of 1,200 hectares.

Table 1

Comparing the cost of homes funded through the Rural Development Programme (RDP) and a BioRegional alternative showed money and land could be saved at the same time as improving the quality of the homes.

RDP *Density 35 homes/hectare*	Cost for 100 Conventional RDP	BioRegional *Density 70 homes/hectare*	Cost for 100 BioRegional
INCOME grant R42K and soft grants R90K	R9,000,000		R9,000,000
COSTS			
Land 3 ha – unsubsidised R15K per plot	R525,000	Land 1.5 ha	R263,000
Infrastructure services (roads, water, sewerage, storm water) R2.2K/unit	R2,200,000	Services reduced by one-third R1.5K	R1,500,000
Electricity – R4K per unit	R400,000	Electricity – R4K per unit	R400,000
Street lights – R1K	R100,000	Street lights – R 0.5K	R50,000
Other – R1K	R100,000	Other – R1K	R100,000
Top structure/materials – R24K	R2,400,000	Cluster/semi-detached/ stand-alone – 10 per cent reduction – R22K	R2,200,000
Green upgrades	-	Rainwater tanks – R0.25K clay block + insulating external render – R4K roof insulation – R1K solar thermal hot water – 6K	R25,000 R400,000 R100,000 R600,000
TOTAL	R5,725,000	**TOTAL**	R5,638,000

However, Cosmo City still relies mainly on a low-density suburban grid plan. This is an expensive way to build and not ideal for creating environmentally or socially sustainable communities.

Could we take some ideas from the compact city and apply them to settlements in South Africa including low-cost homes built under the Reconstruction and Development Programme (RDP)? BioRegional decided to carry out a simple study with Basil Read, the construction company partner in Codevco, the development company behind Cosmo City. The results of the study are summarised in Table 1. We suggested doubling residential density from 35 to 70 homes per hectare and introducing conjoined (semi-detached) and cluster (terraced) homes. In this way we were able to reduce land purchase costs, the costs of road infrastructure, street lighting, services infrastructure and 'top structure' (house) build costs because of shared walls. The money saved would be sufficient to invest in better, greener homes, including wall and roof insulation, higher-quality clay blocks rather than concrete ones, solar thermal panels and rainwater butts. Being insulated, these homes would be far more comfortable in both summer and winter and also have lower running costs. In fact, on paper, the total capital cost turned out to be slightly cheaper.

However, it is not always straightforward to apply these ideas. Government grants work on a fixed budget per home for land acquisition, road infrastructure, services and top structure. Saving money in one part of the budget does not mean this can automatically be invested in other parts. Major changes in the government grant-giving and administration would be needed – something that is not necessarily easy to achieve. Furthermore, a number of people expressed concern that a more compact form of development would not meet the expectations of the people who would be moving to these new suburbs. At BioRegional, we were told many times that the aspiration among the poor in informal settlements is to have a stand-alone concrete house set in its own few square metres of land and, at

Car free is care-free! Personal experience of giving up the car.

I was very nervous before selling my car, having been a car owner for 15 years. My attachment to my car was so great that I did have a physiological reaction – a gut-wrenching half an hour before I finally pulled myself together and said to myself, 'You have been promoting BedZED for 3 years, if you don't sell your car and give the car club a go, who will?' I was like an addict going cold turkey. I can fully appreciate people's irrational attachment to their cars and why challenging car ownership is often seen as a personal attack. However, having sold my car and experienced the car club, I now would not want to go back to personal car ownership.

Before moving to BedZED I used to drive about 12,000 km per year in a 1.9 turbo diesel with estimated 220g CO_2/km = 2.64 tonnes CO_2 per year. After moving to BedZED I drive perhaps 2000 km per year in a small hatchback averaging about 150 g CO_2/km, plus 4000 km on public transport say at 50g CO_2/km = 0.3 tonnes + 0.2 tonnes = 0.5 tonnes CO_2/year. My saving therefore is in the region of 2.1 tonnes CO_2 per annum. This is a saving of around 17% of the 12 tonne per annum average UK CO_2 footprint. (To be fair, I now fly a lot for work which is terrible and greatly outweighs my carbon savings on reducing car use).

One interesting observation is that over time I am using the car less and less. I really cannot think why I used the car so much beforehand. Life tends to gently re-organise and as one's patterns of behaviour change. I get more regular exercise walking and cycling, which I am not sure I would get if I still owned a car. When we go on holiday, we tend to get a train and hire a car at the other end, greatly reducing car mileage overall which I would never have done before. Over time, friends change and I have more friends who live locally because I don't have a car. I now think of driving as much more stressful than taking public transport (reflecting studies which show how stress hormones are released during driving).

In a complete turnaround, I now would think twice before going back to the hassles and costs of owning a car for everyday use and would not want to live somewhere without easy access to a car club. I get all of my everyday motoring needs for £20 per week, whilst the average UK car costs £100 per week to run by the time road tax, depreciation, insurance, servicing and fuel costs are included.

On perhaps 3 occasions in 6 years was I not able to get a car exactly when I needed it because all the cars were booked – I simply went a bit later. It does take a tiny bit of planning to remember to book the car in advance if you really need it at a particular time.

As most car clubs have national networks, it also means you can use cars located across the country. So for example, when I have needed to visit a estate in Scotland because of forestry work, whereas previously I would have driven, I was able to get the train to Edinburgh and use the car club car just outside Edinburgh station. It means a more pleasant journey on the train and with the train ticket booked in advance, much cheaper as well. Driving up in my car alone would have released about 100kg of CO_2, whilst the train released about about 10kg – so this represented a 90% reduction in my contribution to global warming for this journey.

CO_2 emissions per person travelling London to Edinburgh:	
coach	9.2 kg
rail (modern high speed electric)	11.9 kg
car (1.5 people)	71.0 kg
plane	96.4 kg

Source: Department for Transport/National Atmospheric Emission Inventory 2004

However, as a legacy of a mid-life crisis, I do retain a sportscar, kept garaged and brought out for occasional use in the summer. A recycled 1987 Ford Sierra, it has been modified by friends at Cranfield University to run on waste cooking oil – zero carbon, zero waste.

the earliest opportunity, to buy a car to park outside it. Although this may well be the case, sometimes we might do well to challenge aspirations and offer alternatives. Indeed, where small numbers of conjoined houses have been built, such as in the Alexandra township, they have been well received. Indeed cluster housing is common and sought after in middle- and upper-income housing estates.

Simply better

As we progress through the 21st century, as evidence mounts and more people have direct experience of living without a car, we will design and build for compact communities (cities, towns, villages and suburbs) with much lower levels of car use. Reducing environmental impact will be one reason, but increasingly it will be seen as a way to promote better health, higher quality of life, better public space and stronger communities. Projects like Masdar City in Abu Dhabi have started to lead the way. Even existing urban and suburban areas could be transformed by retrofitting car clubs and public transport and providing local services within walking or cycling distance (one example of how this might be done is described in Chapter 14). Communities with fewer cars and car-free cities will simply be better places.

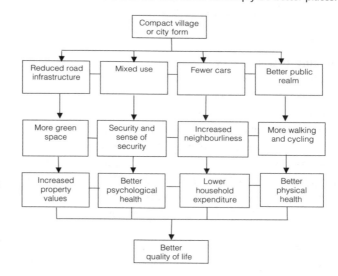

Figure 4

The synergistic effects of compact form and reducing car use inevitably lead to better health, quality of life and ultimately increased property values.

Notes

1   Sultan Al Jaber, CEO, Masdar, 'Green City in the Desert', *Host City* magazine, Cavendish International Group, Spring 2008.
2   Department for Transport, *Petroleum Consumption: By Transport Mode and Fuel Type: United Kingdom:1 1997–2007*, 2008.
3   P Newman and P Kenworthy, *Cities and Automobile Dependence*, Gower Technical (Swansea), 1989.
4   Richard Rogers, *Cities for a Small Planet*, West View Press (New York), 1997.
5   UK Department for Transport, *Encouraging Walking and Cycling: Success Stories*, 2008.
6   UK Department of Transport, Success Stories Case Study 8, *Encouraging Walking and Cycling*, 2009.

Chapter 10

One Planet Living — philosophy, story and set of principles

To create sustainable communities we need a paradigm shift. We need to change the DNA of the design, development and long-term management of communities. We also need to create a 'story' which we can easily communicate to people so that we can maximise the chances of residents understanding and modifying their behaviour to secure the greatest environmental benefits. One Planet Living and the One Planet approach is a concept and framework which fulfils these requirements.

Making sustainability relevant

In Chapter 1 we saw how ecological footprinting can be used to help us think more clearly about sustainability, and our target should be to create a future where people can lead happy and healthy lives within a fair share of the earth's resources – what we might call One Planet Living. I hope from the chapters that followed, it has become clear that we will only build a sustainable future if we create places where it is easy, attractive and affordable for people to adopt a whole sustainable way of living. Green buildings must be complemented by sustainable products and services which link people harmoniously to the local environment and hinterland, creating zero carbon and zero waste cycles. We must create walkable mixed-use communities which will improve health, quality of life, neighbourliness and happiness.

Although it is starting to change, to many people sustainability still remains just one issue among a host of others and one perhaps not immediately relevant to day-to-day living. Added to this, there is often too much information, too many ideas and seemingly conflicting statistics, so that there often seems little hope in finding any coherent way to address all of the challenges – from local to global ones – facing us.

To achieve a transformation to a sustainable future, we need some way to organise our thoughts. A purely rational approach is a good start, but it is not enough. Much as we might like to think otherwise, people – including you and me – rarely make choices in a rational and dispassionate way based on information provided. Our behaviour and our choices are as much, if not more, determined by our expectations, habits and culture. Ultimately it is the personal story we carry about our place in society and the bigger scheme of things which determines what we do.

One Planet Living as a cohering force in sustainability

For any approach to bring change, it must be able to operate and engage people at various levels including:

- Objective level – be rational and consistent with science.
- Personal level – embodying a philosophy which links an individual person to the bigger picture.
- Interpersonal level – carry a simple story so that it can be easily communicated and act to link people.
- Organisational level – be based on a set of principles to align action.
- Spiritual level – inspire a vision which goes beyond personal material aspirations.

As the whole One Planet approach has emerged and evolved, we believe it can operate effectively at these different levels.

One Planet Living finds its objective and scientific base in ecological footprinting. We have seen that ecological footprinting does have limitations, but it provides an insight and metrics which are useful as a benchmark or indicator for decision-making. It can also engage people at a personal level. The philosophy behind One Planet Living is simple: that we live on a planet with limited resources and if we are not to fight over them, we will probably have to have some sense of equitable distribution of resources. The aim therefore defines itself: to create places, products and services where people can lead happy and healthy lives within a fair share of the earth's resources. If we so choose, we can also see One Planet Living as having a spiritual dimension in that it is a call to transcend purely material aspirations and create a world that is better for us all.

At the interpersonal level, One Planet Living is easy to communicate. It does embody a simple story. Indeed Kofi Annan, the former United Nations Secretary General, quoted at the very start of this book, implicitly recognised a real limitation for sustainable development when he described it as an abstract concept. Ecological footprinting does make sustainability easy to understand. The simple question 'How many planets does it take to support your lifestyle?' can elicit discussion and engagement with everyone, not just sustainability professionals or green enthusiasts. One Planet Living has the ability to create a story linking people to the global availability of resources, making it easier to convert the abstract concept of sustainability to something real for people in their day-to-day lives.

A philosophy and story is good to engage with people at a personal level, but it is not necessarily enough to organise action. BioRegional therefore led a process working with WWF (World Wide Fund for Nature) to create a set of 10 guiding principles to turn the philosophy into a useful tool. The 10 principles cover environmental, social and economic themes: Zero Carbon, Zero Waste, Sustainable Transport, Local and Sustainable Materials, Local and Sustainable Food, Sustainable Water, Natural Habitats and Wildlife, Culture and Heritage, Equity and Fair Trade, and Health and Happiness. Anyone working in sustainability would probably create a similar set of principles – the terminology might vary, the emphasis might be different, but the scope would probably be more or less the same. Working with its partners, BioRegional has found that we can

Figure 1
The One Planet principles
can be seen as DNA for
sustainability.

1	Zero Carbon
2	Zero Waste
3	Sustainable Transport
4	Local and Sustainable Materials
5	Local and Sustainable Food
6	Sustainable Water
7	Natural Habitats and Wildlife
8	Culture and Heritage
9	Equity and Fairtrade
10	Health and Happiness

apply these principles more or less universally, as we shall see later in this chapter and the remainder of the book – for example, to the design of a product or service, to project management processes, a supply chain initiative and as a guide to help us to adopt sustainability in our own lives. We can also apply them to estates management or the level of a municipality. The principles are like DNA – a way to embed sustainability deeply into projects and processes so that it is a natural outcome. When sustainability is *really* in the DNA of projects and processes, it *emerges freely*, and almost joyously, rather than being forced through constraining means such as prescriptive sustainability standards and regulations – in Chapter 1 we saw how relying too heavily on regulation and standards can compromise sustainability. Ultimately we should aim to create ways of living and working where sustainability is a natural emergent property rather than something which has to be forced artificially.

Coherence

The holistic nature of the 10 principles and their wide scope also allows us to connect areas in everyday life which are otherwise divided by government standards and regulations and to create a more coherent outcome. It can be used to give us opportunities to drive links between different aspects of sustainability. For example, taking just one principle, Natural Habitats and Wildlife, we can consider how this principle might link to the nine others, as in Table 1.

The One Planet concept and principles are being applied internationally on projects as diverse as property development (One Planet Communities), retail (eg, B&Q One Planet Home) and municipal sustainability strategies (eg, One Planet Sutton). The framework was even used by BioRegional to write the sustainability vision for London's successful bid to host the 2012 Olympic Games. The aim of the One Planet Communities programme is to create a network of pioneering sustainable communities – great places to live – which can also act as inspiration for people, provide learning to the industry and inform government policy. The One Planet Communities network includes One Brighton in the UK, Sonoma Mountain Village in California, Mata de

Table 1
Possible relationship of Natural Habitats and Wildlife to:

Zero Carbon	Use woodchip energy from local coppice woodlands managed for woodland butterflies
Zero Waste	Design reed-bed sewage treatment as wildlife refuge (see Sustainable Water)
Sustainable Transport	Organise shuttle buses for local eco-tourism rather than driving cars
Local and Sustainable Materials	Use timber from local well-managed forests which support biodiversity
Local and Sustainable Food	Buy food from local farms which support wildlife friendly practices
Sustainable Water	Design reed-bed sewage treatment as wildlife refuge (see Zero Waste)
Culture and Heritage	Install bird boxes with webcams for children to learn about local wildlife and ecology
Equity and Fair Trade	Buy fairtrade 'shade' grown coffee using traditional forest gardening which supports a diversity of wildlife
Health and Happiness	When increasing greenery in streets, plant native species and design to create wildlife corridors

Sesimbra in Portugal and Masdar City in Abu Dhabi. A number of other developers such as Tongaat Hulett Developments in South Africa and China Merchant Property Developers in China have also been exploring ways to apply the concept and principles.

The One Planet approach is enabling the science of ecological footprinting to create a common purpose from industry professionals to ordinary people. Monitoring results from the practical application of One Planet projects around the world will start to emerge in 2009, but the initial indications are that creating a coherent story and framework is serving well to align people and projects, technology and culture. The principles are 'freeware', and BioRegional is working with its partners to create simple templates which can help individuals, companies, municipalities and governments start to apply them for themselves.

Table 2
Possible relationship of Natural Habitats and Wildlife to other One Planet principles.

Global Challenge	One Planet Principle	Local Opportunity
Climate change due to human-induced build up of (CO_2) in the atmosphere	Zero Carbon	Create a renewable energy economy Implement energy efficiency in buildings and infrastructure; supply energy from on- and off-site renewable sources

Waste from discarded products and packaging creates a huge disposal challenge while squandering valuable resources	Zero Waste	Generate local employment in recycling and remanufacturing, eliminating the need for landfill Reduce waste generation through improved product design; encourage reuse, recycling and composting; generate energy from waste cleanly
Travel by car and aeroplane can cause climate change, air and noise pollution, and congestion	Sustainable Transport	Improve air quality, improve public transport, reduce congestion, promote low emissions vehicles Provide transport systems and infrastructure that reduce dependence on fossil fuel use, eg by cars and aeroplanes. Offset carbon emissions from air travel and car travel
Destructive patterns of resource exploitation and use of non-local materials in construction and manufacture increase environmental harm and reduce gains to the local economy	Local and Sustainable Materials	Create an economy where products and services have a positive impact on the environment Where possible, use local, reclaimed, renewable and recycled materials in construction and products, which minimises transport emissions, spurs investment in local natural resources and boosts the local economy
Many forms of current agriculture do not support local ecosystems, while over-dependence on imported food contributes to global warming	Local and Sustainable Food	Support the local rural economy, revitalise traditional rural landscapes, improve health Support local and low-impact food production that provides healthy, quality food while boosting the local economy in an environmentally beneficial manner
Local supplies of fresh water are under increasing pressure, often resulting in depletion of existing stocks	Sustainable Water	Maintain good water supplies into the future Implement water use efficiency measures, reuse and recycling; minimise water extraction and pollution; foster sustainable water and sewage management in the landscape such as by using reed beds; restore natural water cycles
Loss of biodiversity and habitats due to development in natural areas and over-exploitation of natural resources	Natural Habitats and Wildlife	Increase biodiversity, restore and create beautiful landscapes Protect or regenerate existing natural environments and the habitats they provide to fauna and flora; create new habitats
Local cultural heritage is being lost throughout the world due to globalisation, resulting in a loss of local identity and wisdom	Culture and Heritage	Build on local cultural heritage to create a sense of place and belonging Celebrate and revive cultural heritage and the sense of local and regional identity; choose structures and systems that build on this heritage; foster a new culture of sustainability
Some in the industrialised world live in relative poverty, while many in the developing world cannot meet their basic needs from what they produce or sell	Equity and Fair Trade	Promote positive impacts on other communities, support a more politically stable world Promote equity and fair trading relationships to ensure the community has a beneficial impact on other communities both locally and globally
Ever increasing consumption is not leading to greater health and happiness, but is causing environmental damage	Health and Happiness	Promote healthy lifestyles and increase quality of life Promote healthy lifestyles and physical, mental and spiritual well-being through well-designed communities and community engagement, as well as by delivering on social and environmental targets

One Planet Living as DNA for a company

BioRegional Quintain Ltd was established in 2005 as a company which would have the One Planet principles in its DNA.

The firm was established by BioRegional Properties Ltd (a company established by eco-entrepreneurs and BioRegional Development Group) and Quintain Estates and Development plc, a London-based property company with major developments such as around Wembley Stadium and the O2 arena. The One Planet principles are embedded in the shareholders' agreement, ensuring sustainability is at the core of the company. Through the insight of Pete Halsall, co-founder and managing director, BioRegional Quintain has pioneered measures to drive the One Planet principles through the whole design and development process. Everyone working on its projects is required to attend a One Planet Living induction. This does mean everyone. The company runs one-day induction days and training courses to orientate not only engineers and architects, but also lawyers, facilities managers, sales and marketing staff, financial analysts and quantity surveyors.

Why might BioRegional Quintain want to induct even its lawyers? It is so that when they are writing sales contracts and leases, they know what BioRegional Quintain is trying to achieve and can consider opportunities or pitfalls of incorporating the sustainability aims into these documents. The company also invites future tenants (where these exist) and other stakeholders such as local authority planning officers and community groups to the induction sessions, so they can understand, engage with and contribute to the vision.

On BioRegional Quintain developments, every worker on site must go through a One Planet induction too, alongside the compulsory health and safety induction, receiving a sticker for the helmet before they are allowed to work on site. The induction explores, in an interactive way, how workers might take the principles of One Planet Living into their own lives as well as how it is being incorporated in the construction process, calling for ideas from the workers on how it might be improved.

Property development and the creation of a sustainable community is the result of a whole process from design, through construction to estates management and community engagement. The product and the outcome is the result of millions of decisions and chains of decisions – from large ones such as the specification of the energy system to individual micro-decisions such as a site worker deciding whether to put a bit of wood in the recycling skip or the general waste. We need to ensure that as many of the decisions and micro-decisions as possible are orientated towards the desired outcome. It is as much, if not more, about changing culture as managing sustainability.

In the next two chapters we look at how the One Planet principles can be applied practically to create One Planet Communities. We explore how the principles can be used to align design, construction, estates management and community governance. The pioneering One Brighton development, being constructed by Crest Nicholson plc and BioRegional Quintain Ltd, will be a key case study.

Rooftop allotments with sea views – available at One Brighton

One Brighton is a mixed-use development of 172 apartments, office and community space, part of the regeneration of the New England Quarter next to Brighton railway station on the south coast of England. The site, a run-down car park with a small number of workshops, had been bought by a major supermarket chain, and an out-of-town-style supermarket with extensive car parking was proposed. Local opposition to the scheme was strong and through a process of community engagement (to which BioRegional contributed) a new masterplan was created in which the supermarket would be retained, but with lower levels of car parking and complemented by a whole mixed-use development including homes, hotels, offices and community space.

Ethical Property Company (EPC), a company purchasing office space and renting it out to community, environmental and social change groups, was engaged by the council to operate the community centre to be constructed within a block with other office and residential space. EPC suggested BioRegional might become the developer for the block as a whole.

The project would require entrepreneurs, financial partners and residential development specialists working together. This ultimately resulted in the formation of a special-purpose vehicle called Crest Nicholson BioRegional Quintain LLP (CNBQ), which secured the option to purchase the site and build it using the One Planet framework. Construction started in September 2007. The development is car-free (with space only for car-club cars, visitor and disabled parking) and the design includes a biomass boiler, rooftop allotments and below-ground recycling bins. Approximately 50 per cent of the energy required for the building is generated on site, with the remainder bought in bulk for residents from large off-site wind turbines via green electricity supply company Good Energy Ltd. To build additional renewable capacity, BioRegional Quintain is identifying possible sites locally for a large wind turbine. First residents started moving into One Brighton during summer 2009.

Chapter 11

Design and construction of One Planet Communities

The One Planet principles can be used to create a sustainability action plan (SAP) for a development. They can also be used as a framework for the construction process and to create a green supply chain.

Perhaps we shouldn't start at the beginning

Building a One Planet Community is a process with many steps – from design, through construction, sales and marketing to long-term operation including estates management and governance. The outcome of the current property development process is 'unsustainability'. The whole process needs to be transformed. If I could leave you with one piece of advice in constructing a sustainable community it would be this: it is not enough just to alter design.

It has been our experience, as well as that of others trying to address sustainability, that it is relatively easy to propose changes at the design stage. The real challenge is making sure that the changes can be built in within predicted costs, and then even more importantly, to ensure that they can be operated and maintained long term. As we explore in the next chapter, we would do well to start at the end and have a really good idea of how the estate and utilities will be *managed* long term – the energy, water, waste, food, transport, community facilities, etc. Added to this, we should carefully consider sales and marketing and the community governance and engagement mechanism which we might introduce to encourage the behaviour change needed to achieve One Planet Living.

Of course in reality, developing a project is an iterative process, where design informs sales, marketing and long-term management, and sales, marketing and long-term management inform design. As building sustainable communities still requires pioneering, the technical and financial success of a sustainable community will be determined by how well this process has been managed. In 10 or 20 years time, when building sustainable communities is the norm, the process will inevitably become easier.

Creating a One Planet Community

The 10 One Planet principles outlined in the previous chapter form a simple framework which can be used to develop a vision as well as plans for action – sustainability action plans, or SAPs. As we shall see in the following chapters, these SAPs can be at the level of a product, service or process and can contain the strategies, key performance indicators and key targets to ensure sustainability is embedded in the DNA.

If sustainability is really in the DNA, then every decision made by anyone working on the project should refer back to sustainability – this is why BioRegional Quintain, for example, trains everyone in the One Planet principles. However, when creating a One Planet Community, to formalise the process, there are four main stages we can identify:

1 Vision – looking at what it will be like to live there, the facilities and services that need to be provided to make it easy, attractive and affordable for people to lead a One Planet lifestyle.
2 Design Stage (or Outline) SAP – creating the overarching strategy and targets for the community embodying the vision for the community and summarising at a high level how each of the One Planet principles is expressed in design, construction, sales and marketing, estate management and governance.
3 Construction SAP – setting down in detail how the One Planet principles are integrated in the construction process.
4 Estates Management and Community Governance Plan – setting the strategy, targets and operational mechanisms for management of the community long term.

In developing the vision and outline SAP it is best to do this as a collective process using all team members and as many stakeholders as possible. It must be developed with not just the architects and engineers, but also with the sales and marketing teams (so they have something they feel they can sell) and the future estate managers. It might well be worthwhile or necessary to involve local government representatives, community stakeholders and future residents or tenants if these are identified. The Outline SAP for the One Brighton development is reproduced in the Appendix 1 p 198.

Creating the vision

Creating an integrated vision with all project team members and stakeholders is absolutely essential. One Planet induction days when all teams and stakeholders involved are brought together are critical. These days provide an opportunity to communicate the aims and ensure everyone is working in unison. It is also possible at these events to engage professionals at a personal level in the creation of the project. Indeed, rather than thinking first about buildings, it is essential the developer and team think about creating a place which supports an attractive and sustainable *lifestyle*. Thinking about *how* people will live there – whether they are a young family, retired couple or young professional – is essential. Role plays can be a very useful way to draw out ideas, make it personal and get the team into the right 'space'. What services might residents require to make it easy, attractive and affordable to lead a sustainable lifestyle? How might these be managed? How might objections to change be overcome in the sales and marketing communications? How will all this be managed long term?

Drawing together the outline SAP

The vision process creates the basis on which an SAP can start to emerge. Using the 10 principles as a framework, for each principle, we can consider:

- global and local context – such as the current energy or waste situation, outlining the opportunities for change;
- ecological footprint and other targets related to the principle which will need to be met to achieve One Planet Living;
- local or international benchmarks such as any standards which might be adopted (eg FairTrade, LEED, BREEAM, FSC, Organic, etc);
- key performance indicators and timeline to meet One Planet Living (eg dates to achieve 50 per cent, 70 per cent and 98 per cent diversion from landfill);
- key strategies to be employed through the whole development process: design, construction, marketing, sales, estates management, governance and community engagement;
- communications and PR strategy related to the principle;
- regulation and policy issues related to the principle – for example, making sure strategies comply with any energy or waste regulations, or social requirements such as provision of subsidised housing for low-income groups;
- mechanisms to achieve wider community and municipal engagement such as Local Agenda 21;
- key partners to enlist (eg renewable energy companies, local or national government, specialist NGOs in social or environmental issues); and
- key cross-cutting issues with other One Planet principles which need to be addressed and/or how synergies might be maximised (eg between local food and culture and heritage; or between zero carbon and zero waste through energy-from-waste).

The outline SAP forms the key sustainability document to inform the whole project.

One Planet principles during construction

As well as during design, the One Planet principles can be used at the construction stage to inform the details of sustainability for the process. The zero carbon principles can be used to decide which generators might be used on site to power cranes, for example, or how waste management might be organised. Local and Sustainable Food and Health and Happiness, might inform the type of on site catering facilities provided for workers. Sustainable Water can direct specification of washroom facilities on site, including low-flush toilets, water-efficient urinals and spray taps.

Constructing a healthy menu

When a canteen for construction staff was needed at One Brighton, BioRegional Quintain started a local campaign in the local press to find a suitable operator. Construction site canteens traditionally serve what can only be called poor-quality food – high in saturated fat and salt, poor-quality meat, mainly fried, and few or no fresh vegetables. Through the local press, a call was put out for a caterer to provide a canteen that would offer local, organic, seasonal produce, as well as vegetarian meals. This is how Wendy came to be running the on site canteen.

The menu includes all the building-site favourites – such as English breakfast – but with a green twist: made from local, organic meat, free-range eggs and served with grilled vegetables. There are other less traditional choices like local mackerel and fish cakes accompanied with a salad, or lentil curry with pilau rice. All tea and coffee is fair trade. Fresh fruit is always available.

The response from the workers has been fantastic. One worker straight out of school said he had not eaten fresh fruit since the age of five. He was now a convert to mackerel and salads. The workers feel the site is different; and the contractor, Denne Construction, even took them on a fishing trip to catch local fish.

Figure 1
Wendy serves construction workers in the
Green Canteen at One Brighton.

Figure 2
Healthier construction.

Figure 3
One Brighton construction workers catching
a healthy lunch off the coast of Brighton.

Reducing CO$_2$ emissions and improving sustainability during construction at One Brighton

At One Brighton, to reduce the CO$_2$ emissions associated with construction, the main strategies employed were to:

- use energy-efficient site cabins;
- ensure all electricity used on site was from guaranteed renewable sources; and
- use biodiesel to power the on site generators.

The design and build construction contractor, Denne Construction, sought out greener site cabins which were insulated and had doors with airtight seals to prevent heat loss. Green electricity was sourced by BioRegional Quintain through Good Energy Ltd, a company which guarantees all electricity comes from renewable sources, mainly large-scale wind turbines.

Attempting to use biodiesel took a considerable effort. We were keen to ensure we were using biodiesel from waste cooking oil rather than virgin biodiesel, the latter being controversial in putting pressure on food prices by taking fertile land out of food production. Not only did we have to secure a reliable source of this waste cooking biodiesel, but we also had to procure generators which were guaranteed for use with biodiesel. In particular, natural rubber seals and pipes can deteriorate with biodiesel, although newer generators tend to use synthetic seals and so it should be easier to secure these generators in future. The biodiesel also tended to cause filter problems, particularly in cold weather as the biodiesel tends to start to solidify.

Denne started at 100 per cent biodiesel when we began construction in autumn 2007, but after a cold winter moved to 50 per cent biodiesel/50 per cent mineral diesel in May 2008. We think the problem was that the generators were not specifically designed for biodiesel. However, with very cold weather in winter 2008, Denne had to move to 100 per cent mineral diesel. The generators were taken off site by Christmas 2008. Overall we used 54,000 litres (95,027 pints) of biodiesel and 34,000 litres (59,832 pints) of red diesel – so we had managed to achieve an almost 60 per cent reduction in use of mineral diesel for the generators.

Green supply chain for construction

In order to deliver sustainability, the supply chain is very important. Without a green supply chain, life is very difficult for a developer. To help to create one which is compatible with the One Planet principles, BioRegional have initiated a not-for-profit service for its members – including developers, housing associations and architects – to help them to select greener products and services. The service is called One Planet Products. Both products and suppliers are assessed against the One Planet principles. In a second phase of development of the initiative, suppliers will be asked to create and implement their own SAPs based on the One Planet principles – spreading the principles as DNA through the supply chain.

Products such as the Natural Building Technologies clay block used at One Brighton are listed on the website www.oneplanetproducts.com, making it easy for members to select them without having to carry out extensive research themselves, serving to spread knowledge and increase understanding in the industry. By increased sales volumes and market penetration of green products, developer members of the One Planet Products service aim to reduce the costs of using such products.

An example of a product review is given in Appendix 3 p 212.

The Role of Sustainability Integrator

To ensure that the SAPs are integrated seamlessly from design through construction to estates management, BioRegional Quintain Ltd has introduced the role of Sustainability Integrator (SI) – see the job description. Each BioRegional Quintain project has one person whose function is to ensure that the sustainability balls are not dropped. Using the overarching Outline SAP as the key document, the SI is responsible for working with the various teams to write the Construction SAP and Estates Management Plan. Ultimately the SI hands over to the Green Caretaker as we will see in the next chapter.

Integration with estates management and sales and marketing

Having considered how One Planet principles might be incorporated into design and construction, in the next two chapters we look at how they can be incorporated into estates management and sales and marketing. Reiterating, to successfully build a sustainable community it is essential that estates management and sales and marketing are adequately considered from the beginning of a project. Sales and marketing must inform the product and vice versa, and without a long-term estates management strategy, the experience offered to future residents (customers!) will be compromised. I speak from hard-earned and sometimes painful experience.

Note

1 Professor Jason Hu, personal communication, 2009.

China – creating a culture of living in harmony with nature

The choices which China makes will be critical to the trajectory of global warming over the next few decades. Fortunately the Chinese government and research institutions are embracing the sustainability agenda and world-class green projects are now being constructed.

China Merchant Property Developers (CMPD) is one of China's largest real-estate developers headquartered in Shenzen, south China. Its head office is a converted Sanyo factory. In a truly remarkable green refurbishment, the factory has been reclad and mixed-mode ventilation introduced. Passive systems including solar chimneys are operational for most of the year, but in the hot humid summer, a very low-energy active cooling system comes into play, based on underfloor cooling using water cooled to only 18°C rather than say typical air-conditioning cooling to 7 to 12°C. Water-efficient appliances have been complemented with rainwater harvesting to flush toilets, and an on site reed bed to treat black water. Hot water is supplied through solar thermal panels and a government grant enabled fitting of photovoltaic panels.

Before: *After:*

Since 2006, BioRegional has also been working with CMPD on its 1 million-square-metre (10.76 million-square-foot) Jinshan ('The Hills') mixed-used development which has incorporated a number of green features including novel passive ventilation, solar thermal panels and on site waste water treatment. The marketing suite includes an exhibition centre which explains and demonstrates the One Planet principles and how they are starting to be applied at Jinshan, attracting a wide range of visitors from senior government officials to local school children. The project was one of five projects worldwide to received a UN Habitat Award in 2009.

Professor Jason Hu of CMPD notes the link between China's culture and heritage and One Planet Living; 'China has always placed great value on its cultural inheritance gained from 5,000 years of civilisation. Family names, family trees, poems and songs – all represent traditions that are very important for Chinese people. We view nature and humans as one and feel that both should live in harmony. As our society becomes more industrialised, we are gaining a deeper understanding of the true value of harmonious growth and sustainable development. Gaining economic benefit at the same time as paying attention to environmental and social development: this is the soul of building a harmonious society.'[1]

Job description: the Sustainability Integrator

The Sustainability Integrator will:

- Work with partners and colleagues to ensure the implementation of all sustainability measures, construction and non-construction related, to enable future residents to make sustainable lifestyle choices
- Work alongside the developer's Sustainability Manager, Construction Project Manager and contractor's Site Manager to oversee the integration of sustainability/OPL principles and targets into the delivery of construction, sales and estates management
- Formulate and implement in conjunction with the professional team Construction Sustainability Action Plan
- Check design and construction documentation for compliance with the requirements of the Construction SAP
- Formulate and oversee the implementation of systems to facilitate the reduction and monitoring of construction site waste and energy consumption etc, in line with relevant adopted systems such as SMARTwaste
- Produce monthly sustainability reports for the developer's Sustainability Manager
- Ensure all partners, contractors and subcontractors working on the scheme are inducted in the developer's sustainability ethos and One Planet Living, running induction courses
- Conduct regular inspections on site to ensure that 'performance metrics' are recorded and sustainability targets met
- Represent the developer's interests on site in dealing with the local community and produce quarterly stakeholder newsletters
- Support production of BREEAM and EcoHomes reports, primarily through the gathering and recording of information
- Oversee acoustic and thermal testing
- Conduct/oversee site noise testing
- Support Sustainability Projects Manager in the preparation of One Planet Living annual reports
- Support Sustainability Projects Manager in the preparation of Green Lifestyles Packages for residents
- Support writing up of the project as case studies for internal learning and dissemination
- Undertake discrete areas of research under the direction of the Sustainability Manager required to promote One Planet Living delivery

Reproduced courtesy of BioRegional Quintain Ltd

Local and Sustainable Materials

Local and Sustainable Materials is one of the One Planet principles. When selecting materials a developer or architect needs to consider using reclaimed, recycled or low environmental impact materials. Factors such as the embodied energy and toxics released in manufacture or use need to be considered. Choice of materials can also impact well-being – for example indoor air quality – either negatively such as 'off-gassing' of formaldehyde from some particle boards, or positively such as 'breathable' walls which reduce the incidence of excess humidity in the building and of the growth of moulds and dust mites. When used as a building material, wood and products such as Hempcrete (see Box in Chapter 6) derived from plants lock up carbon so can be considered a way to remove CO_2 from the atmosphere.

At One Brighton, the One Planet Living principles were used to select the construction materials, including a green concrete frame and natural clay blocks.

The concrete frame poured at One Brighton may well be the greenest in the UK and was delivered within the context of conventional overall cost. It comprises 50 per cent Portland cement and 50 per cent ground granulated blast furnace slag (GGBS), a waste product of the steel industry. This was combined with 100 per cent recycled aggregate – stent – a waste from the China clay industry transported by barge to a nearby port plus locally dredged sand.

The walls at One Brighton have been constructed using aerated clay blocks fired at a low temperature (reducing embodied energy by 60 per cent over conventional concrete block) which have good insulating properties as well as being breathable to ensure good indoor air quality. Currently imported by Natural Building Technologies from Germany, the transport of the blocks reduces the carbon benefit to 40 per cent overall – so still a saving – but it is hoped that by stimulating the market, they can be produced locally in future. Talks have begun with brick manufacturers to establish local UK production, though collapse of the UK property market at the time of writing means the economic climate is not right for establishing any new production capability.

The overall result at One Brighton is eco-apartments which are smart and modern.

Chapter 12

Start with the long term — governance and estates management

More work needs to be done on long-term issues such as governance and estates management which ultimately will be critical to securing long-term benefits. New opportunities lie in getting this right, both in business and environmental terms.

Estates management is as important as design

Sustainability will probably drive the emergence of a new type of property development industry – one that, of necessity, takes a long-term view. Most property developers are traders, selling on the properties when they are complete, and not retaining a long-term interest so the commitment to long-term management is not necessarily strong. As we shall see, this opens up challenges as well as some interesting opportunities for those starting to work on these issues.

Design is important in creating sustainable communities – in reducing energy consumption, making green choices easier and promoting healthy living. However, as important is how the design is managed in the long term – the services required and mechanisms to ensure community engagement and governance. We can put in as many on site renewable systems as we like, but if they are not maintained in the long term, we will reap no benefit. We need to have thought through how the renewable energy services will be maintained and how billing and metering will work – perhaps looking at setting up an energy services company (ESCo). If residents are not fully engaged in recycling, the full potential of installing recycling bins will not be achieved. The same goes for car clubs and local food initiatives.

As we saw in Chapter 1, three things have to come together to achieve One Planet Living: sustainable behaviour, local infrastructure and wider government spending. In the UK each represents about one planet's worth of ecological footprint. We can think of estates management as a way to harmonise local infrastructure with sustainable behaviour, making the green choice as easy, attractive and affordable as possible. Getting this link right is one of the most important ways to reduce ecological footprint as well as being the main way to ensure that people living in a community have a good experience of living there.

Estates management has been undervalued

Estates management (also called property or facilities management) is ripe for reinvention and reinvigoration. The term 'estates management' covers a range of offers from comprehensive services (for example, grounds maintenance, cleaning of communal areas, security, concierge and laundry services) to minimal services such as arranging repairs or insurance to communal parts. In the UK residential sector, estates management is more usually associated with leasehold and rented properties (rather than freehold properties) where the reason for some form of communal service is driven at the start by having a shared building envelope and utility services which require collective maintenance, such as in a block of apartments. Residential estates management serves a range of income groups from social housing estates for those on low incomes to the expensive private estates such as Grosvenor and Bedford Estates in London. However, of course both leaseholders and freeholders do pay for some common services such as domestic waste collection through taxes paid to the municipal authority and the division between these services and what might be provided for on the estate is one which needs to be thought through to achieve the best outcome.

In many cases, estates management has been viewed as the unglamorous relation of property development and property investment sectors and, in the UK at least, is characterised by poor service and a workforce undervalued and lacking in enthusiasm. This is a great shame, as there are huge opportunities for increased customer care and added value. If we use sustainability and community creation as drivers for this industry, we really do start to unlock a new realm of possibilities.

Creating a clear strategy for long-term management

The commentary and strategy below are based primarily on work carried out by BioRegional Quintain in pioneering the incorporation of One Planet principles into estates management. Colleagues at BioRegional Quintain had to work through complexities of laws and regulations surrounding estates management in establishing an energy services company to create a satisfactory governance and estates-management structure. The aim was always to offer future residents a more integrated service, enabling delivery at no extra cost compared with a good practice conventional alternative. This has been achieved, as far as possible, by redefining rather than increasing conventional estates management. Ultimately property law dictates, quite rightly, that residents could, if they so chose, replace the governance and estates-management structures by majority vote, but our intention is to have created a service which residents positively choose to keep. At BioRegional Quintain, we believe this is where we have the opportunity to add most value to residents', sustainability, as well as our own business.

Estates management or community management?

Whereas previously we may have thought about estates management as simply maintaining the buildings and keeping the grounds tidy, if we start seeing places as communities with a positive stance on sustainability, the role of estates management takes on new meaning. The opportunity extends beyond buildings maintenance, grounds maintenance and waste collection to embrace a host of lifestyle services including:

- providing transport services such as car clubs, cycle clubs and travel information;
- promoting local food links and receiving deliveries of local food;
- supplying renewable energy;
- advising residents on energy saving and green choices;
- promoting community spirit and community events;
- providing on site composting and food growing facilities;
- managing leisure facilities such as gyms and office space; and
- managing a community centre.

Perhaps we should call this holistic, people-centred service 'community management' rather than estates management. In this light we see that we can learn a lot from the management of leisure resorts where lifestyle and customer service are drivers for management. Such community management companies, or CoManCos (sorry to introduce a rather ugly acronym) may deliver services themselves and/or subcontract them to a range of service providers such as local maintenance contractors, recycling companies, car-club providers, or even residents who want to take on duties on a paid or volunteer basis.

Of course the range and extent of services which can be provided will depend on the size, location and aspirations of the community. Careful thought must go into the capital and running costs of such facilities, but nonetheless there are huge opportunities for CoManCos to bring coherence to the lifestyle being offered and to ensure cost-effective delivery. Not everything need be seen as additional cost on a service charge to residents. Some of the services can be organised as separate cost centres or independent businesses run within an overarching estates-management strategy. For example, food-growing space, such as allotments or mini rooftop allotments, can be rented to residents covering their costs of maintenance. Community centres can be run as social enterprises, gaining income from renting out space or acting as small business hubs with hot desks and shared office facilities.

Community governance

Sitting alongside community management is community governance. Whereas community management covers the day-to-day provision of services, community governance should address how residents and tenants are involved in maintaining, reviewing and evolving the direction of the community, dealing with problems and identifying opportunities. Such a community governance organisation (CoGO) should also represent the residents and tenants in overseeing the delivery of community management services.

The governance mechanisms put in place for communities can have a profound long-term effect on culture, sense of place, neighbourliness, levels of crime, environmental performance and, ultimately, real-estate values. The balance of functions between on site community governance and other structures such as the municipal authorities and central government will vary site by site and country to country, depending, for example, on context (eg, demographics of residents or tenants), scale (some services may be dependent on having a minimum number of residents), cost issues and central government regulation (energy and estates management service charges may be regulated).

Wider links and outreach

In some situations, there may be a case to establish a body, perhaps more informal than the CoGO, to be a forum for wider community issues – perhaps involving neighbouring estates, key local employers, the police or other stakeholders with a common geographic interest. It might simply be the case of ensuring that the CoGO has a representation on an existing forum for the wider area. Such a body might act in a similar way to a parish or village council and perhaps be a forum intermediate in scale between the estate and the municipal authority.

A question worth considering is whether sustainable communities could or should have a wider role in outreach. Certainly some of the services provided by sustainable communities could be

Governance and management services in a sustainable community

The governance and management structures for a sustainable community should consider three main components:

Community governance organisation (CoGO)

Decision-making structure for residents and tenants. This might be the residents' association, residents' management organisation, tenants' association or traders' association, all preferably brought together as one entity.

The CoGO directs and oversees the work of the CoManCo. It sends one or more representatives to any body concerned with the wider community.

Community management company (CoManCo)

Contracted by the CoGO, the CoManCo is responsible for professionally delivering and/or subcontracting the management services on behalf of the CoGO. These services may include building maintenance, grounds maintenance, running the community centre, managing recycling, running the energy services, organising car clubs, etc.

Wider community engagement

A new or existing forum to engage with the wider area is also worth considering. This can be an informal group or structure such as a community interest company.

Case Study – Community governance and management at One Brighton

One Brighton Neighbourhood community interest company (CIC)

The wider area organisation with representatives from One Brighton Residents, Management Organisation, business tenants in the One Brighton building, business in the wider New England Quarter area and key local people with a wide range of interests. The CIC owns some of the open space which it can use for events and possibly fund-raising. Sign up to One Brighton Sustainability Charter and One Planet principles written into terms of reference.

One Brighton Residents' Management Organisation
(The community governance organisation)

The members of the community governance organisation are the residents (home owners, social housing, commercial tenants and BQL). They elect a chair, treasurer and other officers. They are responsible for representing the interests of the members and the site's manifesto – which includes a commitment to One Planet Living and the Sustainability Charter. They oversee the estates management and other services provided via BioRegional Quintain (BQL), ensuring an annual customer satisfaction survey is completed and a One Planet Living report is created. They also send a representative to sit on the CIC.

The community management company

BQL Communities Ltd works with the managing agents to the estates management to secure services on behalf of the Residents' Management Organisation. It uses One Planet principles delivering services or selecting service providers:

- local food deliveries;
- green grounds maintenance;
- renewable energy services;
- recycling and waste;
- green Caretaker;
- buildings maintenance;
- green insurance;
- car clubs;
- extranet.

offered to the wider area. For example, car-club services could be promoted to residents in the surrounding area – which is of course what now naturally happens. This is mutually beneficial, increasing the viability and profitability of the car club. Other services like farmers' markets or community centres likewise could spread their benefits more widely. Their influence is potentially enormous in changing perceptions and the behaviour of people in the surrounding area through direct contact and by allowing people to experience aspects of sustainable living.

From an altruistic (or enlightened self-interest) perspective, sustainability at its heart is based on a recognition of interdependence. Therefore we need to spread the message of sustainability, and sustainable communities could start to do this. Could new sustainable communities take on a role in proselytising the message, particularly perhaps to local school children? If there is a community centre on site, could it incorporate a public exhibition? Could training courses be run on sustainability? Certainly at BedZED, tours and training courses have proved a way both to manage the 'eco-tourists' who want to visit the site as well as generating income to support jobs and running costs of an exhibition and community centre. At One Brighton, residents and tenants will be encouraged to hold an annual open day for the public, with the help of the Green Caretaker (see Box on page 156), perhaps doing this as a celebration of 'interdependence day'.

Embedding the One Planet approach into the DNA of long-term management

In the same way as One Planet principles can be used to drive coherence through the design and construction process, so can they be used as a cohering mechanism in governance and community management structures. Key mechanisms include:

- ensuring that sales and marketing have incorporated the One Planet principles so that people understand the philosophy and know what to expect;
- producing a short Sustainability Charter or One Planet manifesto for the site, made available to all residents and tenants, to formally set out the context for community governance and management which encourages certain types of behaviour and discourages others;
- introducing terms of reference for the CoGO which include One Planet principles and which encourage the election of One Planet champions from among the residents who, in partnership with the CoManCo, promote sustainability and produce an annual One Planet report; and
- establishing a body to promote interests in the wider neighbourhood to which the CoGO for the estate belongs.

Other strategies such as encouraging certain types of retail or food outlets (eg, encouraging vegetarian or restaurants using local, organic food) on site can also be used.

The Green Caretaker

For successful long-term management, the interface between residents and the community management service becomes critically important. This interface role gives us the opportunity to upgrade the concierge or caretaker to include facilitation of community interaction and as a sustainability motivator – the Green Caretaker. Gentle facilitation of community interaction could include helping the residents and tenants organise seasonal events and welcoming all new residents. We can see the Green Caretaker as the key person carrying on the sustainability baton from the Sustainability Integrator who looked after sustainability during design and construction, and ensured it was integrated into the estates-management strategy.

Figure 1
Estates management offers
new opportunities to
engage with residents.

Job description: Green Caretaker for One Brighton

The Green Caretaker is an innovative role, combining traditional caretaking duties with a new set of duties in supporting residents in sustainable living. The Green Caretaker would be a full-time role employed by the community management company, and paid for via residential and non-residential service charges.

Activities

The Green Caretaker will act as the day-to-day 'face' of the community management company, carrying out general caretaking duties as well as being the first point of call for residents and tenants with regards to the maintenance and general management of the communal areas. The Green Caretaker will also engage in more specific and sustainability-focused activities such as managing the day-to-day operation of:

- the on site composter;
- on site recycling facilities;
- cycle storage and car park;
- general management of communal areas vis-à-vis community events;
- overseeing, in partnership with the community management company, the ongoing provision of the community extranet including day-to-day management of community-specific elements such as the events calendar and circulating general notices to residents; and
- coordinating, in partnership with the community management company and the Residents' Management Organisation, the programme of ongoing monitoring including resident food and travel surveys.

Supporting sustainable lifestyles and One Planet Living

As part of supporting residents in leading more sustainable lifestyles, the Green Caretaker will be trained and supported in One Planet Living by the community management company and will engage in other activities such as:

- encouraging people to recycle;
- supporting residents in using the car club (first point of call only as the car club provider has its own customer support department);
- assisting residents in using their appliances and mechanisms correctly and for maximum efficiency;
- in partnership with the Community Management Company and the Residents' Management Organisation, producing a community newsletter that includes articles on sustainable lifestyles and performance of the scheme;
- supporting residents in organising community events;
- welcoming new residents and introducing them to One Planet Living; and
- issuing Green Lifestyles Packages and Handover Packs to new residents.

Energy and ESCo
The Green Caretaker will take an active role in the day-to-day management of the renewable energy technologies on site. These activities will be supervised and supported by One Brighton Energy Services – the energy services company that will provide energy to the development. It is likely that the Green Caretaker will engage in:

- supporting the ESCo in the deliveries of biomass fuel on a weekly/bi-weekly basis, coordinating the logistics on site and carrying out basic quality control;
- ensuring that the fuel storage is adequately maintained and fuel is kept in optimum conditions;
- via daily basic checks, ensuring that the energy-generation technologies are running adequately and if there are any issues, reporting them to the ESCo; and
- carrying out basic maintenance to the biomass boiler.

Necessary training will be provided by the community management company.
Reproduced courtesy of BioRegional Quintain Ltd.

The role of residents in delivering sustainability

As society has become more anonymous and neighbourliness has decreased, we have almost forgotten how to work together for our own communities. Instead we have become increasingly dependent on services from police to social workers to solve problems which in the past may have been nipped in the bud through natural policing of communities. If community involvement can be fostered – without forcing it – there is much to be gained in terms of quality of life, sense of security, property values and reduced costs to society.

In any community, there are always people who are enthusiastic about something – whether it be organising events, participating in the residents' association, encouraging recycling, gardening or promoting local food. Some people, of course, won't ever be interested in getting involved, but it is always worth putting in place a structure within which residents can express their enthusiasm and knowledge. One way this is being harnessed at One Brighton is by encouraging the Residents' Management Organisation to select a champion of each One Planet principle.

The ESCo

One major new area that developers and housing associations are starting to have to consider is the energy services company or ESCo. Increasingly, renewable energy systems will be installed on site – mainly renewable heating systems initially (solar thermal and biomass boilers), as discussed in Chapter 6, but perhaps in due course increasing amounts of renewable electricity as well, as technologies emerge and are proven. ESCos are local energy providers, selling energy direct to consumers, often through on site energy generation such as from a combined heat and power (CHP) plant. Sales of electricity are regulated by government and there are still some grey areas which will end up being tested by case law over the coming years.

However, in general terms, landlords can establish legal structures to supply heat to residents through a district heating system. Electricity supply is different. For commercial users, the landlord can require purchase from a stated supplier, but for residential users there is more legislation aimed at protecting the interests of consumers. This regulation aims to prevent unscrupulous landlords taking unfair advantage and instead promotes consumer choice and competition between suppliers. However, the viability of much on site renewable electricity generation is dependent on having a secured and stable market. The uncertainty that competition introduces can make the risks of installing renewable electricity generation on site too high to secure investment.

So are there ways for a developer to encourage residents to use renewable energy? As has been suggested above, renewable heat is more straightforward. Of course homes can be fitted with systems such as solar hot water panels. We can also introduce district heating systems running on renewables – biomass boilers, for example. Renewable electricity is more difficult. Of course, developers can provide information on green electricity at the time of home purchase and use a green electricity supplier as the default supplier, which residents may or may not choose to change. For green electricity supply at One Brighton, we are installing a private wire arrangement (ie, where the physical wires supplying electricity to the home are owned by the landlord) and purchasing green electricity in bulk and retailing it to our residents. However, residents cannot be tied indefinitely to purchasing electricity from the ESCo. The aim therefore must be to offer a sufficiently good deal that residents choose not to opt out. Developers might also be able to promote off-site renewable generation to their residents, for example by selling shares in off-site generation. This would enable residents to own a share in their power generation. It could parallel the business opportunities identified by organisations such as Baywind which establishes cooperatives as a way for people to invest in large-scale renewable energy generation such as wind turbines. As we explored in Chapter 6, ultimately as a society we will need to see our whole national electricity supply system becoming green, which will, in due course, alter the emphasis and purpose of ESCos.

The community centre

A social focus for the community is very important for engagement and if a community centre can be incorporated then it can repay the investment many times over. As well as a place for the residents' management organisation to meet, it can be a place for coffee mornings for parents, exercise classes, parties, training courses, conference facilities, a place for weekend markets (for example, local fruit and vegetables, bring-and-buy sales or clothes swaps), generating income to cover costs as well as bringing social benefit.

Often a community centre may be specified by the municipal authority as part of granting planning permission, but thought should always be given to how it will be run and financed in the long term. To save costs and not burden residents with estate service charges (which can be challenged legally by residents), it is often best to cross-subsidise the costs by providing the community centre as a 'by-product' of another service. Community centre functions can be provided synergistically with a range of other facilities, for example:

- a school being used out of hours as a community and sports centre;
- space offered within primary healthcare facilities;
- a business centre serving the community as well; and
- a hotel or pub which could become the focus.

One exceptional example of integrating community centre functions is the Bromley-by-Bow Centre in east London. The centre is a run by a partnership of organisations including a housing association, GP practice, childcare provider, church and government employment training organisation. Another example is the services offered by the Ethical Property Company which runs commercial properties that provide serviced office and meeting space at low-cost rent to community groups and NGOs.

Green leases

The One Planet principles need to flow through into the activities of commercial operators and tenants (offices, retailers, hotels, leisure operators, etc) as well as residents. How can this be done?

As truly sustainable communities remain pioneers, and because it is about creating an integrated 'lifestyle offer', their scope is broader than conventional standards such as LEED and BREEAM. Communities pioneering in sustainability are ahead of tried-and-tested standards and so there is often the need for developers to co-create solutions with operators offering such services as offices, retail, hotels and leisure facilities. New technologies and approaches are emerging continually and our understanding is evolving all the time. At some point in the future the solutions may be codified into formal sets of standards, but for the time being at least (and perhaps to maintain continual improvement long term) a more flexible, less rigid approach is required to secure the best results.

Therefore, if tendering out for an operator, say, for a hotel, a strategy is to:

- Supply the Outline Sustainability Action Plan for the development as a whole.
- Invite tenders in the usual way but with a requirement to respond to the One Planet principles and Outline SAP plus any existing standards which may be adopted (eg, LEED, BREEAM, Pearl, Hotel Association of Canada's Green Key Eco-Rating Program) covering aspects such as fit-out, operations and maintenance, monitoring and feedback, communications and marketing.
- Specify in the tender documents any non-negotiable aspects such as source of energy supply, waste collection, etc.
- Run workshops on the One Planet approach with shortlisted tenderers to explore opportunities and issues.
- Select potential operators on the basis of their formal response to the tender, and in the contract of engagement require successful tenderers to work with the developer to complete a detailed SAP which is mutually acceptable to both parties and which is aligned to the Outline SAP for the development.
- Ensure the successful operator inducts all staff working on the project in One Planet Living.
- Second staff into the operator to support delivery of One Planet principles if required.
- Ensure the successful operator has a process in place to vet the products and services they procure against the One Planet principles.
- Ensure that the successful operator produces an annual report against their detailed SAP which feeds into the overall SAP for the site, including reporting against ecological footprint.
- Require the successful operator to join a forum to review the overall SAP and their contribution to it with meetings occurring initially every three months.

The aim for this process should be complete engagement with the operator and to foster culture change so that the offer to the consumer – the whole lifestyle provided – is as sustainable and coherent as possible. In BioRegional Quintain's experience this is only partly achieved through trying to develop or enforce standards, especially on more complex projects. A 'living' participatory approach of co-creation must be at the heart.

Figure 2
Potential operators of the hotel and leisure facilities at BioRegional Quintain's Riverside One in Middlesbrough are integrating One Planet principles into their proposals.

The community extranet, monitoring and feedback

Systems like an extranet for the estate – an interactive website for residents providing information and forums for discussion – can support communication between neighbours, the Green Caretaker and the estates management company. It can carry key information about transport and food and upcoming community events, and foster clubs such as a book club for residents. It can also become a portal to promote new green products and services to residents, perhaps opening opportunities for special offers and bulk discounts.

Long-term ongoing feedback on the environmental performance and social health of the community can greatly assist its governance and estates management, as well as providing useful and interesting information to residents – for example, on energy efficiency, membership of the car club or the average number of neighbours that residents know. It can also provide useful learning for the developer to incorporate into future projects. Huge opportunities exist to incorporate monitoring and feedback mechanisms into the sustainable communities using estates management, the ESCo and extranet. Wherever possible, monitoring should not add another layer of bureaucracy or cost but be integrated into normal functioning. Reporting against zero carbon, for instance, can be incorporated into the normal annual reporting of the ESCo. Figures for recycling for zero waste targets can be part of monitoring and annual reporting by the Green Caretaker and the estates management company. An annual residents' satisfaction survey – which any good estates management company would undertake – could incorporate a few simple questions, say, on the number of neighbours people know, and travel habits, to track the Health and Happiness and Sustainable Transport principles respectively. All this information can be provided as a summary One Planet Living report to the residents' management organisation.

A long-term opportunity – to create brand recognition based on community creation?

Where residential developers are traders – selling homes rather than retaining a long-term interest – there is little brand recognition. People choose a home on the basis of location and price. In such an undifferentiated market, is there a business opportunity here to create a brand through creating sustainable communities? Given that sustainability is about the long term and that some of the value generated through sustainability likewise is long term, it is highly likely that the most successful business models for sustainable communities will be ones where developers take a long-term interest in the schemes they build. This will inevitably lead to the opportunity to create long-term reputation and therefore to create brands based on value, quality and service.

I hope after reading this chapter some readers will be inspired to reconsider estates management as an opportunity to really advance the cause of sustainability and customer care. None of it is rocket science, but it does require commitment and persistence to ensure that an estate is being managed well and that customers are offered a good experience even as new sustainability services are being introduced. As an undervalued part of the property industry, it is the field which is most open to reinvention and which promises to bring the greatest benefits and rewards long term.

**Estates management can be reinvented –
even cleaning can be given an overhaul and made green and fun**

Greenmop – The Argus Green Awards
Monday 27 October 2008

When Racheal Hughes decided to leave her job in IT to do something completely different, most didn't expect that to mean setting up an environmentally friendly cleaning company.

Greenmop has been up and running for less than a year, but it has already grown into a busy, successful company which actively promotes the benefits of a chemical-free approach to cleaning. Racheal had the idea to set up the company after discovering how chemical cleaning products cause damage to both our natural environment and to our health.

As an allergy sufferer herself, she has found marked improvements in her own symptoms since using eco-friendly products both at home and work. Employees always take their eco-products with them so they never have to compromise on what they use, and everyone gets around on scooters, bikes, on foot and by bus. They also insist regular customers have the big things such as vacuum cleaners and mops so the cleaners can carry everything they need in backpacks to negate the need for cars.

Racheal also runs a regularly updated blog on the Greenmop website which offers information and advice on how to get by without the chemical cleaners we have come to rely on. Greenmop's popularity is undeniable. There is a whole raft of nominations from people saying things such as: 'I'm nominating Greenmop as I believe the company shows that by doing the little things, they add up to big things – and they make your home clean too!' and 'Fantastic independent local cleaning company. Get your house or business cleaned in a 100% ethical and green way. They ride green mopeds, they wear green T-shirts – we love them!'

The Argus Eco-Awards October 2008 — GREEN **BUSINESS** sponsored by — theargus.co.uk

Winner   Greenmop
Chemical-free cleaning

Every employee at Greenmop takes their eco-products with them so they never have to compromise on what they use

Chapter 13

Sell the dream

Green is becoming more of a selling feature, but when buying a home other factors such as location remain major criteria for purchasers. The same is true for commercial purchasers or tenants. Other features of truly sustainable communities such as reduced household expenditure and healthier lifestyles can be promoted. To be successful, developments cannot rely solely on environmental sustainability. They must stand on their own merits as great places to live, work and/or play.

There is of course little point building greener homes if you can't sell them. There will always be a small percentage of the population who will buy green because of their personal convictions and because they want to do the right thing. Selling to them, provided they have the money, is one thing. If we want to expand sales beyond a small niche, selling to a broader market is a different proposition.

When selling homes, the key criteria for selection currently remain traditional reasons for purchase such as proximity to place of work, quality of schools, quality of neighbourhood and access to local amenities such as shops and nightlife. The eco-friendliness of the home itself remains a secondary criterion for the majority of purchasers although there is anecdotal evidence that this is changing. The attractiveness of green homes is likely to increase as awareness increases, fuel prices fluctuate and as legislation and energy labelling for homes kick in.

Richard Donnell, Research Director of Hometrack, recognised as a leading UK residential research service, believes:

'The primary factors that influence the decision to purchase a home are its location, the number of rooms and overall living space as well as the affordability of the purchase. There has generally been little focus on the running costs of a property. Yet higher energy bills and weekly recycling collections make households increasingly conscious of the green agenda. There is not currently a large, mainstream market for green homes, especially if priced at a premium. While many households will talk a good story over going green, when it comes to buying a green home then they will want to see financial benefits such as lower running costs. The problem is that the savings may be small when set against the overall cost of buying a home. Developers need to reinforce the differential running costs as this is likely to become an increasingly important part of the decision making process. This could certainly be accelerated if, or when, the second-hand market is taxed on its energy efficiency. Marketing can also focus on the other benefits of green homes together with a continued growing awareness of the green agenda so the potential market for green homes will grow and eventually become mainstream.'[1]

A percentage of purchasers are very committed green buyers – the type who will always buy organic products and electric cars. This means that although it may be possible to sell a few properties or a small development with a green premium, it is still risky to assume that there is a premium to be secured in selling eco-housing on a mass scale.

However, there are a number of features of sustainable communities as described in this book which do certainly add positive selling points. Depending on specifics of the market (such as supply of other homes in the area, energy prices, lifestyle expectations), the features may or may not increase the price achievable for the home. However, positive features of homes in sustainable communities can, depending on specification, include:

- better build quality of homes protecting long-term investment;
- healthier homes (eg, use of materials which reduce emissions of gases such as formaldehyde which are implicated in sick building syndrome);
- more comfortable homes (eg, a well-insulated home can offer better comfort levels);
- access to lifestyle facilities such as a car club, farmers' market, allotments or community centre;
- better access to green space and the joys of wildlife;
- more space where children can play safely without parents having to worry;
- greater neighbourliness for a positive living experience leading to a reduction in levels of crime;
- lower living costs from reduced energy bills or through membership of a car club – affordable lifestyles not just affordable homes;
- future proofing against rising or unpredictable energy costs;
- opportunities to reduce commuting which is the single greatest contributor to reported unhappiness in the UK;
- easier reselling of homes – for instance as experienced at BedZED; and
- the emerging status symbol of having a green home.

Some of the move to greener homes will be driven by regulation. In the UK, this includes increasing energy efficiency through mandatory Buildings Regulations and the recent requirement for all homes now sold – new and old – to have an energy performance certificate. As purchasers start becoming aware of energy performance certificates, it will certainly start to become harder to sell homes which are G-rated rather than, say, C- B- or A-rated. It is arguable that it is worth being ahead of regulation and planning for greater eco-performance, particularly given the timescales for building homes and communities.

Of course, I have described all the positive features. Some features such as reduced parking may be seen as negatives that can hit hard at a deep cultural and almost physiological level, recalling my experience of selling my car before moving to BedZED. However, there are benefits, not least the overall sense of community spirit, which can be created – something that is so lacking in our modern lives. The task in sales and marketing therefore is to promote the positives

Accordia

The first residential scheme to win the UK's most prestigious architectural award, the Stirling Prize, in 2008, Accordia in Cambridge, comprises 378 homes. The homes are well insulated, passively ventilated and described as being set in a garden. Small private gardens are complemented by large communal spaces improving the efficiency of land use, the sense of greenery and promoting neighbourliness. Accordia was developed by Countryside Properties and designed as a joint project with Feilden Clegg Bradley Studios, Maccreanor Lavington Architects, Alison Brooks Architects and Grant Associates.

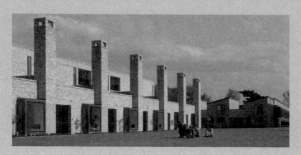

and to overcome initial objections people might have. Once experienced, though, I believe it is hard to go back to living in a place where sustainability and community spirit have not been designed for or are not promoted. I do not want to underestimate the task of the sales job, and certainly the sales staff have to believe in the product, and therefore training of sales staff, which includes direct experience of facilities such as car clubs, is absolutely essential.

Positive selling

There is one big hurdle to overcome. The environmental message is generally a negative one because it starts with the premise that humans are damaging the planet and that we have to reduce our ecological impact. This does mean that environmentalists are often thought of as killjoys and it is hard to get out of this negative frame of mind. But actually the message can be a positive one as there are always two sides to the coin. Just as there are two ways to lose weight – the negative way of reducing calories and the positive way of moving to a healthy diet and getting more exercise – we can present sustainability not as doing without, but as gaining something positive.

At One Brighton and Riverside One developments, the car club, for instance, is not sold primarily as a way to reduce environmental impact, but as a convenient way to get access to a clean, valeted car which also saves money. At One Brighton, working with communications company, Ferrier Pearce, a positive message is created using the One Planet principles, so people can engage in sustainability should they wish to. So, for instance,

'Zero Waste. We ... are helping to reduce the amount of waste being sent to landfill sites by using recycled building materials, reducing construction waste and providing you with the opportunity to separate and recycle your domestic waste easily. You ... can reduce the amount of waste you create by purchasing products with minimal packaging and recycling your domestic waste using the community's recycling bins and composters.'

This creates a mutually beneficial compact with customers, where both parties are doing their bit.

Table 1
Always look on the bright side

Olive Drab	Vera Bright
I need to reduce my carbon footprint by 90 per cent by 2030.	I am buying state-of-the-art, energy-efficient goods – and renewable energy from these fantastic new clean technologies such as wind turbines and concentrated solar power plants – cool.
I need to radically reduce my meat and dairy consumption and stop wasting so much food.	I feel so much healthier since I increased the amount of fruit and vegetable protein in my diet. I have also lost 7 kilograms – and got two marriage proposals. I think it is good that supermarkets stopped those Buy One Get One Free offers – what a change in attitude we have towards waste now. It was that campaign in the schools that did it.
If we want to reduce our transport impacts sufficiently, we need to stop travelling so much, and we certainly can't fly any more. We need to give up our cars and develop more locally based communities and services.	The street life is so much better since they pedestrianised the whole of central London – it's all like Covent Garden now. I can't understand why I was happy to spend so much time cooped up in a car and stuck in a traffic jam. Real shame air travel has become so expensive – never mind – the fortnight in the south of France is not too bad. I am saving up for a six-month overland trip to India in the bio-bus though. However, planes powered by hydrogen from massive solar plants in the desert are on the horizon.
I need to reduce my water consumption down to 80 litres a day and then I also need to think about the 3,000 litres a day that is embedded in the products I buy. I wonder how I can reduce that too?	I didn't even realise my house is fitted with water-efficient appliances. Great the manufacturing companies have taken Corporate Social Responsibility so seriously and reduced the amount of water it takes to produce our goods and services. Another thing not to worry about!
Jewellery has surprisingly high environmental impacts in both carbon and ecological footprint. We need to stop buying gold and precious metals for unnecessary luxuries.	Bling was so 20th century.
I only buy second-hand clothes and furniture because it reduces my impact.	Quality is so important. I can't get it with cheap new furniture, so I buy real, craftsman-made second-hand furniture.

The existing UK housing stock needs massive investment in order to retrofit it to be thermally efficient.	Via the mortgage companies, the Green New Deal offered low-cost loans to householders to improve energy efficiency.
The payback period for a lot of energy-efficiency measures or renewables is a very long time, but we need to take these measures anyway, regardless of the cost, in order to cut our carbon emissions.	The government introduced 'budget neutral' green incentives – increasing VAT on non-renewables, taking off VAT on renewables and removing Employers' National Insurance contributions so labour-intensive activities were not penalised.
We need to ensure that products we buy are manufactured in a clean and non-polluting way and avoid products that don't have proper environmental management systems in place.	The revolution in clean technology in the first half of the 21st century created masses of new jobs.
Western developed countries have caused the climate-change crisis and so they now need to cut right back on their emissions in order to allow developing countries to invest in their own infrastructure and quality of life.	The US didn't want to be dependent on Middle Eastern oil and Western Europe didn't want to be on the end of a gas pipeline from Russia – so we just got on with promoting renewable energy introducing green infrastructure.
Most environmental damage has been caused by us in rich countries so we need to pay poorer countries a stewardship fee to keep their forest resources intact or to leave the oil in the ground.	People just changed. Countries decided for themselves that renewable energy and bioregionalism was better. The Stone Age didn't end because we ran out of stones – so the Fossil Fuel Age was replaced by the Age of One Planet Living.

Can a green premium be achieved?

Reflecting Richard Donnell's view at the beginning of this chapter, there remains little good evidence of widespread premiums for green homes. Values achieved at BedZED are 5 to 20 per cent higher than the immediate surrounding area. A great deal of this additional value is explicable through the relatively low quality of housing in the area around BedZED; BedZED is more comparable to prices in a good residential area a few kilometres away. Our experience at BedZED, though, is of very good re-sales rates – with people positively wanting to live at BedZED. Moreover, a number of BedZED residents have sold and moved to other properties within the development when some have started families and needed a larger home.

BedZED and the Barbican (a mixed-use development in central London which includes extensive arts facilities and communal services) are unusual in London in the degree to which people single them out as developments where community spirit and character are positive features. BedZED's strong design and the fact that the properties are sold leasehold (there is still some customer resistance to houses sold leasehold, although it is standard for apartments to be sold this way) does divide opinions. Ushers, BedZED's local estate agent which has dealt with a number of BedZED properties, say: 'BedZED is like Marmite – you either love it or hate it.'

Certainly in the case of BedZED, sales interest is on the one hand increased by its strong visual identity, but on the other hand, decreased by it as well. Much like cars, a strong statement can be very successful usually in a particular niche, but the volume car market is filled by more pedestrian designs. However, tastes do evolve over time and the populace is becoming more design-conscious – witness the growth of companies such as Ikea.

At BioRegional Quintain Ltd we assume no green premium, but use the features as positive selling points that may express themselves, for example, in better sales rates, which are as valuable as better sales prices. Particularly in an economic downturn such as the one being experienced as I write this book, the features are a differentiating factor and important in a difficult market. We believe that this is generating greater levels of interest in our developments than rival schemes.

Is green the message, or might it be health or quality of life?

'Green' is an interesting and evolving label with both positive and negative aspects. Being green is seen overall as positive, but it can still carry residual connotations of worthiness – of eating lentils, refusing to drive cars and taking pleasure in telling others about it. Greenness can result in customer resistance if sold too hard, as the top-line message of the label carries certain perceived responsibilities with it: 'If I am green then I should not fly for my holidays.' Anecdotes from our sales staff yield some interesting insights such as customers saying: 'I am not green, but I want to live somewhere which doesn't damage the environment.' Selling green too hard can therefore hinder sales.

Although major selling points remain location, access to work and schools, other messages like quality of life and health which are real benefits of sustainable communities might actually be stronger selling points than 'green'. At the Riverside One development in Middlesbrough, the main message is unambiguously one of modern urban living in a town where no such offer currently exists. Environmental sustainability is an important but secondary message. While

Creating a sense of community to maintain re-sales value

Tom and Jannette bought a one-bedroom apartment at BedZED in 2002, just as they were expecting their first child. With their family growing, in 2004 they sold up, buying a three-bedroom maisonette a few doors away in the estate. 'First we bought because of the affordability and the design, but mostly it is the people and sense of community that makes it a nice place to live, and that has kept us here ...'

sustainable communities require a degree of innovation, sales can be modulated to appeal to the less conservative and those attracted by the new – a focus perhaps on 21st-century living. However, clearly the messaging for successful sales needs to be tailored to the specific project, its features, its competition, the cultural context and the target market. Building green or sustainable communities does not reduce the importance or subtleties of conventional marketing, and sales strategies needed to ensure good sales.

The committed developer – green lifestyle upgrades and a pact with residents

A committed developer, however, may take the opportunity to move potential residents further along the green path. Moving home is a good opportunity for people to have a lifestyle makeover and make a fresh start – offering opportunities such as getting rid of a car or energy-inefficient appliances. We can capitalise on this opportunity in a few ways which might include:

- offering green products in upgrade packages such as low-energy flatscreen LCD televisions, designer hemp upholstered furniture or solid wood FSC-certified kitchen units;
- providing green incentives in welcome packs such as discounts on energy-efficient appliances, free car-club membership, cycle vouchers or vouchers redeemable at a local vegetarian restaurant;
- welcome inductions to explain sustainable lifestyle features of the development; and
- possibly even offering a lifestyle coaching session on, say, exercise, diet and ecological footprint.

Selling commercial and retail space

In a sustainable community, the range of facilities and services required by residents are at one level very similar – food shopping, restaurants, convenience retail, childcare, etc – but the 'flavour'

Possible green incentives or welcome-pack contents
Energy-efficient appliances such as LCD televisions and wind-up radios.
Green insurance (eg, home content insurance with naturesave).
Free car-club membership.
Hamper of fair-trade food.
Free three-month trial of a local organic vegetable box.
Book on healthy cooking.
Vouchers to local green restaurants.
Free one-year membership of local Wildlife Trust.
Tickets to local arts cinema.
One Planet Lifestyle workshop.

of these services might need to be slightly different. Ideally, for instance, food retail will offer more local, organic and seasonal produce, restaurants might have more vegetarian options and childcare might be within walking distance. Because of market pressures, developers may not have the complete freedom to choose or dictate the types of commercial or retail businesses which choose to locate in the development, but they can influence the mix and require all tenants to sign up to the sustainability ethos. Indeed more and more companies are positively looking for green office space to reflect their commitment to corporate social responsibility. Tatiana Bosteels, Head of Responsible Property Investment for Hermes Real Estate Investment Management Ltd comments:

'Green issues are not going to go away. There are two main drivers for more sustainable commercial properties. First, there is government regulation which will push buildings towards being greener. Second, there is the opportunity for differentiation, especially when it is a sellers' market. In addition, there is a cultural shift starting to appear where, for example, trustees of pension funds are seeing sustainability as an important aspect of discharging their fiduciary duties.'

For large companies some issues will need to be worked through such as purchase of heat and/or power from any ESCo on site, as some companies may have energy supply agreements covering multiple sites. Initially it might be that creative and small businesses are more keen to adopt green working wholeheartedly – perhaps opening opportunities for serviced green office hubs and e-office concepts.

More niche opportunities may exist such as rental space for 'social change' organisations such as NGOs and community groups, as well as for niche green retail and restaurants. It might be hard to encourage in some retailers such as supermarkets whose retail model is based on attracting shoppers by car – but perhaps the opportunity exists to engage with these companies to use their expertise to create a more sustainable retail model.

The developer itself could exploit potential opportunities through new community management services. For example, could developers make agreements with companies offering comprehensive home deliveries of groceries to residents, bypassing supermarket retail? Could this be linked to the community extranet?

The sort of transformation change required for One Planet Living may take time to achieve as suitable sustainable services and offers emerge – but the scope for innovation is huge together with the opportunity to *sell the future*. Ultimately, the strength of the original vision, together with persistence, will determine the degree to which a clear and positive experience is created and conveyed to customers – one example is being planned at Sonoma Mountain Village in California.

Notes
1 Richard Donnell, personal communication, 2009.
2 Geof Syphers, personal communication, 2009.
3 Dr Jennifer Fosket, personal communication, 2009.

Reproduced by permission of Richard Donnell.

'Five-Minute Living' at Sonoma Mountain Village

Clustered around a new town square and daily farmers' market, Sonoma Mountain Village in California is planned to ensure every resident is no more than a five-minute walk to the cinema, groceries, restaurants, offices, daycare and shops offering local, sustainable and fair-trade products and services. The streets are narrow, pavements are wide. Children can walk to school and play safely in the streets. By combining new urbanism with deep sustainability, Sonoma Mountain Village will turn an old factory into a living neighbourhood of almost 1,900 units of housing including live-work, condominiums, row houses, small and large detached homes and tiny affordable cottages.

Geof Syphers, Chief Sustainability Officer of Codding Enterprises, the developer of Sonoma Mountain Village, explains:

Of the 36.9 tons of greenhouse gases emitted each year by the average Californian household, 8.7 tons come from building and powering homes. However, the majority of household greenhouse gas emissions – 28.2 tons – are a result of lifestyle choices, including car and airline travel, the use of services and solid waste. We have a five planet lifestyle and need to get down to one planet. The way our cities are designed actually makes environmental responsibility inconvenient. We need to reach beyond the highest national standard of LEED Platinum because even if each building at Sonoma Mountain Village achieved that standard, the community would still generate 16,870 tons of CO_2 each year just from energy use in buildings. We would need four million trees to sequester that carbon – a forest 64 per cent larger than the city of Rohnert Park.[2]

The development is reusing over 700,000 square feet of existing buildings and includes a $7.5 million, 1.3 megawatt photovoltaic array and, in 2007, Codding founded the Sonoma Mountain Business Cluster, a non-profit business incubator for sustainable resource technologies that assists start-ups with training, management, investment resources and support networks.

The developer has also established Codding Steel Frame Solutions' 50,000 square foot manufacturing facility which is completely solar powered. The framing company uses recycled steel to manufacture framing for residential and commercial construction. President and CEO Brad Baker says: 'We take about six old SUVs out of the junkyard and recycle them into a 2,000-square-foot home, saving 50 trees in the process. The steel is not only made from recycled materials, it also is recyclable. In 100 years, it can be taken apart screw by screw and reused to create another building, or to create more recycled steel.'

And Dr Jennifer Fosket, a sociologist at McGill University, says: 'Sonoma Mountain Village's emphasis on job creation and social capital can help create a more genuinely wealthy community. Long working hours and commutes are cited as major reasons for dissatisfaction. By encouraging on site work opportunities the project can help alleviate those sources of unhappiness. And by creating opportunities for volunteerism, care-giving, and civic and environmental action, Sonoma Mountain Village will make it easier for residents to participate in the greater good – a different kind of wealth in a better place to live.' *(Reproduced by permission of Geof Syphers)*

Personal Footprint					Personal Share of Societal Footprint
Food	Housing	Mobility	Goods	Services	Gov't/Infrastructure

Chapter 14

Retrofit One Planet lifestyles

New communities are only part of the story. We will need to retrofit sustainability to existing communities. Just as with new communities, this is not just limited to making buildings more energy efficient, but rather creating a whole sustainable lifestyle. The One Planet principles are being applied to a number of initiatives aimed at individuals and existing communities. Because of CO_2 already released into the atmosphere, the planet is locked into some degree of climate change so we will need to adapt our buildings and activities such as farming for different weather in future.

So far in this book I have concentrated on what we might do when we build new communities. Of course this is hugely important, particularly at a global level with massive urbanisation in countries such as China and India. To achieve One Planet Living, we must also have a strategy for existing communities, which deserves a whole book. For instance, in the UK housing stock turns over at about 1 per cent per year, which means that it will take about 100 years to be replaced (some buildings will of course long outlast this and we may choose to retain many buildings for their historic value). Given the urgency of climate change, we cannot afford simply to wait for this stock to renew itself and to build new sustainable communities in their place; we have to consider what to do with existing stock and communities. Researchers at the Environmental Change Institute at Oxford University have gone so far as to suggest that we should accelerate the demolition of the least energy-efficient existing homes fourfold and rebuild them to better environmental standards in order to meet CO_2 reduction targets.[1] But as we have seen in this book, it is not just the energy consumption of homes we must consider as our environmental impact arises from the whole lifestyle we adopt. Can we apply the One Planet framework to retrofit existing homes or communities?

Retrofitting energy efficiency and renewable energy systems
Of course we can start by retrofitting existing homes to make them energy efficient. Considerable energy savings can be achieved, sometimes with very short payback periods, particularly in the oldest and least energy-efficient homes, through simple measures such as loft and cavity wall insulation, draught-proofing, double-glazing (and perhaps triple-glazing) and energy-efficient lighting.

In the UK, energy supply companies are required to reduce carbon emissions by supporting energy efficiency in the home, which has resulted in campaigns such as offering free energy-efficient

Case Study: Parity Projects, Carshalton Grove, south London

Built in 1870, the property at Carshalton Grove is a single-skinned (non cavity-walled) house and was in need of renovation throughout. Owner Russell Smith has used eight different types of insulation to compare their performance and pros and cons: sheep's wool, recycled cotton/hemp, recycled newspaper, multi-foil, polyurethane, polyisocyanurate, expanded polystyrene and wood-fibre board.

Russell has also installed solar thermal panels. He has avoided on site electricity as he believes micro-wind turbines and solar voltaic panels are not yet cost-effective for mass installation. He has, however, installed a weather station on the roof of the house to show just how much natural resource is available for such technologies and to monitor how each insulation material reacts to changes in external conditions.

To reduce water consumption he is harvesting rainwater and has installed water-efficient appliances with the aim of achieving a 60 per cent reduction.

light bulbs through supermarkets and free loft insulation to the over-70s. Going beyond this, there are a number of homes that have been retrofitted to high energy-efficiency standards. Just one example is Parity Projects, Carshalton Grove, in south London.

Retrofitting renewable energy systems is usually not as easy or cost-effective as basic energy-efficiency measures, but there are opportunities and these will grow as new technologies come to the fore. Solar thermal panels are becoming relatively common and are definitely worth considering, but payback periods still remain between 10 and 20 years. Wood and wood-pellet stoves are also gaining market share, particularly as a supply chain for wood pellets has emerged. At the level of individual homes, wood and pellet stoves are often selected for the lifestyle benefit and the inarguable homeliness of a real fire – home is where the hearth is! In places where homes don't have access to mains gas, wood-fired systems can be a cost-effective option if replacing oil or electric heating; and some municipal authorities like Barnsley, a former coal-mining town in the north of England, have converted their coal-fired district heating systems to run on woodchip from local forestry and tree-surgery waste.

Uptake of photovoltaics has been slow even with government grants, which is not surprising as capital costs remain very high and payback periods in excess of 50 to 75 years. We will need to see a tenfold reduction in cost – or a massive hike in energy prices – before photovoltaics make economic sense. Unfortunately, the evidence emerging from installations of building-mounted wind turbines is that they are not very efficient because of the turbulence and reduced wind speed around buildings, as well as the need to structurally reinforce buildings to support them. However, technologies do change and we should retain an open mind for all these technologies in future. Heat pumps potentially have an important place in retrofit – particularly air-source heat pumps as they don't require the extensive underground piping required with ground-source that remains expensive to retrofit. At a community scale there is considerable scope for retrofitting district heating which has been done on a large scale in countries like Denmark. Possibilities exist in the UK, such as proposals to take the waste heat from the gas-fired power station at Barking in the London Thames Gateway. Barking Power Station was commissioned in 1995 and uses relatively modern combined cycle gas turbine (CCGT) technology to generate a massive 1,000 megawatts of electricity – sufficient to power almost two million homes. However, 40 per cent of the energy in the natural gas (some 400 megawatts) is lost as waste heat. Plans from the London Development Agency involve piping the heat as hot water ultimately to around 120,000 homes.

Retrofitting One Planet lifestyles

From the early chapters in this book, we know sustainable living is more than reducing CO_2 emissions from homes – we need to think about food, waste and transport as well. It is possible for anyone to start pulling together a One Planet lifestyle for themselves, but this is not always very easy. People can try to give up their cars, but this can cause difficulty if there are no car clubs nearby. Can we start bringing together the products and services more coherently to make it easy for Jo(e) Public?

Of course we can. There is no reason why we can't systematically and comprehensively retrofit green lifestyles by providing car clubs, farmers' markets, recycling, local vegetable box deliveries, organic food, green energy supply and recycled products.

Colleagues at BioRegional have been working on a few initiatives to start making it easy. These include:

- creating a One Planet tool which helps people measure their footprint and helps them to develop a plan for themselves based on the 10 One Planet principles;
- working with the UK's largest home improvement (DIY) retailer, B&Q, to promote the One Planet Home, directing consumers to products in store which can help them reduce their ecological footprint; and
- working with local authorities such as the London Borough of Sutton to use the 10 One Planet principles to create a municipal-wide sustainability action plan.

Other municipal authorities are now looking to follow Sutton's lead in adopting One Planet. These include Middlesbrough Council, Brighton and Hove City Council, and the City of Rohnert Park in California.

One Planet Living Footprint Calculator

The One Planet Living Footprint Calculator is for anyone. It involves an online questionnaire developed using modelling data from the Stockholm Environment Institute at York (SEI York) to calculate an individual's ecological footprint and carbon emissions. There are two options: a quick and easy version (five minutes) or the full calculator (15 minutes), which gives more accurate results and a detailed action plan.

After calculating impacts, a personalised sustainability action plan can be produced, packed with practical things to do to achieve One Planet Living. This includes links to useful information and products to make it easier to shrink one's footprint. Users are invited to create an account and log in to tick off daily tasks which help to reduce their footprint such as:

- Do a weekly shop at your local farmers' market to find food sold by the producers in your local area.
- When buying everyday products look for recycled materials, such as foil, toilet paper, stationery, furnishings and tableware.
- If you get panniers or a basket for your bicycle you'll be amazed at how much shopping you can carry (without much more effort!)
- To attract wildlife to your garden leave an undisturbed area of it and try drilling holes in pruned branches and logs to provide insects with shelter and nesting space.

Courtesy of BioRegional Development Group – www.bioregional.com

One Planet
Living
Footprint
Calculator

Work out your
ecological
footprint
and get a
sustainability
action plan

Get started

B&Q One Planet Home

Britain's largest DIY retailer, B&Q, recently launched the One Planet Home product range to help its customers to live more sustainably, and to reduce their ecological footprint by up to 10 per cent. The One Planet Home product range consists of over 2,000 products which have been assessed by BioRegional against the 10 One Planet principles.

B&Q has introduced a One Planet Home Starter Kit which should have an immediate impact on household bills. For an initial outlay of £333 on B&Q's new One Planet Home range, the firm claim you could save over £1,000 a year on household expenses. The One Planet Home Starter Kit includes five basic components that could save an average three-bedroom terraced house with a garden £1,050 on energy, water and food bills. These include loft insulation to equivalent 270 millimetres, energy-saving light bulbs for the entire house, a water butt, a washing line instead of tumble drying, and vegetable seeds that go towards your 'five-a-day' recommended fruit and fresh vegetable intake.

BioRegional and B&Q have also worked to make sure that customers are supported in their eco-choices. A range of One Planet Home information leaflets and an insulation DVD are also available in stores. An online One Planet Living Footprint Calculator is also provided so that people can work out their ecological footprint and get a personalised action plan to help to shrink it.

The public response has been very good – and sales of loft insulation have been going through the roof!

One Planet Sutton

The London Borough of Sutton, home to BedZED, was the first local authority to adopt the One Planet Living principles. In May 2005, the borough's Strategy Committee, working with BioRegional, made the following statement: 'Building on Sutton's reputation as a greener, cleaner borough, the new Environmental Sustainability Team is recommending that we set a vision for Sutton to be a One Planet Living borough within the next 20 years.'

A workshop with departments will develop a sustainability action plan (SAP) to common international targets set by BioRegional to achieve a reduction in ecological footprint to the One Planet level. The sustainability action plan was submitted for borough-wide consultation via public meetings and a website. Having received resident feedback, the revised plan was presented to the borough Executive Committee for scrutiny by its various departments.

A number of initiatives have been established to promote One Planet Living in the borough. For example, urban regeneration plans for the Hackbridge area have been drawn up using the One Planet Living framework and any planning applications now have to make reference to this. A website has been created where residents can find out about One Planet Living, the 10 principles and how the borough's One Planet plan has been developed. Residents can also see targets of each of the principles, see how they can help to support those targets and find out about case studies from around the world so that they can see that they are not alone in their move towards sustainability (see Appendix 2 p 209).

Municipal retrofit in Freiburg

In 1986, Freiburg, a German city with a population of over 200,000 people, adopted a renewable energy strategy. Since then, the municipal council has introduced a scheme to insulate existing homes, and all new houses built on city land must meet energy-efficiency design standards. Concentrating on solar power, Freiburg now has over 400 photovoltaic installations, as well as solar thermal systems and sun rooms or 'winter gardens'. The city has also introduced widespread cycling plans, constructing over 500 kilometres of bicycle paths and promoting 'bike and ride' schemes linked to the tram system as well as a low-cost flat-rate 'Environment Ticket' on the buses. Freiburg is now often described as Germany's ecological capital and has become home to a number of environmental institutions and businesses. The city recognises it still has a long way to go, with solar energy generating only 2 per cent of its energy needs, so it is now looking at major wind developments and woodchip from the Black Forest.

Sustainable suburban retrofit – and the concept of the suburban village

Arguably suburbia is the least sustainable model of living we have with high ecological footprints driven by high car-dependence and relative affluence.[2] Suburbia also has a massive land take and its anonymous character has been the subject of much criticism, though obviously a high proportion of people choose to live in it. Our challenge is to marry the benefits of suburbia, such as green space, with sustainability. High car-dependence in the suburbs may seem hard to tackle with the low densities making public transport and car clubs difficult to operate cost-effectively. What might be a solution? We often talk about urban villages and of course we have rural villages, but could we develop the concept of the suburban village?

Perhaps we can take existing, extensive, even-grained, monotonous suburbs and punctuate them every kilometre or so with 'suburban village centres' – of higher density with key facilities such as convenience stores and a mix of community facilities, childcare centres, offices and apartments. By creating such centres, we can provide facilities within an easy walk of 500 metres – creating convenient five-minute living. These suburban village centres could be home to car clubs and local business hubs, and hold farmers' markets.

Targeted intervention to create a One Planet suburban village

A short concept study was carried out by BioRegional Quintain and architects Feilden Clegg Bradley Studios. Typical suburban densities at, say, 20 houses to the hectare fail to build communities, lead to excessive energy use for running both households and cars, make poor use of the scarce availability of the land, and do not provide a sustainable future. In particular there is a wastage of space devoted to cars – streets become roads, ie spaces for cars and not people – and quite often back-garden space is underused and unproductive.

Could a set of key interventions be developed to enable such a transformation to One Planet Living? One possible set of measures could be as follows:

- Introduction of a community centre and e-business hub with 30 apartments to add a sustainability heart and to generate funds through development profit.
- Use some of the funds from development to remodel the streets and gardens.
- Turn over half the road infrastructure to shared gardens, reducing parking space, introducing car clubs (including electric and biodiesel vehicles) and releasing land for composting and food growing.
- Install solar thermal on individual homes and biomass heating (either individually to homes or via a district system from a boiler in the community building with pipework running through newly created semi-public space or streets).
- Use the opportunity to install high-speed optic-fibre internet cables.
- Offer low-interest loans to residents as a way to fund green upgrades to homes.
- Establish a community renewables fund to invest in renewable electricity production via off-site large-scale wind generation to make the homes zero carbon.
- Reduce private garden size and open up space for communal leisure, secured play space for children, orchards and allotments.

The intervention almost doubles the density of the site, creating a 'village edge' to a formerly suburban street and a new 'heart'. Modern living often does not allow time for people to manage large suburban gardens and so many might well positively enjoy small private space and more communal space. As we saw in Chapter 9, this sort of living will increase neighbourliness, reduce fear of crime and improve psychological and physical health, particularly of children. Creating such communities would increase the sense of security and enable parents to let their children play more freely in the communal areas.

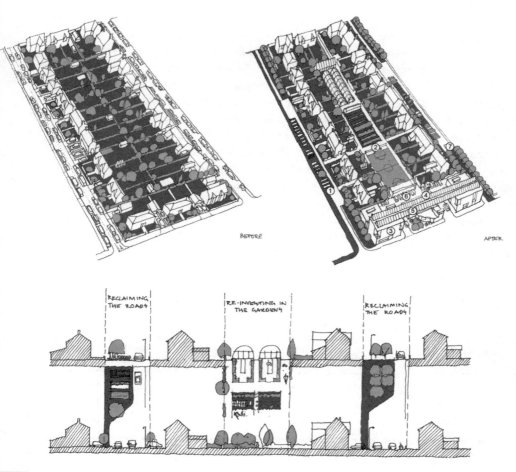

Figure 1

Concept retrofit to create a One Planet suburban village

1. Reduce number of cars and road width and relocate parking centrally. Access roads can be retained for emergency access and deliveries, but parking is provided centrally.

2. Create communal productive shared garden space for community greenhouses, allotments and secure shared play space by reducing back-garden space.

3. Remove three semi-detached houses to be replaced by 30 apartments, plus community resource building. This results in effectively almost doubling the density of the site and creating a more urban edge to a formerly suburban street.

4. Biomass heating and potentially future CHP is installed within the new development with pipework running through newly created semi-public space or streets, together with ultra-high-speed fibre internet cables.

5. New development allows for roof-space solar thermal domestic water and/or photovoltaics to service studio apartments and community building.

6. Car club run from community building with electric cars possibly charged by photovoltaics.

7. Roads reduced in width to create space for community orchards and allotments.

A simple financial analysis, as in Table 1, demonstrates how such a retrofit could be financed and that it does lead to an opportunity to reduce household expenditure of residents. Capital cost for the communal areas can be offset by income from development and green upgrades to homes via low-interest loans. As there are costs to the municipality for disposal of waste and government targets to reduce CO_2 emissions, there should be some incentive via reduction in local taxes (called the Council Tax in the UK). There are also other benefits which are real but harder to quantify such as avoided health cost, increased social capital and increased happiness.

Of course, making the concept real is another matter. Technically it is simple, but it would require the support of residents and agreement of the local authority. In a democracy we cannot underestimate the difficulty of the people issues – climate change might have come and gone before it could be achieved! However, if oil and gas prices rise substantially, and supply starts to come under severe pressure, a different sentiment may well emerge. There may also be some communities which would positively choose the sort of option outlined above and act as examples for others to follow in due course. It would be good to identify such a community.

Table 1
'Back of the envelope' financial analysis for 100 suburban homes.

Intervention	Cost per household	Communal cost	Cost per 100 households	Income
Cost of developing 30 apartments, e-business and community centre including land purchase paid for by development		£4,000,000		
Gross development value £5,000,000				
Percentage of development profit invested in local retrofit fund				£350,000
Capital costs for communal retrofit elements				
Car club start-up subsidy	-	£10,000		
Allotments	-	£10,000		
Composting area and in-vessel facility		£30,000		
Landscaping and road remodelling		£200,000		
Project management fee contribution		£100,000		
Total			**£350,000**	

Retrofit cost per household				
'Green upgrades package' to residents – funded by 10-year low-interest loan paid out of household expenditure savings				
Insulate homes	£1,000			
Solar thermal unit	£3,000			
Pellet stove and installation	£3,000			
Water-efficient makeover including butts	£500			
Community turbine investment	£1,000			
One Planet induction and training for each household	£100			
Total	£8,600		£860,000 loan for 100 homes	£1,000,000 repayment over 20 years

Weekly household expenditure	Three Planet suburbia	One Planet suburbia
Housing and mortgage	£100	£100
Home green-fit loan	-	£10
Transport (from 2 cars to 1 car, car club and public transport)	£150	£100
Energy	£20	£15
Water	£10	£7
Food (change from high meat and veg to low meat plus high-quality veg)	£60	£60
Leisure and eating out	£100	£100
Council Tax refund for reduced waste and CO_2 savings (£100 per annum)	£20	£18
Clothes, furniture and other consumables (move to fewer but higher quality)	£60	£60
Other	£50	£50
Total	£570	£520
Weekly health and happiness account		
Avoided health cost		(£10)
Increased social capital		(£10)
Increased happiness		(£10)
Overall balance	£570	£490

Climate change adaptation

Some level of climate change is inevitable because of CO_2 already released into the atmosphere. This locked-in climate change will require society to adapt to increased temperatures, intense periods of rainfall, rising sea levels and increased frequency of extreme events such as droughts, floods and storms. The severity of these is likely to increase over time. The UK government has recognised this, stating: 'It is essential that we build the potential for adaptation into design and construction methods ... Green infrastructure, for instance, has a key role to play in ensuring developments are resilient and adaptable.'[3]

The North East Climate Change Adaptation[4] study is the most detailed of its kind, providing an action plan against the projected impacts for the region. Table 2 outlines some of the considerations arising from the report.

Table 2
Summary of Actions from the North East Climate Change Adaption study

Climate change	Impacts	Area for adaptation
Increased rainfall and sea levels	Flooding	Sustainable Urban Drainage Systems
Increased rainfall and sea levels	Pollution leaching from contaminated land	Pollution control, land remediation
Warmer summers	Overheating	Natural cooling/ventilation + IT systems
Warmer summers	Pests	Waste collection/storage
Warmer summers	Tourism	Recreational use of local beaches and uplands
Warmer summers	Food	Broader range of local produce
Changed seasons	Wildlife cycles	Habitat construction and maintenance activities
Increased extreme weather	Transport services and road disruption	Transport links, updates and work-from-home options
Increased extreme weather	Debris in drainage systems	Robust drainage
Increased extreme weather	Damage to building fabric/structures	Careful consideration of materials and maintenance

The future

The impacts of climate change are almost definitely going to create major challenges for us in the 21st century. The more we prepare now, the greater the chances of us being able to face with confidence the changes that will be needed. Certainly there is the opportunity to rise to the challenges in a positive way. The next chapter speculates on how some exciting developments in technology and thinking might support us in our endeavours, possibly opening a new era for us as human beings.

Australia – urgent need for action

Australia is the driest inhabited continent and predicted to be one of the first countries in the world to suffer serious effects of global warming. With an ecology balanced right on the edge between viability and desertification, major environmental catastrophes are already being experienced. For example, years of drought combined with high levels of water use for agriculture and urban centres are resulting in the collapse of the Murray-Darling river system. So much of south and eastern Australia are dependent on this system and yet water consumption continues to rise. It is sometimes described as an Easter Island scenario unfolding before our own eyes.

Even with obvious environmental problems, Australia has not been setting a good example on the global stage in relation to reducing carbon dioxide emissions. Emissions have been growing and now stand at an enormous 21 tonnes per capita per annum, aggravated by the heavy reliance on brown coal for electricity generation. Things do not look set to improve in the near future. For example, to address the shortage of fresh water in the state of Victoria, commitment has been made to building a coal-fired desalination plant.

However, in Australia, as in many other parts of the world, there are pockets of good practice emerging due to the commitment of certain individuals and organisations. Melbourne is one city with a number of good case studies. Council House 2 has been built by the City of Melbourne and includes chilled beams, storage of coolth in phase change materials in the basement, evaporative cooling towers, automatically operated window shutters made from recycled wood and black-water treatment using ceramic filters. In the suburbs, the community at WestWyck has refurbished a former school, converting it into a green home, and constructed a new small eco-village of five townhouses and seven apartments. On a wider scale, Moreland Energy Foundation has been working with households and businesses to promote energy audits and helping to fit renewable energy systems such as solar thermal panels. Major developer Lend Lease and government land owner VicUrban have been working at the docks in

Melbourne, promoting the Flexicar car-club service and green buildings, such as 6 Green Star offices and a 'children's hub' including a playground on the roof of an energy-efficient Safeway supermarket.

In 2009, Sustainability Victoria in Melbourne launched the Zero Emissions Neighbourhood (ZEN) scheme. Recognising the importance of precinct-scale solutions rather than focusing purely on individual buildings, the scheme aims to showcase innovative precinct-scale water, waste, transport and energy solutions, such as local renewable energy supply, sustainable masterplanning and design, and energy meters to help track usage.

Notes:
1　Brenda Boardman et al, *40 percent House*, Environmental Change Institute, University of Oxford, 2005.
2　Anna Francis and Jo Wheeler, *One Planet Living in the Suburbs*, BioRegional and WWF, 2006.
3　HM Government, *Strategy for Sustainable Construction*, Chapter 9, 2008.
4　http://www.adaptne.org/.

Chapter 15

Keep one eye on the future

New green technologies will emerge, but we will also fundamentally change the way we live. By embracing change with an open mind, we can improve sustainability at the same time as increasing our levels of health and happiness. We might even be able to create communities which positively promote the health of the planet.

'The best way to predict the future is to create it.'

Anon

Green will not fade and new technologies will emerge

The world is rapidly changing. Globalisation is mixing people and cultures, often for the good, but occasionally causing conflict. There is increasing economic volatility as oil, gas and other commodity prices fluctuate, sometimes wildly.

Society's thinking on what is truly sustainable will also evolve and there won't be single solutions or right answers – the right solution in any given case will be context dependent. The future is impossible to predict in detail, but because environmental sustainability will undeniably become increasingly relevant to our societies, everyone will need to be conversant with some of its basic concepts. We will need to create a common language for sustainability. Although things will change in many ways which we cannot imagine, hopefully the philosophy and principles underpinning this book will be more enduring.

New technologies

There is huge investment, activity and enthusiasm in new, green, clean technologies. Some of these technologies will be 'disruptive', completely redefining the way we might live or work – just as mobile phones have done over the past 20 years. Indeed, we are seeing major advances in renewable energy. Progress in thin film photovoltaics and concentrated solar power promises to reduce the cost of solar generation to make it competitive with brown electricity. Plans are being drawn up for solar farms in the deserts of North Africa with this solar electricity transported to Northern Europe via massive DC copper cables with minimal loss of energy.

Algal bio-oils are being developed to offer cost-effective alternatives to fossil fuels for vehicles and because they can be grown in saltwater, without competing for land needed for food growing.

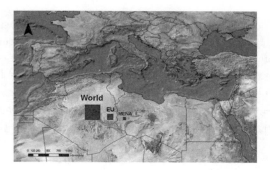

Figure 1
The area needed to provide all of the world's, Europe's or the Middle East and North Africa's electricity needs via concentrated solar power.

Figure 2
The Sahara Forest Project proposed by Exploration Architecture Ltd, Max Fordham LLP and Seawater Greenhouse Ltd uses solar power to convert seawater or briny groundwater to fresh water for growing fruit and vegetables. Such desert farms can export electricity as well as food.

Electric and hydrogen vehicles are being launched by major car manufacturers. Massive offshore wind farms are being constructed. Peak load reduction strategies and storage technologies such as advanced batteries, compressed air and high-performance flywheels are being developed to overcome limitations of the intermittent nature of renewable energy generation. Farms are being proposed which take briny groundwater in the Sahara to generate tonnes of fruit and vegetables. New materials such as bioplastics and carbon ceramics are being advanced from renewable rather than fossil resources.

Some green technologies being heralded today won't stand the test of time and parts of the clean technology boom will collapse in the way of the dot.com bubble. We will also always need to be alert to greenwash.

Will technology deliver the solutions?

There is no doubt that technology will play an important role in creating a sustainable future.[1] Technologies are also being proposed to prevent climate change and 'save the planet' – everything from mirrors in space diverting solar energy from the earth, to machines creating artificial clouds to prevent the surface of the planet from overheating. However, by itself, technology will not be enough. We have a growing population and steadily growing ecological footprint, so even if we generate all our energy from renewables, it does not mean, for instance, that there will be enough land on the planet to feed us if we rely on intensively reared meat. In order not to lose the benefits of new clean technologies, we will need to ensure technology is integrated into a whole sustainable lifestyle with concomitant behaviour change, creating a way of living and a culture integrated more or less harmoniously with natural systems.

One Planet principles can add coherence

It will be important that we create a common language in what has become the noisy and confused world of sustainability. One Planet Living is a simple philosophy, a story and a set of principles which can act as DNA from which sustainability can emerge, not least to create One Planet Communities. Its principles can be used to help create a clear framework for sustainability for a person, estate or municipality; and they can guide the development of products, services and processes or companies – creating a linking framework (Figure 3). One Planet Living can potentially bring together behaviour change, local infrastructure and government spending, which as we saw in Chapter 1 are the three determinants of a person's ecological footprint. One Planet Living also provides an easy and visual way to communicate the message of sustainability, enabling everyone to understand the end goal. It will be interesting to see how One Planet Communities emerge and spread in the coming years. I hope in reading this book, you will see value in the One Planet concept and its principles and use them yourself.

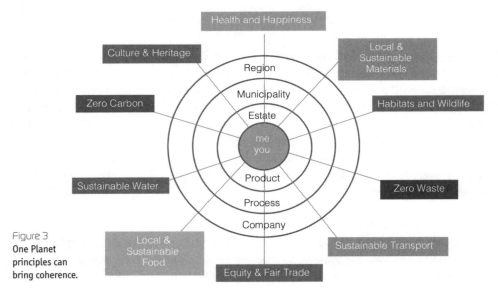

Figure 3
One Planet
principles can
bring coherence.

The need for elegant regulation

How can we make sure that sustainability flows through our society systemically and that we phase out less sustainable ways of doing things? Many organisations, private and public, have been slow to respond to the environmental agenda. This has led many environmental NGOs to lobby for increasing regulation and more environmental standards.

However, greater regulation and more standards are not always better. They have their place, but all regulation and standards have perverse effects. We need to understand these perverse effects so that on balance the positives far outweigh the negatives. One example might be a requirement for all wood products to be Forest Stewardship Council (FSC) certified. However the cost of certification is high so the small-scale local independent woodland worker who might be managing his or her woodland extremely well may be barred from supplying the market even though his or her product might be the most sustainable option by far. There are small-scale farmers who have experienced similar issues with certified Organic Standards. We must always leave room for discretion and common sense.

In the case of buildings, independent standards such as BREEAM, LEED and the UK's Code for Sustainable Homes are increasingly being written into regulations and adopted as planning requirements. At the higher levels of these standards, particularly, say, the Code for Sustainable Homes in its current iteration, the requirements can be so prescriptive that the right solution is not implemented. For example, requirements for on site or directly connected renewable energy generation are forcing the creation of homes which are actually *less* environmentally friendly. We saw in Chapter 1 how the proliferation of green regulations, standards, codes and guidelines – from individual buildings and components to planning and environmental issues – is not only compromising good design and innovation, but adding unnecessarily to costs. BioRegional Quintain's own experience is that we are finding ourselves spending more time and money on writing environmental reports than installing green technologies. It is almost criminal. To some extent contradictions in regulations and standards are inevitable, but increasing the level of detail will not improve the situation. It will simply make everything more complicated, innovation more difficult, planning more expensive and the process totally joyless. It is only the practical experience of innovating which enables one fully to appreciate how the good intentions of regulation have made the system so incredibly irksome and counterproductive.

We must take this opportunity to start simplifying and rationalising. If we really wish successfully to create sustainable communities, we need to recognise that industries such as property development are complex dynamic systems which need to evolve. In complex dynamic systems not everything can be measured or managed. We must therefore not rely too heavily on the approach favoured by so many professional managers and politicians who say: 'If you can't measure it, you can't manage it.' Complex and dynamic systems are not amenable to this arguably impoverished outlook which leads to the straitjacketed, uncreative and unresponsive world of performance indicators, targets and standards. It may be true that you can't manage what you can't measure, but not everything of value is measurable. It is not easy to measure innovation or creativity and difficult to set targets for it. We might evolve a better approach; much like bringing out the best in children, or raising trees, perhaps we should try not so much to manage the development industry as to nurture it.

Taking this nurturing approach, how then should we look at standards and regulation? They can have an important role to play, but I suggest it is primarily to maintain *minimum* standards, ensuring that what is unacceptable does not happen: 'regs for the dregs' as it is sometimes described. Standards may well have a role in improving general levels of performance, but we must recognise that true excellence, which is what we need for real change – and involves pushing boundaries – can *never* be driven through standards or regulation. Trying to legislate for this will only add to green tape and hobble those wishing truly to excel. Therefore government and NGOs should not try to define or force excellence, but should work with committed practitioners to ensure that regulation is simple, clear and carefully targeted (what we might call 'elegant regulation'). Excellence on the other hand is best brought out by encouragement and nurturing – through incentives like grants and concessions (for example, grants for innovation or releasing public funds specifically for pioneering projects), competitions, and financial and fiscal incentives (such as reducing or eliminating VAT on green products). Taking this approach, over time, the industry will change and we can make progress by using the learning from excellence to raise the minimum standards. This approach gives the time and space for the system to evolve, for knowledge to be internalised, and for supply chains to align and the solutions to emerge.

We need a common language and coherence, but as we have seen this cannot be imposed purely in a top-down fashion through regulation and standards. We need to change from the inside and this will only be successful by embedding sustainability – by changing the DNA of the design and development process, as well as the culture and knowledge of every single person working within it. If we can do this, we will have created a system where sustainability emerges naturally – as an emergent property of the system. If we want to build a sports car, it is better to start from scratch, than to take an off-road vehicle and try to convert it. The same can be said about sustainable communities. We will always end up with an unsatisfactory product if we take a conventional approach and bolt on solutions and regulations. We need new DNA and ultimately I hope some seeds of this – based on the work of many people – are contained in this book.

Stepping back: beyond One Planet Living?

It is always useful every few years to step back, reflect on assumptions and check your bearings by starting from scratch again. In 1998, we started working to make BedZED a reality. In 2002, as BedZED was being completed, we had started to learn its lessons. Going back to the drawing board led us to build on what we had learnt, but to realign to zero carbon zero waste concepts and develop the One Planet Living approach. In 2008, six years on and with the first One Planet Communities under construction, we started this review process again.

The One Planet Living approach does appear to be powerful. Using ecological footprinting as a key indicator is giving us a good perspective on where to invest our efforts. It is enabling us to deliver high levels of sustainability cost-effectively, such as at One Brighton. However, emerging scientific evidence is telling us that the environmental challenge is greater than we thought. The scale of the challenge of climate change is gradually dawning on us. Levels of CO_2 in the atmosphere are 40 per cent higher than they were in the Ice Age.[2] In 2000, the Royal Commission on Environmental Pollution proposed an atmospheric concentration of greenhouse gases of 550 parts per million (ppm) as a target to contain climate change within 2°C.[3] Lord Stern's report for the UK government in 2006 looked at a target of stabilising greenhouse gases of 500 to 550 ppm.[4] However, the UK's former Chief Scientific Advisor is recommending no more than 450 ppm as the safe limit.[5] We are already at 430 ppm and locked into continuing rises for the foreseeable future. To reflect this change in our understanding of the threat of climate change, our horizons must change. What are the new frontiers which come into view?

Starting from the beginning, sustainability itself is an odd concept. The planet has always been dynamic and changing. So it is not that we should preserve nature or the status quo, because life on the planet is a process of irreversible change and human beings are inextricably part of that change. Do we need to look at our place on the planet in a new light?

Human society's great scientific and technological achievements – from ancient cities to the moon landings – disguise a fundamental truth which only becomes apparent when we look back on ourselves from space. Our tenure as human beings on this planet is a precarious one. If we represent the earth as a circle one metre across, the breathable atmosphere is thinner than the pencil line used to draw it. It is not some comforting bubble around us; rather, at less than 4.8 kilometres deep it is no more than a thin film. The whole biosphere – the living part of the earth – is a tenuous fabric, not much more than an ephemeral dividing line between a hot planetary core and a deeply cold and hostile space.

No one has seen and expressed this view of life and earth better than Professor James Lovelock, the originator of the Gaia Hypothesis.[6] A brilliant chemist and, in a profession now as rare as hen's teeth, an independent scientist, he started to evolve a view of life which brings together biology and geology – and a recognition that each has co-evolved with the other on earth – creating a complex, dynamic, highly interdependent and somewhat self-regulating system. Lovelock started to form this view when, as a scientist engaged by NASA, he was asked to consider how to identify life on another planet. His key insight was to ask the question: 'How would we know there was life on earth if we were alien beings scanning our solar system?'

The answer lay in the observation that the atmosphere of earth is not in chemical equilibrium. The earth's atmosphere exists *because* of life, life does not exist because of the atmosphere as we might usually assume. Indeed the composition of the earth's atmosphere is very far from what one would expect on an inert planet – most notably the presence of high levels of oxygen is a key indicator of the presence of life at this stage of its natural history. The composition of the atmosphere is dependent, for example, on the photosynthetic activity of plants, but plants themselves would not have come into being without calcium having been removed from the seas by the action of bacteria in the primordial seas. The *history* of life on earth is as significant as the presence of life. Over eons, the land and sea has been shaped by a complex interaction and co-evolution of life, rocks and atmosphere – bacteria and methane, algae and carbon dioxide, phytoplankton and limestones, stomatolites and animals, formaninifera with plate tectonics. This science has become known as geophysiology, from which has evolved the idea of seeing the planet at some level as a single regulating system, or more controversially, a single organism – the Gaia Hypothesis, named after the Greek goddess of the earth.

In the context of our current fears of global warming, the surface temperature of the planet is far cooler than we would expect of a dead planet. If our planet were dead – without life changing its composition – its equilibrium temperature would be 40°C at which temperature there would be much less life on the planet.[7] In fact, the planet is on average 20°C, at which temperature our land and seas support an abundance of fish, fruiting plants, big cats, dinoflagellates, comb jellies, great apes and an inordinate number of beetles. It is on this natural abundance that we have built our civilisation. If we tease apart the living fabric of the earth, the composition of the atmosphere changes and the temperature will flip to a higher state, just as happened at the close of the last Ice Age when temperatures rose 5°C in the space of a few years, at the end of the period known as the Younger Dryas.[8] The next stable temperature is 5°C hotter than the current temperature of the planet. At this higher temperature we lose many of the currents in the ocean which mix nutrients and keep it healthy. Much of the land in the tropics turns to desert. Sea levels rise 20 to 30 metres and we are left with thin strips of the planet suitable for human habitation near the poles and a planet which can support maybe not much more than 500 million people.

What might this mean for us as we seriously consider how to build the communities of the future? The shape and extent of large planned city extensions such as the Thames Gateway might need to be rethought in the light of more rapid changes in sea level than previously predicted. Low-lying populations from New Orleans to the Maldives may have to move (as they are already doing), but more rapidly than we thought. The effects of climate change are already with us. The devastating forest fires in Australia in 2009 follow record-breaking heatwaves on top of drought. It has even been suggested that troubled areas of the world such as Darfur have been created in great part by climate change leading to pressures on land and food precipitating social strife. What happens if, as some predict, the monsoon rains start to fail for countries such as India that are already reaching the limits of food production?

Runaway climate change is a real possibility as certain feedback loops start to kick in, such as the thawing of the Siberian tundra releasing millions of tonnes of methane, enhancing global warming and in turn resulting in further release of methane. The geopolitical consequences are unimaginable.

But there may still be hope! Where might this hope come from? We have discussed some of them in this book, but as we move forward, the key observations I suggest we use to guide us are:

- We have got richer but not happier. Can we fundamentally design and run our communities and societies to promote health and happiness rather than the growth in material wealth which is devastating our planet?
- As we have seen so clearly from the events of 2007–8, an over-globalised economy is a wrecking ball, where the natural controls based on personal trust inherent in local trade have been lost in faceless international transactions. The naturally resilient communities of the future will need to have a large part of their economy based on local trade.
- It is now not enough to create communities which don't damage the planet. Communities must now positively create a healthier planet which is conducive to supporting human life. We might call this 'earth repair', but it should not be a separate function, an 'end-of-pipe' solution, putting right ongoing damage. It must be a natural function and outcome of the everyday activities of our communities.

We can look at each of these three areas in turn.

Happier communities

We have seen how we can create happier communities, for instance, by reducing car dependence and creating places for neighbourly interaction. This approach brings about the best in human nature and is more suited to the nature of human beings. We have also seen how material wealth, beyond the basics, does not increase happiness but instead – promoting competition and consumerism – results in avarice and unhappiness. We have also seen how more equitable communities are generally happier.

It is not difficult for us to create low-car and car-free communities with good public spaces. We can try ourselves to become happier and less consumerist, and to spread this attitude informally to those around us. More formally we can educate people and children in particular perhaps – building One Planet Living schools – on how to be happier and less consumerist. If necessary, we could simply and strictly control advertising, for example, or in some cases ban it. We can promote equity through education and culture supported by fiscal policies such as progressive taxation. We can promote and celebrate entrepreneurship where the rewards are not seen as purely financial, but also social and environmental.

But could we go further? I remember in my school days in the 1970s with computers just coming into everyday use, the greatest challenge we thought we would face would be what to do with our leisure time. How wrong we were! We are working longer hours than ever before. Instead of technology assisting us, in many ways we have become slaves to technology. Can we reclaim our position? In a less materialist world where we are not striving to earn more all the time, we could have the freedom to move communities to a four-day working week, making the fifth day a community and family day which would benefit the economy long term.

Economies integrated into local ecology and promoting health

Although we have been warned many times in the past, we still rely too heavily on conventional economic indicators such as GDP. Robert F Kennedy famously and eloquently put it as follows:

> We cannot measure national spirit by the Dow Jones Average, nor national achievement by the Gross National Product. For the Gross National Product includes air pollution, and ambulances to clear our highways from carnage ... The Gross National Product includes the destruction of the redwoods and the death of Lake Superior. It grows with the production of napalm and the missiles and nuclear warheads ... It includes the broadcasting of television programs which glorify violence to sell goods to our children.[9]

Conventional thought on economic development is not currently linked to the health of natural systems, nor indeed to how people naturally operate. This fundamental disconnection is a problem. The collapse of the global financial system is in great part due to loss of trust, blamed on a failure of governments to regulate sufficiently. However, we accept that the artifice of regulation of trade and financial systems can never replace the natural policing offered by personal trust. It might be worth looking at the success of micro-credit schemes such as that offered by the Grameen Bank to villagers in Bangladesh, where the security of loan repayment is primarily based on the peer pressure of neighbours.[10] This drives us again to a more balanced local trading model as discussed in Chapter 7. When this local trade is based on the use of local renewable and recycled resources, we have bioregional economics, wherein lies the seed of hope for an integrated and sustainable economy.

Could we cement this form of economic development with local currencies as proposed, for example, by Richard Douthwaite in his book *The Ecology of Money*?[11] The fundamentals of conventional economic thought are now very much out-of-date and belong in the 20th century when the challenges and aspirations were different. It is based too heavily on assumptions such as that humans make rational decisions which is simply not consistent with our everyday experience, and creates a way of thinking which is divorced from how people behave.[12] New ways of looking at economic systems such as complexity economics are starting to create models which are closer to reality. Conventional economic thought also promotes global markets and global competitiveness – but for what purpose? To create wealth? We know that it has mainly moved resources from poor countries, such as Africa, to rich ones and not made rich countries any happier. That is not to say we shouldn't have international trade, but a locally based economy can be better for people and the environment.

Creating a healthier, happier and more sustainable society does ultimately have economic benefits. Increasingly we are seeing economic arguments used to justify moves for building communities less dependent on the car, for instance. Perhaps we might also find ways to harvest the financial benefits of health and happiness to incentivise developers to take on the ideas and strategies.

There are ways in which the avoided costs in physical and mental healthcare, waste management and climate change could be converted to income streams. Of course, we have carbon trading. More incentives for recycling such as rebates perhaps on local taxes could offer great opportunities for estates-management companies. Could rebates also be offered based on increasing walking and cycling or the sale of healthy food? Using data from actuarial analysis as a basis for calculating health and life insurance premiums might be interesting. Indeed, health insurance companies like PruHealth have been offering to pay membership at Virgin Active gyms. To quote PruHealth: 'If you're making an effort to lead a healthy lifestyle we believe you're likely to live longer and make fewer claims. So we think it's only fair that we help you pay for your gym membership.'

So there are ways to cross-market and cross-subsidise, even on a business-to-business basis, to promote health.

Oil to soil: communities that create a healthy atmosphere
Communities now must not only reduce or eliminate CO_2 emissions, but go further to removing CO_2 from the atmosphere. We saw in Chapter 5 that we can describe cities and communities in terms of their metabolism. We can create sustainable communities by replacing fossil fuel energy with renewable energy from sources such as wind, solar and biomass, and moving to zero waste through closed-loop recycling of waste streams. Developments such as One Brighton and Masdar City, built on a compact city form, go even further in being car-free communities, and this increases their energy efficiency. Can we conceive of cities and communities of the future which have a physiology where the metabolism is such that they contribute positively to the health of the planet?

One possibility is cities run with a base load of energy coming from the carbonisation of agricultural and forestry wastes (such as wheat and rice straw and sawmill offcuts), or even possibly algae – providing heat and power with charcoal as a by-product.

Plant material heated in the range of 270°C to 500°C yields wood gases and tars, leaving the carbon skeleton of the plant as more or less pure carbon – or charcoal. The wood gases can be used to generate electricity and heat, for example, through a gas turbine. The yield of charcoal is between 30 and 50 per cent of the dry biomass weight. Charcoal has interesting properties. If mixed in the soil its large internal surface area adsorbs nutrients and moisture and acts as a substrate for microbial activity. The soil-improving properties of the charcoal can be enhanced by 'charging' the charcoal with compost, manure or urine. In tropical regions this can increase the fertility of the soil, as was recognised by Indians of the Amazon who produced the so-called Terra Preta, or dark soils.[13]

Charcoal is resistant to decomposition in the soil so that each tonne of charcoal stored in the soil removes between 3 and 3.7 tonnes of CO_2 from the atmosphere. Considerable work is being done in this area, for example, through the International Biochar Initiative. With biomass yields of, say, 3 to 10 dry tonnes per hectare, each hectare could generate 1 to 5 tonnes of charcoal per year, locking away the equivalent of, say, 3 to 15 tonnes per hectare per year.

Taking a low figure for biomass production of 3 dry tonnes of biomass processed through a 'charcoal, heat and power' plant as proposed by engineers such as Dr Gabriel Gallagher and his colleagues at Sustainable Energy Consulting and BioEnergy Devices Ltd, would mean a hectare could yield 1,350 kilowatt hours of electricity, 5,400 kilowatt hours of heat and 4 tonnes of CO_2 sequestration per year. This is enough to meet the energy needs of one person leading a high-quality life in an energy-efficient home as well as allowing for carbon offsetting for personal travel.

Can we then imagine cities of communities getting their energy from biomass, creating charcoal as a metabolite which is buried in the soil to increase its fertility and generate more biomass? Such a city, just going about its everyday business, would pump excess CO_2 out of the atmosphere. In effect, the city would be converting CO_2 in the atmosphere, released by burning of fossil fuels, into a product to improve fertility of the land – oil to fertile soil. Indeed, Professor Lovelock believes that burial of carbon is our best chance of avoiding major climate change.

It will be tight. With a total of about 9 billion hectares of forest, cropland and pasture on the planet, we would have about 1 hectare per person by the time population growth levels off. However, we might be able to combine the biochar approach with other key strategies such as biodiesel from algae, car-free cities, low-impact food and integrating forestry and farming (so-called agroforestry) to reduce land requirement fourfold. If we are lucky we might not only be able to drive down CO_2 from the atmosphere, but also free large tracts of land to be left to wildlife for its own devices and provide what might be an essential function in self-regulation of the planet as postulated in the Gaia Hypothesis.

Although it sounds revolutionary, one day all this might come to be seen as mundane. However, from where we are now, the result would be a fundamental change in the physiology of human society – much as happened once with forest clearances by earlier farmers and again following the Industrial Revolution. However, this time, rather than a physiology which destabilises Gaia and the atmosphere, such a society could positively contribute to the health of the planet.

Could we even consider ourselves emerging into what would amount to a new species, one which has positively and consciously changed its physiology in recognition of its place as part of a wider living system on which it depends for everything including climatic regulation? *Homo sapiens indraensis* perhaps – after the Hindu god of weather, and supreme god, Indra, whose palace was hung with pearls, with every pearl reflecting every other pearl demonstrating the interconnectedness of things.

Notes:
1 Chris Goodall, *Ten Technologies to Save the Planet*, GreenProfile (London), 2008.
2 Gabrielle Walker and Sir David King, *The Hot Topic*, Bloomsbury (London), 2008.
3 Sir Tom Blundell, *Energy – The Changing Climate*, Royal Commission on Environmental Pollution, 2000.
4 Nicholas Stern, *The Economics of Climate Change*, HM Treasury Cabinet Office, 2006.
5 Gabrielle Walker and Sir David King, op cit.
6 James Lovelock, *The Ages of Gaia: A Biography of Our Living Earth*, Bantam (New York), 1989.
7 James Lovelock, *The Vanishing Face of Gaia*, Allen Lane (London), 2009.
8 Jeffrey Severinghaus et al, 'Timing of Abrupt Climate Change at the End of the Younger Dryas Interval from Thermally Fractionated Gases in Polar Ice', *Nature* 391, 1998, pp 141–60.
9 Senator Robert F Kennedy, Presidential Campaign Address, University of Kansas, 18 March 1968.
10 www.grameenfoundation.org.
11 Richard Douthwaite, *The Ecology of Money*, Schumacher Briefing No 4, Green Books (Totnes), 2000.
12 Eric Beinhocker, *Origin of Wealth: Evolution, Complexity, and the Radical Remaking of Economics*, Harvard Business School Press, 2006.
13 J Lehmann, 'Black is the New Green', *Nature*, 442, 2006, pp 624–60.

One Brighton Sustainability Action Plan

Zero Carbon	Reducing carbon dioxide emissions by optimising building energy demand and supplying from zero carbon and renewable resources
Strategy	
Over-arching Zero Carbon Plan developed	•Strategy developed that facilitates a net carbon-neutral development through addressing demand and supply issues •Zero carbon strategy to ensure percentage energy saving in excess of 40% site-wide target for New England Quarter •Targets developed in line with One Planet Living Communities international targets •Targets developed with reference to EcoHomes and BREEAM standards which support achieving 'Excellent' ratings overall •Target for net CO_2 emissions associated with providing heat and power for proposed development to be zero •Target for CO_2 emissions (as defined under EcoHomes) for residential elements of proposed development to be < 25kg/m^2/annum •Target for space heating demands for residential elements of scheme to be less than 30 kWhr/m^2/annum •Target for energy consumption for hot water heating for residential elements of scheme to be less than 45 kWhr/m^2/annum •Target for electrical consumption (including ventilation) for residential elements of scheme to be less than 45 kWh/m^2/annum

Approach	D	C	D/C	Mechanism	Notes
High thermal performance standards of built form	√ √ √			•Insulation levels to be in excess of 2002 Building Regulation minimums. Proposed external wall construction has U-value of 0.21 W/m^{2}K (40% above 2002 Building Regulations) and window U-value of 1.3 W/m^{2}K (sufficient to preclude unwanted cold down-draughts) •Window surface area for residential elements to be greater than 0.15 m^2 per m^2 of floor area •Target for air tightness of 5 m^3/hour/m^2 @ 50 pa.	
Energy-efficient appliances and fittings	√ √			•Provide A-rated appliances in homes and information to occupants on purchasing energy-efficient goods •Energy-efficient light fittings specified internally and externally to secure maximum relevant EcoHomes and BREEAM credits, and to help ensure efficient lights are used in perpetuity	
Low/Zero carbon energy generation	√			•Centralised renewable energy system providing a carbon-neutral solution *Heating and hot water*: •Biomass-fuelled boiler coupled to accumulator with back-up gas boiler. Summer-time temperatures to be limited by facade design, exposed thermal mass and night-time purge by ventilation unit *Electrical*: •PV power generation via array of small-scale building-mounted systems •Commitment to feasibility study investigating twinning development with new larger-scale wind turbine array in Brighton area •Remainder of electrical demand met via 'green tariff' supply contract between renewable utility provider with sub-metering via private wire to individual residents (currently exploring approach via 'opt out' of 28- day rule). REGO (Renewable Energy Guarantee of Origin) certified 'green tariff' selected to support the creation of new renewable capacity	Undertaken in partnership with ESCo (energy services company)
Ongoing management strategy		√		•Energy services company (ESCo) established to manage sustainable energy supply. ESCo to maintain/upgrade infrastructure and provide affordable sustainable energy to community	

Zero Waste	Reducing waste arising, then reclaiming, recycling and recovering
Strategy	
Over-arching Zero Waste Plan developed	• Strategy developed in partnership with waste contractor(s) and other local stakeholders, which supports a long-term vision for a zero waste community • Targets developed in line with One Planet Communities international targets • Target for household waste arisings to be 400kg/person/annum within 2 years of development completion (compared to 512kg/person/annum for UK in 2002/03 – Defra), with ongoing incremental reduction per annum • By 2020: 98% of household waste to be diverted from landfill (could include recycling, composting, clean energy-from-waste)

Approach	D	C	D/C	Mechanism	Notes
Reduced levels of construction waste	√ √ √ √		√ √	• Target for construction waste to be less than 15 m³ per 100 m² floor area (refer to Constructing Excellence EPI) and less than 0.2% of construction cost • Development of comprehensive construction waste management plan, potentially with use of BRE SmartWaste system. • Trust to seek opportunities to liaise with and support EcoSys (www.greenbusiness.org.uk), local schools and organisations, including retail and commercial outlets, to promote waste minimisation • Proposals developed to coordinate with local authority sustainable waste management strategy • Provide space and storage within individual homes for the storage of segregated waste • Guidance notes, collection schedules and performance details available on community extranet	In partnership with building contractor
Composting facilities	√		√ √	• Subject to securing appropriate licensing etc, it is proposed that green waste (and hopefully kitchen waste) would be segregated for either on-site treatment using the 'Bokashi Rocket' system (or similar), or for collection by local operator. • Kitchen design and storage facilities to support collection and storage of organic waste • Target to establish links between on-site non-residential occupants and existing local 'scrap stores'	
Ongoing management strategy		√ √		• Negotiation with local authority of the terms for engagement of third-party waste management contractor • Community management to take responsibility for waste/recycling obligations and undertake ongoing waste monitoring with annual reporting	

Sustainable Transport	Providing sustainable alternatives to private car use and reducing the need to travel
Strategy	
Over-arching Sustainable Transport Plan developed	• Strategy developed which supports a long-term vision for a community with minimised transport impacts • 2010 target for annual total travel distance for residents of 20% below DfT NTS benchmark, or equivalent • 2020 target for annual road vehicle travel distance for residents of 80% below DfT National Travel Survey benchmark, or equivalent • Ongoing target to reduce transport-related carbon emissions, based on a local benchmark, to level consistent with 'one planet' level by 2020

Approach	D	C	D/C	Mechanism	Notes
Reducing the need to travel	√ √		√	• Homes provided with conduits for the installation of broadband infrastructure • Development sited within close proximity to a range of existing facilities and employment opportunities • Communal internet ordering point and collection facilities for on-line orders, e.g. food boxes	
Alternatives to private car use: public transport	√ √		√ √	• Development sited within close proximity to established public transport hub – Brighton station • Information on public transport options provided as part of residents' packs and via community extranet • Work with car club and public transport operators to explore opportunities for offering limited discounted public transport travel as part of an over-arching sustainable mobility package – as part of ongoing process • Proposal to provide two charging points for electric vehicles for use by car club and/or disabled drivers vehicles	
Alternatives to private car use: car clubs	√ √ √	√	√ √ √ √	• Car club established to serve residential and commercial users • No private car parking provision – spaces provided for car-club vehicles and disabled provision only • Secure and sheltered cycle storage provided for residential and non-residential users. Cycle parking provided for communal/casual use • Showering/changing facilities provided within commercial space to secure associated BREEAM credits – as part of fit-out • Information on opportunities to walk and cycle for day-to-day journeys provided as part of residents' packs and via community extranet • Discounted cycle purchase/service vouchers offered to residents as part of over-arching Green Lifestyles Package options • Personalised sustainable travel planning session offered to residents as part of Green Lifestyles Package (potential link with local cycle group – www.bricycles.org.uk and/or to Sustrans) • Proposal that Green Transport Coordination role undertaken by Green Caretaker	With ethical property company

Sustainable and Local Materials	Materials chosen for buildings and infrastructure to give high-performance in use with minimised impact in manufacture and delivery
Strategy	
Over-arching Sustainable and Local Materials Plan developed	• Strategy developed which supports a long-term vision for a community with optimised material life-cycle impacts • For further information on Sustainable and Local Materials strategy refer to Design Statement • Targets developed in-line with One Planet Communities international targets • Plan to include a method statement on the opportunities for designing for deconstruction • Target for embodied CO_2 to be less than $700kg/m^2$ (excluding any energy/ventilation plant, eg wind turbines) • Target for 25% of materials to come from recycled/reclaimed sources (including recycled aggregate)

Approach	D	C	D/C	Mechanism	Notes
Materials with low embodied energy	√ √			• Life-cycle methodology and 'whole life costing' approach to be used alongside other parameters to inform selection of materials • Embodied energy/CO_2 audit to be undertaken	With building contractor
'Healthy' and non-toxic materials	√			• Within the materials specification: PVC use will be minimised, MDF containing formaldehyde will be prohibited, materials with greater low levels of volatile organic compounds (VOCs) will be prohibited, materials with ozone depleting potential or a global warming potential >5 will be prohibited	With building contractor
Specifying sustainable timber	√			• All timber products will be specified in accordance with securing maximum credits under BREEAM and EcoHomes, with priority given to FSC-certified timber	With building contractor
Specifying local materials	√			• Subject to life-cycle analysis, the use of local construction products (considered to be within a 50-mile radius) will be optimised within the materials specification	With building contractor
Reused and recycled materials	√			• Construction specification developed to optimise opportunities for including materials from recycled and reclaimed sources, as well as those derived from waste products	With building contractor
Multi-skilling approach	√			• BioRegional Quintain is committed to adopting a 'multi-skilling' approach to construction to facilitate increased efficiencies arising from reduced build time and wastage. The proposed Brighton development would be used to support the evolution of the approach	
Ongoing management strategy	√			• Through its One Planet Products initiative, BioRegional Development Group is seeking to establish a buyers group for developers to bulk-purchase 'green' building products to secure the associated economy of scale benefits. BioRegional Quintain is fully supportive of this initiative and will seek to join any such buyers group when established	

Sustainable and Local Food	Consumption of local, seasonal and organic produce, with reduced amount of animal protein and packaging
Strategy	
Over-arching Sustainable and Local Food Plan developed	• Strategy developed which supports a long-term vision for a community which enables people to choose low-impact produce • Strategy developed with reference to Spade to Spoon – Brighton & Hove Food Strategy and Action Plan • For further details of Sustainable and Local Food strategy refer to appendices • Targets developed in-line with One Planet Living Communities international targets • 2020 target for at least 25% of food consumed (by weight) within the development to be sourced from within a radius of 50 km (or equivalent area) • 2020 target for at least 10% of food consumed (by weight) within the development to be from certified organic and/or fair-trade sources

Approach	D	T	D/T	Mechanism	Notes
Opportunities for on site food growing	√ √			• Roof-top mini-allotment areas to provide space for growing selected plants for food • Balconies, where provided, will include integrated planters suitable for growing selected plants for food	
Opportunities for off-site food growing			√	• Establish community garden as food growing and land restoration project	
			√ √	• Residents able to receive trial membership of local food box schemes as part of Green Lifestyles Package • The community space will be designed to include a communal internet ordering point and a secure 'drop-off' point and storage for receiving food box deliveries	
Low-impact and fresh food issues promoted			√	• As part of the community facility, a café operated by a local community group using local and seasonal produce	
Supporting fresh food preparation	√			• Encouraging fresh food preparation will be an important driver for residential kitchen design – residents to be offered steamers and juicers as part of Green Lifestyles Package	
Supporting sustainable food waste management	√ √		√	• Kitchens to include spaces suitable for compostable waste storage • 'Bokashi Rocket' composter(s), or similar, to be provided for communal use. Subject to appropriate licenses etc. Refer to Zero Waste section for further details • Resulting compost to be made available to residents with sky gardens, and for use on communal grounds where appropriate	
Ongoing management strategy		√		• The ongoing implementation and development of the Sustainable and Local Food Plan will be led by the community management	

Sustainable Water	Reduced water demand with rain and waste water managed sustainably
Strategy	
Over-arching Sustainable Water Plan developed	• Strategy developed which supports a long-term vision for a community with optimised water usage • Targets developed with reference to EcoHomes and BREEAM standards which support achieving 'Excellent' ratings overall • Target for residential water use to <100 litres/person/day from outset. Represents a 25%+ reduction on 139 litres figure for metered homes (OFWAT, Security of supply, leakage and efficient water use, 2004–05)

Approach	D	T	D/T	Mechanism	Notes
Water-efficient fittings and appliances	√ √ √			• All units to be fitted with low-flush, dual-flush WCs and water-saving taps/fittings • No 'power' showers will be specified • All provided washing machines to be higher performing water-efficient models	
Rainwater management	√ √ √			• Rainwater collected on southern block to be used for irrigation of roof terraces (as appropriate) and sky gardens. Additionally, collected rainwater used to flush demonstration WC(s) within community facility • Rainwater collected on northern block to be collected in butts for use in irrigating communal external areas • Soakaways, porous paving and other landscaping treatments to facilitate high levels of surface water attenuation	

Natural Habitats and Wildlife	Existing biodiversity conserved and opportunities taken to increase ecological value
Strategy	
Over-arching Natural Habitats and Wildlife Plan developed	• Strategy developed which supports a long-term vision for a development which optimises ecological value within an urban site • Strategy developed with reference to Brighton & Hove Sustainability Natural Environment document 2004–06, and SEEDA's Building for Nature

Approach	D	T	D/T	Mechanism	Notes
Interventions to enhance ecological biodiversity	√			• Development site is adjacent to a proposed 'greenway' which will run through the New England Quarter to provide a pleasant circulation route as well as a range of wildlife habitats Envisaged features/characteristics include: • Incorporating bird boxes and feeding points into buildings and the surrounding environment • Including areas of wildlife planting using native species where appropriate • Finishing sections of the roofscape with 'green' and/or 'brown' roofs to encourage biodiversity	
Ongoing management strategy		√ √		• Ongoing implementation of the Natural Habitats and Wildlife Plan will be managed by the community management who will advise in the appointment and remit of landscaping contractors. It is envisaged that this will include working with partners to facilitate monitoring of biodiversity levels • Green Gym opportunities with the British Trust for Conservation Volunteers (BTCV). Green Gym projects	With local wildlife groups

Culture and Heritage	Cultural heritage acknowledged and interpreted. Sense of place and identity engendered to contribute towards future heritage
Strategy	
Over-arching Culture and Heritage Plan developed	• Strategy developed which supports a long-term vision for a culturally rich community • Targets and showcased case studies developed in line with One Planet Living Communities international targets

Approach	D	T	D/T	Mechanism	Notes
	√		√ √	• Community centre provided to support community cohesion and interaction • Community extranet developed. The proposed system would have inward- and outward-facing roles. The system could be used to provide: • supporting information on sustainability issues to residents and some access to wider community • mechanisms to establish a time bank • booking mechanisms for community facilities • information on upcoming events • guidance on sustainable travel options • An events programme will be developed and supported by the community management to support engendering a sense of community identity	
Culture of sustainability		√		• The One Planet centre, provided as part of the community facility, will have support, outreach and dissemination roles. The Brighton community will be part of a growing network of international communities inspired by the One Planet Communities initiative.	
Integrating art	√			• Engage with process for site-wide New England Quarter art strategy, as appropriate	
Ongoing management strategy		√		• Requirement to review the plan periodically to ensure that it both reflects the culture and heritage of the area, promotes a culture of sustainability to all, and strives to ensure that facilities and services are promoted which support the future culture of the community	

Equity and Fair Trade	Create a sense of community. Provide accessible, inclusive and affordable facilities and services
Strategy	
Over-arching Equity and Fair Trade Plan developed	• Strategy developed which supports a long-term vision for an equitable community • Strategy developed with reference to Brighton & Hove Fairtrade city status campaign materials

Approach	D	T	D/T	Mechanism	Notes
Affordability				• In addition to working with a housing association to provide an allocation of social units, the range of private properties being developed offers opportunities for the intermediate market. In particular, the eco-studios are aimed at enabling young people in getting on to the first rung of the property ladder	
Accessibility				• All of the homes will be designed in accordance with the Lifetime Homes standard • Ramps provide high levels of accessibility for the disabled to external areas, including link to adjacent greenway. Lifts proposed to serve all internal areas	
Encouraging the local workforce				• A construction stage plan will be developed, and incorporated into construction contracts, which promotes the use of local contractors, suppliers and workforce in the development • Contractors will be required to demonstrate investment in training, apprenticeships and staff development • One Planet construction training pack will be created to disseminate the development ethos	In partnership with building contractor
Fairtrade city status				• Brighton and Hove has Fairtrade city status	
Ongoing management strategy				• Ongoing implementation of the Equity and Fair Trade Plan will be the responsibility of the community management	

Health and Happiness	Promote health and well-being. Establish long-term management and support strategies
Strategy	
Over-arching Health and Happiness Plan developed	•Strategy developed which supports a long-term vision for a healthy and happy community •Strategy developed with reference to Brighton & Hove Sustainability Economy and Work, Air Quality and Community Safety documents 2004–06 •Target to be established for night-time noise levels in line with guidance currently being developed by the World Health Organization (WHO)

Approach	D	T	D/T	Mechanism	Notes
Buildings and infrastructure designed to promote well-being	√ √			•Issues of noise pollution, access to daylight and indoor air quality are drivers of the building design •Material specification, thermal and ventilation strategies implemented to achieve 'healthy' internal environments/air quality	
Establishing a community trust			√	•Community management structure established as key vehicle to support ongoing fair and equitable community governance	
Ongoing management strategy			√ √ √ √ √	•Car club established to serve residential and commercial users •Production of 'green lifestyles' induction information, establishment of 'green' benefits package for residents and the provision of ongoing support via the community trust, extranet and Green Caretaker •Commitment to develop a programme of ongoing monitoring of building performance and occupant satisfaction to be undertaken by the community trust in partnership with other stakeholders •Gathered information would be used to both inform changes to the operation of the development in the future and help to inform future sustainable community best practice •One Planet Centre provided as part of the community centre facility	

Living at One Brighton in 2009

Young professional at One Brighton

One Brighton provides me with an excellent base for my busy lifestyle. I regularly need to travel to London and around the South East for work, and living here I have excellent access to transport choices available to me. With the train station being so convenient, my door-to-door journey for those days when I commute to London is around 80 minutes; this is comparable to when I was renting in south London. The broadband connection enables to me to work from home when I can, and the meeting room facilities and café in the community centre mean that I can also meet with clients easily. The good range of local facilities in Brighton and the network of cycle paths mean than I can cycle to most places I need to day to day, although I have to admit that I am a fairweather cyclist and I take the bus when it's raining. The community extranet helps me to organise my travel arrangements. From it I can find out the running times of local trains and buses, identify the best cycle routes to take, and can even book a car-club vehicle for the occasional times when I need a car. It also allows me to see how much energy and water I am using in running my home. This facility has sparked some friendly competition with my neighbours over who can reduce their consumption the most. Even with our very efficient homes and low-energy appliances and lights, it is amazing how a little thought about how I live can save energy and water. I like to eat healthily and order my organic food boxes and items from the supermarket over the internet. My orders are dropped off at the community centre downstairs for me to pick up on my way back from work or from being out with friends. This is really convenient for both me and the delivery people as I don't have to spend hours food shopping and they can deliver in bulk and save on time and fuel. One Brighton is a great place to live; from my apartment I get great views over Brighton and towards the sea. I can have a high quality of life and reduce my environmental impact at the same time.

Local first-time buyer at One Brighton

I have lived in Brighton all of my life and since graduating I have been trying to get on the property ladder. I am very pleased with my eco-studio; I never thought that I would be able to afford to buy my own home in the city, let alone a brand new one. The high-speed broadband lets me indulge my on-line gaming addiction! It is also in such a central location and it is easy for me to walk or cycle to work, to get to the shops or the beach, and to get back after a night out with friends. For my daily local trips I use the folding bike I bought with the voucher I got free with my flat, but at weekends I borrow a mountain bike and head for the Sussex Downs. This year I plan to rent one of the roof-top mini-allotments. I think it will be fun to grow some of my own vegetables using 'home grown' compost, and in preparation I have taken some gardening and cookery lessons which were offered as part of the Green Lifestyles Package I received when I moved in. The city has such great variety and diversity, and there is so much going on. There are also regular events here in the courtyard; in the last few months there has been a fair-trade market, performances by local arts groups, and a cycle maintenance workshop. There is a strong sense of community here, and I know many more of my neighbours than where I lived previously. I think that this is partly due to the design of the development with the community centre and the range of communal spaces. The layout and design of my eco-studio is really clever. It is compact, but perfectly formed, and the storage wall provides enough space for all my bits and bobs, including my bike. Along with the other eco-studio residents, I also get access to one of the innovative skygardens and exclusive use of space within the community centre to relax and meet with friends.

Semi-retired couple at One Brighton

We moved to One Brighton from a bigger family home further along the coast. Now that our children have their own families, we wanted to move somewhere which was easier to look after and less isolated, being centrally located with good access to services. Our apartment overlooks the wonderfully planted greenway and last summer we had some lovely evenings out on the balcony enjoying the sunsets. We have two bedrooms which is great for when we have the grandchildren to stay with us. They think that Nan and Granddad live in a very exciting building, with solar panels on the roof and gardens in the air. Although we are both partly retired, living so centrally means that my wife can easily get the train if she needs to be in London, whilst I hop on a bus to the nearby school where I work. We sold our car when we moved here and we haven't really missed it at all. For those times when we do need one we can make use of the car club downstairs. In addition to not having the hassle and expense of running our own car, we have noticed that our energy and water bills are lower here too; much lower than those of our friends. I think that the efficient design and having our own communal heating will help to save us more in the future as utilities continue to get more expensive, and as we become pensioners! The quality of the indoor environment is important to us as I suffer from asthma. The materials and paints used were carefully selected to minimise the levels of toxic chemicals, and the ventilation system provides us with filtered fresh air which is heated if required. Our home is warm in the winter and cool in the summer; it is also doesn't get stuffy like many other new homes we have been in. The community extranet has played an important part in supporting a sense of community here. Through the time bank facility, I have been able to get computer lessons from neighbours in exchange for giving gardening guidance to some of the younger people who are growing food up on the roof.

Young family at One Brighton

We moved to One Brighton because the children's grandparents bought an apartment in the development. Having lived in Spain for many years, we weren't worried about living in an apartment with young children – it is the norm there in cities like Madrid. Our private garden terrace is great for the children, but so are the communal skygardens and the greenway. With the high-speed broadband we are able to work from home more, spend more time with the kids and take them to the beach. Having the grandparents in the same building makes our lives really easy. We don't have to travel much as everything we need is close at hand – within walking distance. Our budgets are tight so not having to own a car is good. It is also good for the environment. But the best thing, which we hadn't realised before, is that we now have so much more time with the children. We are not rushing around in the car. We are able to lead our lives at a much better pace, but have all the facilities of a city at hand. One of the most important things for us is thinking about the future. It needs to be greener or else what sort of world are we creating for our children? Since having children we have become eco-warriors! It started with buying organic baby food, but moved on from there. We joined Greenpeace and got into all the issues from renewable energy to recycling. At One Brighton, all those things are just second nature – we hardly have to think about them at all. We also get involved in the annual open day here – talking to other parents from the wider area on how they can be greener, especially as their children come home from school with all the green propaganda taught to them by their teachers! It is important for us to lead lives which are compatible with our values. One Brighton makes it easy, attractive and affordable to do just that.

One Planet Living in Sutton

ONE
PLANET
SUTTON

Healthy, happy, low impact living in the London Borough of Sutton

Welcome!

This site is about creating a Sustainability Action Plan for Sutton.

If everyone in the world lived as we do in Sutton we'd need three planets to support us. We need to reduce our impact - our Ecological Footprint - by two thirds to a sustainable and globally fair level. We call this One Planet Living.

We are working with residents and businesses in the London Borough of Sutton to find ways of reducing our ecological footprint by 65% while strengthening our community and improving our quality of life. This is a hugely ambitious project but together we can make it happen.

Sustainability action plan

Vote

Would you like to see an area set aside for self-build developments in Sutton?

100% voted Yes! 0% voted No! of 1 vote

Please login or register to vote.

News

B&Q selling loft insulation for £1 per roll!

The average loft requires 22 rolls to become fully insulated, and B&Q estimates an average household could save £205 on its heating bill each year through this. The retailer said it is aiming to sell a million rolls, saving the British public more than £9m. The offer is available in all mainland UK stores from February 13 while stocks last. Last year the home improvement retailer launched a One Planet Home range designed to help people reduce the environmental impact of their home and help them save money.

Consultation on plans for new eco-buildings in Hackbridge

Sutton Council, as part of One Planet Sutton is working with the community to turn Hackbridge into the UK's first truly sustainable suburb. In From 11 February to 25 March 2009, we are seeking your views on these detailed proposals for the future of Hackbridge. The document is available to view via the Council's website at www.sutton.gov.uk/hackbridge together with a summary leaflet and online questionnaire. Click on events to find out more.

ONE PLANET SUTTON

Healthy, happy, low impact living in the London Borough of Sutton

Sustainability Action Plan
Sustainable Transport

about this principle | the Action Plan for this principle | case studies

The Challenge

The transport sector is responsible for 25% of UK carbon emissions (and that doesn't even include flying!)

Sutton has already won awards for sustainable transport including 'most sustainable school' and 'best council travel plan'. The sustainable transport principle would build upon these successes and will also tie in with the Smarter Travel Sutton initiative, providing alternatives to private car ownership such as car clubs and encouraging a co-ordinated approach to transport through, for example, work travel plans. This could involve developing safer cycling and pedestrian routes in some areas and could also include developing provision of alternative fuels such as oil recycling schemes for biodiesel production and electric charging points powered by renewable energy.

BioRegional have written a report outlining different scenarios for making transport in Sutton more sustainable. You can download a PDF of the report here.

Zero Carbon

Zero Waste

Sustainable Transport

Local and Sustainable Materials

Local and Sustainable Food

Sustainable Water

Natural Habitats and Wildlife

Culture and Heritage

Equity and Fair Trade

Health and Happiness

ONE PLANET SUTTON

Healthy, happy, low impact living in the London Borough of Sutton

Sustainability Action Plan

The Sustainability Action Plan is divided into the 10 Guiding Principles of One Planet Living, and it's all driven by your ideas.

The One Planet Living programme is based on ten guiding principles of sustainability. The 10 principles cover social, economic and environmental sustainability, so One Planet Living is as much about your happiness as the planet's. We use the 10 principles to create Sustainability Action Plans, for individuals, organisations, new housing developments and cities, towns or boroughs. This is a Sustainability Action Plan for Sutton.

> Use the Principle buttons to look at the Sustainability Action Plan

Everyone is welcome to contribute ideas, through this website, through workshops, or by calling us on 020 8404 5924. This is a celebration of Sutton's sustainability as well as a plan to move things forward so please feel free to promote good things that are already happening. The Sustainability Action Plan includes things that we can all do - like choosing to walk and cycle more, or turning the TV off at the wall instead of using standby - to big ideas like providing Sutton with renewable energy, or making major changes to our transport infrastructure. You can look at the Sustainability Action Plan by Principle, and also filter the plan to only look at Big Ideas or ways that you can Take Action.

your ideas
Have a browse through some great ideas, each one getting us one step closer to One Planet Living in Sutton. We hope that the ideas will inspire you to take action!

your profile
Have a look at your profile and see a record of all the contributions you have already made, the votes you have cast, and edit your details.

Zero Carbon

Zero Waste

Sustainable Transport

Local and Sustainable Materials

Local and Sustainable Food

Sustainable Water

Natural Habitats and Wildlife

Culture and Heritage

Equity and Fair Trade

Health and Happiness

Example of Product Review

ONE PLANET PRODUCTS

ONE PLANET LIVING
Assessment

Product: The Greenhouse Effect - Structuran Cladding

Product Type: Recycled Glass Facades

The Greenhouse Effect Ltd
The Coach House
East Sussex
BN26 5TD

Supplier Score: 2 Stars

Supplier Questionnaire completed ☒	Date: 11th Feb 2009	Country of manufacture: Germany
Product Questionnaire completed ☒	Date: 16th Mar 2009	Certifications: CWCT Accreditation testing in progress

ONE PLANET LIVING CATEGORY	DETAILS
Zero Carbon	The facades are sintered (see Local and Sustainable Materials) in ovens that derive 1/3 of their energy from biogas.
Zero Waste	Glass used in the manufacture of Structuran is sourced from float glass manufacturers' waste cullet. It is more energy efficient to turn the waste cullet into Structuran, which is frosted in appearance, than it is to reheat it to produce clear glass. Sintering requires only 1/3 of the energy that would be needed to process waste cullet into new glass.
Local and Sustainable Materials	Recycled glass bonded through crystallization negates the need for a resin bond. Resins have high embodied energy and make end of life recycling more difficult. This is done through a process of sintering and controlled cooling. The cullet pieces are held together by the crystallization of the glass. Sintering requires only 1/3 of the energy that would be needed to process waste cullet into new glass.

SAVINGS			CREDITS	
ENERGY (EMBODIED)	75	kWh	CODE	15 Primary 6 Secondary
ENERGY (IN USE)		kWh/year	ECO HOMES 2006	16 Primary 6 Secondary
WATER		l/p/d	ECO HOMES 2005	16 Primary 0 Secondary
CO_2e (EMBODIED)	16	kg	ESTIMATED LIFETIME	50 years
CO_2e (IN USE)		kg/year	PAYBACK PERIOD	n/a years

ADDITIONAL INFORMATION (CALCULATIONS)
Using recycled glass instead of virgin glass saves 1.1 tonnes of raw materials per tonne of product and reduces energy consumption by 40%.

1 tonne of virgin glass has 15,000MJ of embodied energy (4165 kWh) and 850 kg of embodied CO_2. Using recycled glass instead saves 315kg of CO_2 per tonne of product, which brings the total CO_2 impact down to 535 $kgCO_2/m^2$.

For $1m^2$ of 20mm Structuran façade this equates an embodied energy of 125 kWh and 25 kg of CO_2 (instead of the 200 kWh and 41 kg of CO_2 that would be required for virgin glass).

The emissions associated with transporting the product from Germany equate to 65 $kgCO_2$ per tonne of product (or 3.2 $kgCO_2$ per square metre).

Index

Photo Credits

The author and the publisher gratefully acknowledge the people who gave their permission to reproduce the visual and written material featured in this book. Every effort has been made to reprint such material in its original form but the author and the publisher cannot guarantee that such material will be error free. The publisher would be grateful to hear from any copyright holder who does not deem themselves to be fully acknowledged in this book and will undertake to rectify any errors or omissions in future editions.

Front cover: © Marcus Lyon; p 5 © BioRegional, photo Marcus Lyon; p 8 © Rob Howard/Corbis; p 10 © Bob Krist/Corbis; pp 13, 77, 98, 118, 132-3, 144(tr), 168, 188 © Pooran Desai; p 18(t) © Global Footprint Network. Global Footprint Network, National Footprint Accounts 2008 edition, www.footprintnetwork.org; pp 18(b), 21, 34, 36-42, 45-6, 48, 93, 100-101, 110,129, 136, 156, 176-8, 207-12 © BioRegional; p 22 © Ove Arup & Partners; p 23 © University of York. Data from REAP Version 2, Experimental Release 15/10/08, published by Stockholm Environment Institute, available from www.sei.se/reap; p 27 © Tom Chance; pp 29, 30, 33 © Zedfactory Ltd; pp 32, 110, 136, 139-40, 144(l), 145, 149, 160 © BioRegional Quintain Ltd; p 35 © Courtesy of Maxine Chung; p 43 © David M Triggs; p 44 © Marcus Lyon; p 53 © Gideon Mendel/Corbis; p 54 © Bob Sacha/Corbis; p 55 © Construction Photography/Corbis; p 58(t) © Boyd & Evans/Corbis; p 58(b) © Permanent Publications, www.permaculture.co.uk (Ben Law - www.ben-law.co.uk); p 59(t) © Hockerton Housing Project Trading Ltd; p 59(b) © Richard Mullane, Living Projects www.living-projects.co.uk; p 62 © Phil Shemmings; p 64(l) © Caroma Industries Ltd; p 64(r) © Manjit Lall, CME Sanitary Systems Limited; p 66 © Food Photomedia; p 68 courtesy John Wiley & Sons Ltd; pp 70, 73(t), 74, 79 © Foster + Partners; p 72 © Fulcrum Consulting Ltd; p 73(b) © Narinder Sagoo/Foster + Partners; pp 83-4 © Courtesy of Parliamentary Office of Science & Technology; p 92 © ENVAC UK LTD; p 94(l) © Adnams; p 94(r) © Lime Technology Ltd; p 99 © New Economics Foundation. Image source: www.pluggingtheleaks.org, nef (the new economics foundation); p 104 © British Sugar plc; p 106 © Image Source/Corbis; p 109 © Pelicano Investimento Imobiliário, SA; p 112 © New Economics Foundation; p 113(tl) © Radius Images/Corbis; p 113(tr) © Karen Kasmauski/Corbis; p 113(bl) © Fred Derwal/Hemis/Corbis; p 113(br) © Cultura/Corbis; p 115 © Ed Blake – RIBA Building Futures; p 119 © Adrian Wikeley/Land Use Consultants/Gillian Cartwright; Eden Project; p 120(t) © David Butow/Corbis; p 120(b) © Julia Wright @ Garden Organic; pp 121, 181 © Feilden Clegg Bradley Studios; p 124(t) © From Newman and Kenworthy, Cities and Automobile Dependence, Gower Technical, 1989; p 124(b) © Atlantide Phototravel/Corbis; p 128 © Carlos Cazalis/Corbis; p 144(br) © Boicu Vasile; p 147 © China Merchant Property Developers; p 162 © The Argus; p 165 © Peter Cook/VIEW; p 172(t&bl) © Sonoma Mountain Village – SOMO; p 172(c&br) © Greg Searle; p 174 © Courtesy Parity Projects Ltd; p 179 © Karl-Heinz Haenel/Corbis; p 185 © Lend Lease Development Pty Ltd, photo Gollings Pidgeon; p 187(t) © The DESERTEC Foundation; p 187(b) © Michael Pawlyn; p 194 © Hamiltons Architects